Whose Story?

Reporting the Developing World After the Cold War

Edited by

Jill Spelliscy
Gerald B. Sperling

School of Journalism and Communications
University of Regina

Detselig Enterprises Ltd.
Calgary, Alberta, Canada

Cover Design by Mike Siggins

Canadian Cataloguing in Publication Data

Main entry under title:

Whose Story?

Proceedings of a conference held at the University of Regina, Regina, Sask. in October, 1992.
ISBN 1-55059-077-4

1. Journalism – Developing countries – Congresses. 2. Press and politics – Developing countries – Congresses. 3. Developing countries in the press – Congresses. 4. Journalism – Social aspects – Congresses.
I. Spelliscy, Jill. II. Sperling, Gerald B.
PN5648.W56 1992 079'.1724 C93-091955-6

Detselig Enterprises Ltd.
210, 1220 Kensington Rd. N.W.
Calgary, Alberta, Canada T2N 3P5

Distributed by:

Temeron Books Inc.
210, 1220 Kensington Rd. N.W.
Calgary, Alberta T2N 3P5

Temeron Books Inc.
P.O. Box 896
Bellingham, Washington, USA 98227

Printed in Canada SAN 115-0324 ISBN 1-55059-077-4

Acknowledgments

We wish to thank everybody around the world who made this book possible. They were also instrumental in the realization of the conference, "Reporting the Developing World After the Cold War." Clearly we cannot list them all. Derek Ingram not only made a magnificent address, reproduced in this book, to introduce the conference, he carefully read every word of the manuscript and played a key role in the organization of this seminal event. Without him, neither this book nor the conference would have happened.

Sat Kumar, director of the School of Journalism and Communications at the University of Regina worked closely with the staff of Gemini News Service to develop the concept for the conference. Bethel Njoku of Gemini News Service, along with the entire staff of that organization, must be acknowledged for their sterling work in the U.K. and in Canada in preparing the groundwork for the conference. Most importantly, Bethel helped construct the delegate and participant list.

Nick Russell, Jim McKenzie and Larry Todd of the School of Journalism and Communications gave of their time and intellect to the conference. Wendy Tebb, secretary of the School, patiently slaved for hours on the computer, writing to delegates and transcribing papers. She also organized the conference facilities, invited delegates closer to home and ably handled the countless details that go into the preparation and execution of such an event.

Leanne Swyanyk of the Department of Political Science at the University of Regina cheerfully, as usual, helped with the word processing of the manuscript of this book. Don Hall, a brilliant photographer, took many of the photographs which appear in this book.

Noele Hall, the Regina singer-songwriter, welcomed our delegates from around the world with songs of love and struggle. At the dinner, she and her partner, Jan Harvey, entertained delegates and friends.

Gillian Forrester, a graduate of our School and a Gemini fellow introduced delegates from the developing world to Saskatchewan. She made their stay an unforgettable experience.

The Canadian International Development Agency merits a special thanks for its generous financial assistance and for the vision which turned the germ of an idea into reality. Roger Dumilie of CIDA was especially encouraging.

In a very real sense this book is dedicated to the Gemini News Service for its 25 years of commitment to the people and stories of the developing world.

Jill Spelliscy and Gerald B. Sperling
Regina, Saskatchewan
October, 1993

Detselig Enterprises Ltd. appreciates the financial assistance for its 1993 publishing program from the Department of Communications, Canada Council, and the Alberta Foundation for the Arts, a beneficiary of the Lottery Fund of the Government of Alberta.

The Gemini Fellows

Back Row: Gillian Forrester; Elaine Shein (Western Producer, Saskatoon); Brenda Kossowan (Red Deer Advocate); Allan Thompson (Toronto Star); Teresa Mazzitelli (Family Physician, Toronto); Tina Spencer (Ottawa Citizen); Scott Simmie (CBC); Marcus Schwabe (CBC); Darren Foster; Rick Boychuk. Front Row: Stefani Langenegger (Canadian Press); Gavin Wilson. Others in the picture: extreme left, Bethel Njoku, Gemini general manager; extreme right, Derek Ingram, Gemini editor. Front left (in jeans) Louise Behan, of the International Development Research Centre, Ottawa.

Too Much Too Fast

Black Africa, She move in the street
White whip try to bring defeat
To a people older then the earth
Look what mamma Africa she birth
What mamma Africa she birth.

Chorus

They say, "Too much too fast."
They say, "Too much too fast."
"You want too much to fast."
I say "Give me what's mine or I take it!"
"Ya give me what's mine or I take it."

Third World she ache in her heart.
War and famine tear her apart
Nobody ask for this deed.
Who reap the product of this seed?
Reap the product of this seed.

Chorus

Is your back yard clean and right?
Do you hate gays but act polite?
Those women scare you with their demands.
Are peace and justice only crazy plans?
Peace and justice only crazy plans.

Chorus

You say "Too much too fast."
You say "Too much too fast."
I say, "Give me what's mine or I take it!"
"Ya, give me what's mine or I take it."

Song by Regina Singer-Songwriter, Noele Hall
Noele Hall
2451 Winnipeg Street
Regina, Saskatchewan
S4P 1H5

Contents

1

Introduction

Jill Spelliscy and **Gerald B. Sperling**
University of Regina

Musing aloud in a speech in Washington, D.C. in April 1993, Václav Havel, revolutionary democrat, playwright and now president of the Czech Republic, noted that many people, just three years after the collapse of communism in Eastern Europe were feeling ". . . a little nostalgic for a world that was, after all, slightly more transparent and understandable than the present one."[1] Many of the Third World journalists attending the "Reporting the Developing World after the Cold War" conference in Regina in October 1992, had witnessed not only a drastic deterioration of the economic situations in their countries since the fall of the Berlin Wall, but also a severe limitation in the political options open to their countries.

It is more important than ever to distinguish the differences amongst the countries of what has come to be called the "developing world." For example, while the economic problems facing the People's Republic of China remain immense, the country has been experiencing astounding growth rates since 1979 and more particularly since 1989. The concern of such eminent Chinese journalists as Zhu Yinghuang of *China Daily* is the apparent lack of empathy of the western media with the course of *political* reform in China. His country seems to have the economic clout to play in the same sandbox with "the big boys" of world trade.

On the other hand, many other "developing" nations are facing horrific economic and social problems. "Since 1990, sub-Saharan Africa has seen its debt rise by $30 billion (U.S.) to $183 billion. . . ."[2] And all of this debt is setting the stage for increasing economic and *political* dependence of these countries of the west or more accurately the *North.* As the president of Uganda, Yoweri Museveni, recently put it, "We have been condemned to perpetual dependence on a world market in which we have little or no influence."[3] Furthermore, the successes of the West in intervening in a massive way militarily almost with impunity in the developing world, Iraq and Somalia, for example, to impose a post Cold War "order" has raised fears for the concept of sovereignty in many developing nations.[4]

> I get terribly angry when journalists take the phrase, which is completely manufactured, "New World Order" – it's absolutely meaningless. Personally, I don't think there is a New World Order. I think we have the same world order, but without the Soviet Union which was never a major part of the world economy. And if you live in Katmandu or Kampala, there is no change.
>
> (Danny Nelson, former associate editor, Gemini News)

A provocative comment – coming as it did towards the end of three days of sometimes friendly but often heated exchanges amongst dozens of journalists from all over the world. The place was Regina, Saskatchewan; the time was October, 1992. The weather was unseasonable. There was no sign of the dreaded prairie winter. In fact, the conference occurred during a late fall hot spell.[5]

This chapter is a summary of how the dozens of delegates from the four corners of the earth saw their world and their journalism after three days of intensive exchange and dialogue. As the reader works her/his way through the remainder of this book, she/he will find these summary ideas expanded and developed. We have tried in this introductory chapter to let the words and thoughts of the delegates speak for themselves, but as all journalists know, the very act of selection involves editorial choice and opinion. We bear full responsibility for the contents of this chapter. Throughout this chapter and the book we have tried as much as possible to reproduce the words of *all* the speakers at the conference as they spoke and wrote them.

There was debate about what had changed and what had not changed in the world following the break up of the Soviet Union, the popular struggles in Eastern Europe and the ongoing struggles in the former Yugoslavia. It was a revealing backdrop for analyzing media coverage of the developing world. It was as if there were a competition in the running – that the countries of Africa or Latin America or Asia would now have to come up with equivalent media-draws to get the attention of the world.

The conference took place in an atmosphere of perplexing questions. People were looking for answers with an outmoded language. As Daniel Nelson pointed out, we do live in a world easily manipulated by the power of words and images. The words and the agendas of the powerful are absorbed easily into the popular lexicon – weakening the capacity to be critical and the ability to distinguish between reality and illusion. It is the corporate world which talks of a new economic order.

Nelson and others criticized this clarion call as ideology, insisting that, in fact, "we have the same world order." Indeed, poverty in the developing and in the developed world is increasing to alarming levels.[6] The gap between rich countries and poor continues to widen – debt, environmental problems, the AIDS epidemic, cultural colonialism through the increasing domination by the Western media – the same problems are there and are even exacerbated.

This world order, built upon the world economy of the multi-nationals and Structural Adjustment Programs designed to speed the development of capitalism in the Third World – these realities and this world order are the same. The thawing of the Cold War is uprooting old power struggles and alliances, leaving the aligned-nations (particularly those formerly linked to the old Soviet Union) adrift and the non-aligned countries searching for a meaningful role and new ways to attack the old and the new problems.

The difference between how people live in the West (North) and how people live in the developing world (South) remains unchanged. Injustice remains. In the midst of all this, journalists from the developing world see the Western media turning attention away from the South, bored with the famine stories, looking for new hot spots of conflict and disaster.

Thus, underlying or perhaps more accurately, hovering over the conference, there was fear, fear of disappearing from world news as new wars and new economic conflicts emerge to push stories about the Third World even further onto the back pages and beyond the camera's range.

The delegates wanted more coverage in the Western media. They questioned news values – the West's, as well as their own. They wanted stories told of human achievement, stories about reparation for the devastation of the slave trade, stories, like the one about a Botswana woman who was fighting the courts for the rights of women to pass citizenship onto their children, stories about the slow fight toward multi-party rule and democracy. These were the stories they wanted to tell the world.

No doubt, these are the stories the world wants to hear. However, the media conglomerates have their own agenda, an agenda which emphasizes destruction, when people are looking for social progress and construction, context and connection. Nobody was getting this message from the media during the Cold War. Why would anyone expect to get it after the Cold War?

But things have changed. Delegates from the Third World said they were competing against new forces, new rivals in the fight for coverage in the Western media. Famine, drought, and war were stories overdone by Western media. They created stereotypes of the Third World: images of helplessness, dependence and stagnation. These were hardly the stories developing countries wanted in the international media, but that coverage was perhaps better than none at all. The delegates insisted there were important stories to tell about their countries – stories about development projects, economic strides – success stories. No one was naive about the power of the media and the importance of getting media coverage. Stories can catch the eyes of the powerful – governments who have foreign aid money to loan, corporations searching for investment opportunities, institutes with funds to encourage research. Information has become an integral part of the 'world economy.'

Fear turned into anger as delegates expressed frustration with the Western media and its lack of coverage of the Third World. Many pointed out that this media disinterest comes at a time when many developing countries are fighting for democracy and a freer press. Now more than ever, they argued, was the time for the media to follow these stories of struggle towards self-reliance and social construction.

Both Western and "Southern" delegates charged the Western media with having joined efforts to maintain the status quo. The level of crisis in the developing world at this moment cannot be overstated. Even with the hope of democratic rule and the promise of progressive leadership, the tide is turning against the people of the South.

Western governments are cutting aid to the developing world. Delegates to the conference noted that the Canadian government has decided traditional recipient countries in Africa, Asia and Latin America will be getting a smaller piece of the pie. More money is going to former communist countries in Central and Eastern Europe and to newly independent countries from the former Soviet Union such as Ukraine. The Mulroney-Campbell Canadian government cynically believes the economies of the old Cold War adversaries will respond more quickly to economic assistance than those "tiresome" Third World nations. For example, the Canadian International Development Agency is cutting aid projects in five African countries. The funding is to be re-directed to Eastern Europe. One delegate noted that the Tanzanian Ambassador to Canada has expressed his deep concern about the future of his country's economic development. He sees the Canadian government's move as a portent of worse things to come for Tanzania and for the rest of sub-Saharan Africa.

Both journalists from the developing and from the developed world seemed to have a fading hope for democracy and a real fear about structural transformations demanded of the Third World by the International Monetary Fund and the World Bank. Such structural demands were seen by many as the 'reward' for steps taken towards democracy. Some delegates questioned the assumption implicit in the Structural Adjustment Programs – that capitalism and democracy were synonymous – that is, you could not have one without the other.

These journalists from around the globe had come to Regina to discuss popular perceptions and media coverage of the developing world in the wake of the Cold War. The result was what Rex Nettleford, the distinguished communications scholar from the University of the West Indies, would call "creative chaos."

Gemini News Service's stalwart Derek Ingram opened the conference by setting the context of a different world, a unipolar world, a place in which the Third World's voice may be heard even less than it was before. He argued that there is an important new role for the Non-aligned Movement to give the developing world a stronger voice in the world. The Commonwealth could be used to create a new dialogue about how to narrow the gap between rich and poor countries in the developed world. Old institutions and mechanisms for cooperation and for dialogue would have to be re-thought and new mechanisms found to foment change.

Delegates listened and learned. They learned that there are still profound differences over how to report the developing world in the Western media. Norman Webster, editor of the *Montreal Gazette*, talked about the importance of avoiding "parachute" journalism. He thought it crucial that Western journalists live in the countries they cover. But he also stated quite forcefully that journalists are in the business to inform their readers at home. The stories they write, he said, must have resonance and relevance for people in Canada.

The delegates tackled the subject of using stringers as a means to increase coverage of Third World issues. Norman Webster was somewhat dismissive of stringers. On the other hand, a newspaper such as the *Guardian* was said to rely on its stringers. In fact it had fifty to one hundred of them.

Indeed, as delegates from Gemini pointed out, that is what the Gemini News Service is all about. Gemini uses stringers from the Third World to tell stories of the Third World. These people act as informants to the Centre and as local correspondents inside the countries. Gerry Knight of the *Guardian* pointed out that his paper's stringers were the mainstay of its world coverage.

> It's obvious from listening to people here that a lot of you don't know the *Guardian* stringers [in your countries]. I think one of the things you ought to do is to find out who these people are because they're meant to know what's going on locally. And if they're any good, one of the ways they will know what's going on locally is by knowing you because you know something. That's worth doing. So you really ought to go and find out where they come from.

This suggestion brought Padmaja Padman from Malaysia to her feet with a pointed comment:

> The *Guardian* stringers ought to try to get to know us as well. This is what we've been talking about all day. Not for us to go to you all the time; *you* come out to us. You know where we are. Our establishment, our newspaper organizations are established and looking for your stringers – where do we find them?

There were other suggestions about ways to enhance media coverage of the developing world and to open access for Third World journalists to Western media. Bill Cunningham, the original organizer of the Canadian Global Television's network news, experimented at one time with a way to move away from the centres into the margins in a Canadian context. To get the voices of rural Ontario into the news, Cunningham recounted how he created regional field producers who would go out to all the little towns in Ontario and approach stringers who worked for the radio station or the newspaper. The field producer would find out from the stringers what the story was. Then the field producer would work with the stringer in the telling of the story. The stringer would tell the story, the field producer would produce it for television. Cunningham elaborated:

> It did several things. It had regional authenticity in the sense that if the person had an accent from that particular area – the Ottawa Valley, for example, has a certain kind of accent, which you can hear. It also puts those other voices and those other faces on the air. By using both the stringer and the field producer creatively, we turned the stringer's story into a television package that meets the needs of lighting and screen direction and picture quality and so on, but does not destroy the authenticity of his story.

Cunningham saw this process as one which would work well in covering stories in the Third World.

Many of the delegates wanted to discuss practical ways to gain access to Western media. Mohamad Hamaludin, editor of the black weekly, *Miami Times*, encouraged people to avoid trying to get their stories into the big papers. He said alternative media offered a much more realistic option for Third World journalists.

> I have a problem with us trying to get a news service into CBC or into the *Toronto Star* or the *Globe and Mail* or *New York Times* or Associated Press. There are 200 black newspapers in America which are dying to get information about Africa. Where do they get it from? Associated Press, Reuters, AFP and the like. You have probably five or six thousand and more other ethnic newspapers in America covering every single spectrum of the Third World because those are "ethnic communities" that were transplanted from different parts of the world: you have a Philippine community, you have a Cuban community, African community, a Nigerian community, if you want to segregate them. All of those have newspapers and the better ones have television stations and they have radio broadcast facilities.

Hamaludin said any idea of the media as a monolithic institution – "that has this huge capacity to control the minds of people and direct the flow of information" – was a misconception. In his opinion, people have the power to exert influence upon media coverage.

> The Ross Perot phenomenon has indicated that it is the grassroots people who at the local level have a capacity to influence public policy in the way they choose their national representatives. So I think one way of trying to get access to them is, in fact, to get access to those smaller community newspapers, TV stations, broadcast facilities, and work to bring pressure at the local level, which then can generate into a national debate.

There were delegates who insisted that developing countries had to become more realistic about the kind of news coverage they could get in the Western media. Gerry Knight, from the *Guardian*, said the market for news from overseas is limited because newspapers cover stories closest to their readers – the things which affect you day by day are the things which are happening around you.

> I think it would be [bad] to raise false expectations that there's any realistic way that there will be a lot of news from around the world, in other parts of the world, because there just isn't the capacity to put it in. I'm sorry to say that.

The bigger demand for news, Knight said, was for the financial and economic stories. He went on:

> Someone [at the conference] said the other day, "Oh, the Western media is not reporting that dams are being built." But you have to remember that people assume that dams can be built – it's not a story. You've got to remember what newspapers are about. They're about interesting the reader. People are interested in a dam if it's the biggest dam in the world or if it's fallen down. Economically, though, people will be interested in what's going to be the fruits of producing the dam. That's where the real story is.

The notion of the media's role in providing information for social change was raised at the conference in the context of the move towards democracy and multi-party rule, particularly in Africa. Bethel Njoku from Nigeria (Gemini News Service) thought these developments gave the media a new responsibility:

> The role of the media in the newly emerging nations should be to sufficiently sensitize the rural and the local people to the issues that abound there so that if ever they are given an opportunity to vote, they can vote for those things that can sustain development.

Far too often, Njoku said, the media gatekeepers of the West do not clearly understand this role.

One thought that came through strongly in the panel discussions at the conference, as well as in the written submissions, was the need to pursue the human side – the miracle of people's survival. William Saidi, the editor of the *Sunday Times* of Zimbabwe, talked about the success stories that pass us by. Bernard Proulx of Radio Québec turned an economic story into a human tale with a wonderful reference to a cellist in the Nicaraguan orchestra who had gone into retraining by learning how to mend watches. This was a new angle on the old strains of structural adjustment and recession.

Anjum Niaz of *Dawn* in Pakistan, mentioned the need for the media to provoke change in her country. She also spoke of how she came to the conference looking for answers. In her first area of interest, development reporting, she said Pakistani papers carry a lot of political statements – the day to day reporting of who said what. Niaz feared journalists were losing touch with the lives of ordinary people. During her stay in Regina, she was pleasantly surprised by what she saw in Canada's "national newspaper" about the developing world:

> I must confess I was impressed by the *Globe and Mail*, that on the front page they have carried stories on development issues for the last two or three days.

> That I think is really excellent. We need to convince our editors of these kinds of issues and that they should be given the proper display.

These were words Joe Thloloe, an editor of the *Sowetan* of South Africa, could relate to. He has struggled for many years to get the real stories of South Africa out to the world.

There was much legitimate criticism of the Western media and its coverage of the Third World. But some delegates from the developing world urged their colleagues to quit wasting time – time that could otherwise be spent doing journalism in their own countries. Anjum Niaz captured this sentiment by telling the delegates to "stop moaning about the West. You won't change the West, but what's important is fair, accurate reporting, and let readers decide."

Self-reliance was discussed at length; there were ideas such as creating regional news services similar to the Gemini model. Kuldip Nayar, the well-known Indian journalist, talked of the wise men coming out of the East to save the souls of the West. Ngozi Anyaegbunam of the *Daily Times* of Nigeria talked about the frustration of being ignored - about Nigeria working hard for democracy with scarce attention from the rest of the world.

Projects for media self-reliance, news exchanges and cooperative networks such as Caribvision have worked well in some parts of the world, but there have also been problems. A survey has been done under the auspices of the various efforts that were made after the new world information order debate. It analyzed what went wrong with the various institutions set up for the exchange of news. The survey found stumbling blocks facing these worthwhile attempts at South-South news exchanges:

> Each institution that's been set up has the same problems: inadequate technical equipment and lack of trained staff; low staff pay and poor morale; lack of journalistic professionalism; small markets; and failure of subscribers to pay for the services provided.

Questions about the so-called "new world order" raised a number of memorable comments. Rex Nettleford refused to be taken over by the dogmatic and the exclusive. Instead he insisted that we should all be in the mainstream of designing this New World Order. Theresa Mazettelli, a Canadian with substantial Third World experience, took the notion of change and new world order to another level by raising the problem of sexism in the media and in the newsrooms, and by raising the larger issue of change within patriarchal systems. Padmaja Padman from Malaysia was also concerned about fighting old attitudes inside the newsroom, "Someone said yesterday their newsroom is full of old, white men. I said that my newsroom is full of old, brown men, so we all have this problem."

Padman emphasized how hard it is to change attitudes of her management which is composed mostly of "old brown men." It was important, she thought, to fight for change from the bottom up.

Technology and shifts in transnational economic interests have been creating waves of unemployment causing mass migrations of peoples in search of subsistence. These are economic refugees. The consequences of environmental degradation and disaster are environmental refugees – vast numbers of people with no place to call home. As Luis Tricot, a free-lancer from Chile pointed out, "It is not so crazy to think there will be wars over water in 30 years – maybe sooner than that."

While the focus of the conference was reporting the developing world after the Cold War, delegates were quick to raise the problems facing the developed world as well. Rick Boychuk, formerly an environmental reporter for the *Montreal Gazette*, said one phrase he had heard at the conference kept ringing in his ears, and that was Joe Thloloe asking whether there is a process of disintegration sweeping the West. The question had resonance for many, but for Boychuk, it summed up his most recent experiences as a journalist:

> I spent most of the 1980s chronicling industrial excess and people's environmental anxieties for a newspaper in Montreal. I came to the conclusion after the years of writing about environmental problems that people do have very deep anxieties about science, about what progress is, about industrial advance that haven't really been addressed by our institutions, political, economic or otherwise.

Boychuk argued that the largest social movement in modern history has emerged in the past 20 years in the industrial world – the environmental movement. He urged journalists from the developing world to turn their attention to environmental issues.

William Saidi from Zimbabwe pointed out that in many parts of Africa, the question of the environment is being raised. Resources to fight the problems are scarce but time has run out for excuses:

> The argument has been that we can't follow all those guidelines because we are only developing and if we start behaving as if we had the resources to apply the measures the developed world suggests, our development would be retarded. So give us time. Some of us object to this [approach] because what it means is, "Give us time to pollute the rivers, destroy the forests – until we are a barren landscape." Then we can say, "Okay, we'll apply these new measures." By then there will be nothing left.

Delegates, like Boychuk, shared this sense of time running out, but he believes the environmental crisis has transformed the way people think about what constitutes progress. And he encouraged journalists in the developing world to find a place within this movement to tell new stories:

> I think that one of the things that people are looking for in reportage coming out of the Third World is examples of development that work, development that is sensitive to the fabric of life. I think that people in the West understand in a way that they didn't understand before that development is a matter of options – that people do have choices.

Optimism about a world ready for significant change was not shared by all of the journalists present. Daniel Nelson was quick to question such a rosy picture of a world turned conscious:

> There are the beginnings of things going terribly wrong. For God's sake, we've got holes in the sky now, and the sky is actually falling in. There are signs coming that things are going wrong. But on the whole, I think people are still sticking with this idea that this is basically okay. And I think in developing countries, if you can see that, it's something to aim for. The standard of living here is so amazingly high, even with unemployment, even with everything else, you look around and you can't actually think that this isn't going to work. It's still works.

Nelson was irrepressible. He expressed a hope that that the growing awareness of environmental degradation might translate into an awareness of human degradation that is occurring on a global scale:

> I think, actually, the key problem, the most interesting issue now is whether everybody in the world can have this standard of living. And if, as some people in the West are now thinking, it's not possible, that we ourselves can't have it because it's based on exploitation on a massive scale and will collapse and that in any case there aren't the resources and all the other things for everyone to have it, then we're living the most incredible lie because the whole development industry is based on the assumption that we're all going to hit this level. That actually is a terribly interesting story out of which lots of other stories come. And I do think there is a major crisis in development.

This crisis in development has broadened in the wake of the end of the Cold War amidst the ongoing changes in Eastern Europe. The rich countries of the industrialized world are re-examining their commitment to foreign aid and re-defining notions of development. Again Daniel Nelson:

> The World Bank, the bilateral agencies have absolutely lost confidence in development. Aid is probably dead. In ten years I would say there will be hardly any international aid left. I don't think people know what they're doing with it anymore.

This, Nelson told delegates, is today's big story. And he went on:

> The Bush speech where he questioned the whole basis of aid, and said that it probably isn't necessary – it'll just be support for markets and capitalism – I think that's what's going to happen. It seems to me that the nearest thing we have to a world government is the World Bank. It is not the United Nations,

> and that's why I get personally terribly angry about when journalists take the phrase, which is completely manufactured, "New World Order" – it's absolutely meaningless. Personally, I don't think there is a New World Order. I think we have the same world order, but without the Soviet Union which was never a major part of the world economy. And if you live in Katmandu or Kampala, there is no change. The world is exactly the same today as it was five years ago, and it will be the same in five years – your life is ruled by the bank. That is the most powerful institution. That perception of change or the lack of change is what I think is not being reported. I don't think it is being covered.

Roger Dumielle of the Canadian International Development Agency (CIDA) did not take kindly to the argument that international development is dead, that the World Bank rules and that there's no real change in the world. Dumielle argued profound and deep changes were occurring. The kind of change "that will take more than one or two years, it's going to be very fundamental." He continued:

> We went overseas and consulted with our partners to look at this new reality that we're now living in. We recognize that the words that we're using, North and South, no longer make sense. We developed what we call the sustainable development framework. We did that so we could have a new language, new concepts that we could build into the way we're doing things. Some of the pillars of this sustainable development framework are environmental and economic sustainability, but the new ones for us are things like political sustainability, cultural sustainability and social sustainability. Now these are just words, and you have to look at what's behind them to really understand what is going on and how profound it is.

Dumielle said international development agencies like CIDA have now become very interested in the media's role in development and democracy, in culture and in cultural changes.

But for most delegates, change was the World Bank and the Structural Adjustment Programs, not something called sustainable development. And they questioned the lack of coverage of the World Bank and its economic policies in the developing world.

Wafulu Oguttu asked why journalists in the North are ignoring the fact that much of the Third World has a problem with these institutions of economic restructuring:

> We want you to appreciate that they say Uganda is a success story because we have taken these Structural Adjustment Programs of the IMF. We began by borrowing $100 million. Now we are borrowing $800 million. Servicing the debt was taking about 50% of our G.D.P. Now servicing the debt is taking nearly 100%. How shall we get out of that? How can we unite – a global village – a common sensibility – if we don't understand each other? We're asking, please - we are the people in the South who try to understand the North. Perhaps

> this is the greatest missing story in the world – the way the World Bank makes decisions, how these decisions are implemented, and how those decisions affect the lives of millions and millions of people.

A changing world requires a changing language. But there were warnings at the conference. Language is not a benign, static entity. It can be a vehicle for power and misinformation. Rex Nettleford from the University of the West Indies was one of the delegates who cautioned:

> I do think it's very important, that these new words which come into the vocabulary, that we ourselves be very watchful about them. I mean, sustainable development has hit us like anybody's business. We are grappling with that in the Caribbean. Does it mean preserving the trees or does it mean cutting them down and putting up marvellous high-rises as in Hong Kong, so that you can be economically prosperous? So it's nowhere as simple. The most endangered of the species are we human beings.

Journalists are highly vulnerable to the manipulation of language which can turn the craft of exposé and imparting meaning into vacant misleading jargon. Daniel Nelson believes the language of reporting and the ease in which media vocabulary can become ideology had a particular resonance given the context of the post Cold War period and the discussion about media responsibility and social change:

> The politicians always get us going. They'll make a phrase like New World Order and we run with it because it's a good phrase and you can get it into headlines and intros, but it's actually taking us away from where the real power is and where the real decisions are that affect most people in the world.

At various points during the conference, discussion turned to the role of the young journalists in attendance, who expressed great interest in the affairs of the Third World. Ngozi Anyaegbunanm of Nigeria thought it crucial to expose young journalists to the environments of the developing world:

> So, if you think you are living well here because some other people are being exploited, maybe you will want to sometimes put yourself in their position and you will begin to empathize and that way the global village we are living in might become more humane.

But the delegates could not forget the Cold War. William Saidi took issue with the statement that the Cold War was more illusion than real. For the people of Southern Africa, for Zimbabwe, the Cold War was reality:

> A few years before 1979, Henry Kissinger said he didn't think that the United States should continue to support regimes such as Ian Smith's which were white supremacist. From then on it was inevitable that Zimbabwe would become independent. I know that Ian Smith tried various strategies to retain power. But I think he realized that as long as the Americans were no longer prepared to support him, there was no chance. The game was up. When there was the

conference in Lusaka in 1979 and Robert Mugabe and Joshua Nkomo and all the people who had been called terrorists were welcomed as heroes, Smith himself must have realized that this was the end. What had sustained him throughout the fifteen years of his illegal regime was the assurance by the West that as long as he remained anti-communist, he had their backing. That was the reality of the Cold War.

The end of the Cold War has had a profound effect upon people in Angola, Mozambique and Namibia. William Saidi, again:

> Angola and Mozambique have now changed completely from what they were during the height of the Cold War. Angola and Mozambique were born at the height of the Cold War. They were supported by the Soviet Union and the people who fought against them were supported by the United States. That was a typical example of the Cold War. Thousands of people were killed in Angola. Thousands of people were killed in Mozambique. It wasn't just because the Mozambiquans and the Angolans themselves hated each other. I don't believe that. It was the Cold War. The Cold War was being fought in Mozambique, in Angola, it was being fought in Namibia until Namibia became independent.

For William Saidi and most of the delegates from the Third World, down playing the Cold War was like ignoring years of tangible struggle following colonial rule and the battle between the super-powers:

> I don't think that we can brush off the end of the Cold War as a non-event. As far as we are concerned, it's an event that's worth noting because even in Zimbabwe, the independence struggle in Zimbabwe was fought with the aid of the Chinese and the Soviets. They didn't do that because of some gushing goodness coming out of their hearts. It was because of the Cold War. When we won independence, we unwisely, as it turned out, tried to continue the Cold War by insisting on the policies that were identical to the policies followed by the so-called masters. But we realized in the end that we were neither Chinese nor were we Russians, nor Yugoslavians, nor East Germans. We were Zimbabweans and we had to do things our own way, which we probably are now. It just won't cut it to say that the end of the Cold War is not significant. It *is* significant.

But even in the context of this Cold War discussion, the issue of media and language came up at another level – telling stories in mother languages. Sat Kumar, Director of the School of Journalism and Communications at the University of Regina, was the first to admit the dominion of English in the communications and in the exchange of world information, but he thought it important to encourage people who do their work in the indigenous languages:

> The vast majority of people in India do not read or speak English. The songs, the music, the literature, the poetry are in other languages – that's where the creativity is. As much as one can try and capture that in another language, I think it's not possible. I think it is important that in the kind of work we are

> doing here, we keep in mind that there is a constituency out there of indigenous press in various countries that we must somehow be able to connect with.

Wafulu Oguttu also brought out some of the more interesting contradictions between the words and actions of the developed world – contradictions which raised questions about the rationale for de-emphasizing development news in Western media:

> The farmers want news from the Third World or news from the world because they are farmers and they want statistics and the movement of wheat and what have you. Then we heard views of your women. Is there nothing universal about the Indian woman and the Ugandan woman and the Canadian woman? The Nigerian woman was telling us about the women in Nigeria. Is it not possible that native women in Canada would like to see in graphic detail the women of Nigeria? So what is this business about the audience not being interested?

Other journalists and guests at the conference echoed Oguttu's questions. One woman said she thought one of the biggest barriers to reporting on the developing world in Canada is the attitude of the press that ordinary Canadians are not interested in what goes on in the rest of the world. She told of requesting coverage of some issues and being told repeatedly that the people in Saskatchewan were not interested in the Third World.

A Canadian journalist pointed out that the *Calgary Herald* had just started an exercise where reporters go into the community to talk about community needs and issues, and to get feedback on the paper's coverage. Roman Cooney of the *Herald* thinks this is an important first step. Repeatedly, newspaper and television surveys of audiences come back saying people want local news, not news about faraway countries. Perhaps the face to face process will more accurately determine how the readers look at news and how interested they are in stories about the developing world:

> We go into their environment and say, "What are we doing right? What are we doing wrong? What do you want to see?" And you're right. What we're finding is that there's a little bit of a shift between what the polls and surveys say and what people actually say when they're comfortable and they're talking with their shirt sleeves rolled up and they feel comfortable. So we're hoping that that process will get us a little bit closer to what people want. It may, in fact, turn out that people do want a broader spectrum, and that there are approaches that that really do touch on their lives.

Often it is not the journalists who block reporting on the developing world. Given media formats, paper and program mandates and deadlines, it is difficult to get a story of context and meaning out to the world.

Scott Simmie of CBC Television news spent time as a freelancer in Beijing. He told a story about the time he contacted CBS to do a story about Tiananmen Square:

> I had a name, I had worked for CBC, Pacifica, etc. They said, "This is how you sign off, we like some sound. You have a total of twenty-eight seconds to provide us with a story." Twenty-eight seconds including sign off and a sound bite. So, in the case of Tiananmen, what can you say other than, "Students demonstrated again today. They say they want freedom. 'A clip of a student,' 'I want democracy.' The government says they should leave. Scott Simmie, Beijing"? And there's your 28 second story. And it really was frustrating as a journalist, and this is a very powerful and large media outlet in the United States. I think it was symptomatic of some of the problems, some of the battles we face in getting out these stories.

Journalists, especially from the developing world expressed concern about the lack of detail and analysis in stories about their countries. The success of Gemini News Service in tapping into the Third World and in presenting in depth understandings of the issues had many delegates chastizing Western papers for not using the service. Scott Honeyman shared this concern. But it should be noted that his *Vancouver Sun* does not subscribe to Gemini. However, he did commiserate:

> I think that it's disappointing in a way. I think many foreign editors at newspapers in Canada, for example, regard Gemini as the news service with the heart of gold. But the copy just doesn't get into newspapers here - or very rarely. And I think that's a shame. I think it should get into newspapers here, that there are valuable voices to be heard and that there is a demand, if some foreign editors would give the service a chance as opposed to just calling up the computer and looking at Reuter's or some other option.

At first Joe Thloloe, editor of the *Sowetan*, worried about feeling disillusioned about the discussion and the debate. He had become tired of "the people from the developing countries bashing the Western media and the people in the Western media seeing us moaning again." He feared the conference was just another waste of time – a gathering of people who had arrived with pre-conceived ideas. But he changed his mind. And he credits people like Rex Nettleford, Kuldip Nayar and Abby Tan for making him realize that there had been a breaking of the old mold.

> When a story from India crosses my desk today, I will not look at it the same way as I looked at it before I came to this conference, simply because I met Kuldip and I spoke to Kuldip. Or when a story from the Philippines comes through, I will remember Abby Tan and I will look at it with a different pair of glasses. It's a slow process of creating new perceptions, but for me I think it has been a tremendous achievement.

Notes

[1]Václav Havel, "The Post-Communist Nightmare," *The New York Review of Books*, May 27, 1993, page 8.

[2]John Stackhouse, "Africa the cruel continent," *Globe and Mail*, May 15, 1993

[3]As quoted in Ibid.

[4]See for example Linda Hossie, "Plan to keep world order threatens sovereignty," *Globe and Mail*, May 25, 1993.

[5]What follows is a summary of the last day's session of the conference marvelously distilled by that session's Chair, Clyde Sanger, long time journalist and currently, Director of Communications for the North-South Institute. We are indebted to Mr. Sanger for the masterful direction his comments at this session gave.

[6]For a recent discussion of this problem, see John Stackhouse, "Growth of poverty alarming, UN states," *Globe and Mail*, May 18, 1993. This *United Nations 1993 Human Development Report* makes special mention of the United States. "... If the United States were divided into three countries based on race, the white population would rank No.1 ahead of Japan, while black Americans would fall to 31st spot alongside Trinidad and Tobago. Hispanics in the United States would rank 35th, below the Bahamas, South Korea and Estonia." Canadians, whether journalists or ordinary citizens, should not feel smug about poverty in the U.S. Indeed another UN committee has taken the Canadian government to task "... for allowing poverty and homelessness to persist at disturbing levels in one of the world's richest countries." See Geoffrey York, "UN body chastizes Canada on poverty – Lack of progress appalling, report says," *Globe and Mail*, May 29, 1993. It is probably true to state that Canadian mainstream journalism is more diligent reporting on famines in Africa than on food banks in Canada.

2

The Changed World

Derek Ingram
Editor, Gemini News Service

A Challenge to the Media

> The media in the West should not allow itself to be news managed by those who want a single order and a single focus that may all too easily be leading to a new form of colonialism.

When Gemini News Service was founded in 1967, Lester Pearson was in his last year of office as Prime Minister of Canada. Harold Wilson was in 10 Downing Street. Menzies had only recently ceased to be Prime Minister of Australia and Lyndon Johnson was in the White House. De Gaulle was in Paris, Mao was in Peking, Tito in Belgrade, and in the Soviet Union, Brezhnev was at the start of his long, dreary reign.

These were the years of the Beatles and the Vietnam War, the so-called "swinging sixties." For a second decade, the world was living on the edge of nuclear war. Man had not yet walked on the moon. No one talked about the environment. Newspapers were still being produced with hot metal as they had been for the best part of the century.

In many parts of Africa and Asia, the Western journalist struggled for hours, even days, to get through on the telex or to dictate his copy on a crackly, echoing line. The magic of fax and laptop was to be read about only in science fiction. Although the world was politically polarized and frozen by the Cold War, in 1967, however, we were in a decade of huge change. It was a decade when decolonization reached its climax. India, Indonesia, Malaysia had come earlier, but in the early 1960s almost all Africa had become independent and so had other places like Jamaica and Trinidad and Cyprus. Terms such as "non-alignment," "Third World," "New World Economic Order," were to be followed by "New World Information and Communication Order." All those groups – the Group of 77 (which I think is now 129 at last count), and the Group of 7, and now the Group of 15, were followed by the formation of all those regional bodies – whose acronyms made new words ASEAN[1], CARICOM[2], SADCC[3], and ECOWAS.[4]

In all this ferment of change, the fact of the conflict between East and West dictated the course of most political events and dictated the way they were reported. The independent struggles and the characters of the people who led them were handled cynically by the two superpowers and their allies as part of a relentless ideological war.

Journalists of every nationality were very much part of this conflict, used, as they so often are used (as they were in the Gulf War), without their realizing it.

The Cold War ended symbolically with the pulling down of the Berlin Wall in 1989, but I suppose historically with the end of the communist party. After the coup in Moscow little more than a year ago, the world was turned on its head.

Have we as journalists begun to grasp the implications? I doubt that we have. And that is the question we shall try to address in the next two days because almost every working journalist today – even those just beginning their careers – have been brought up, educated, and worked in a Cold War environment and all that that implies. That meant, for example, that the world was always divided into goodies and baddies whose roles were reversed according to which pair of glasses your country was looking through. Whether it was about Julius Nyerere or Fidel Castro or Gamal Nasser or Mobutu Sees Seko or Samora Machel, each of us had picked up the appropriate conventional wisdom, whether we were Tanzanian or Indian or British, from our earliest days. There's nothing unusual in this.

Indeed, it was inevitable because we are the products of our environment. We can try to look through other people's eyes, but we'll never really be fully able to achieve that. That was part of the philosophy underlying Gemini from the outset – there was more validity in the reporting of events in India by an Indian than there was by an American journalist doing so, and more validity in the reporting of events in the United States by an American journalist than there was by an Indian. Both outsiders would, however, have plenty of interesting and important things to say and, of course, must go on saying them. Because of the power of the journalists from the richer countries, the facilities available, the wider education, the ability to travel, it was the Western pair of glasses which was usually worn.

It was difficult in those days to find political or economic reporting from the so-called Third World that was not affected by the Cold War. Domestic policies on educational health, nationalization, or the negotiation of an overseas commercial deal – all would be seen in the light of the tilt of a country's leadership towards the Soviet Union or the West, or indeed Communist China. I never liked much the talk of "balanced" news coverage, so fashionable during the years of the UNESCO debates, because human beings are not balanced and it would be a very dull world, indeed, if we were. But a more conscious effort on the part of all of us who look through the window, and not merely at ourselves, is possible.

And in this post Cold War world, we have a much better opportunity to do this in relation to our reporting of the developing world. We need to become more aware of the general perceptions that come through in the Western press about the developing countries and to counter them.

The judgments are still almost automatic that the Third World is incompetent in handling its affairs, invariably corrupt, prone to violence, and somehow we go on believing that everything and everybody is more decent in the industrialized countries. Although Western incompetence is all around us, it's different; the corruption is there but that's all right unless it comes to light. The human rights abuses are there, but they're not on the same scale.

Yet, corruption on a huge scale regularly comes to light in the U.S., Britain, in Italy, and elsewhere at the highest level, as well as at local government level in the field of property, in business transactions, and so forth. Human rights abuses are to be found in Ireland, in the United States, in Australia, and the violence in Europe while we sit here is as bad as anything ever seen in the developing world. Less than 50 years ago, we sometimes care to forget, the whole of Europe was awash with blood.

Much of the Western press is happy to focus on what the South African government has cleverly labelled, "black on black" violence. But when did anyone ever mention "white on white" violence in Europe?

In the days of the Cold War, the massive corruption of the Mobutu government and the lack of human rights in Zaire was acceptable because Mobutu was anti-Soviet. Once Said Barre had switched from the Soviet Union to the Western side in Somalia, he was a goody, regardless of his human rights record. The fact that to his own ends he was fueling the clan conflict that was to lead to the destruction of the whole people was by the way. In the end, the whole disaster would be seen as just blacks fighting each other again – more corruption and incompetence. The fact that the superpowers had loaded the entire country with massive amounts of weaponry was passed over.

One lesson of the Cold War is surely that the Western press – and not just the Third World press – was all too often taken for a ride. The general impression created by our journalism was that although the Soviet Union was up to every kind of dirty trick in the book, the West was different.

When a senior Bulgarian in exile in London was pricked in the street by a poisoned umbrella spike and died, there was general horror that such a diabolical act should be perpetrated by the Communists. But we all know now, if we did not then, that just such assassinations were plotted and carried out by the CIA, by MI6 and other Western intelligence agencies. The myth, however, was maintained by our media that we in the West did not behave like the other side.

I know it's argued, and perhaps I might agree, that this was, in fact, a war situation, albeit not a hot war, for most of the 40 years. The argument can be made that the end justified the means. The West won.

But now we're out of that and into a situation that, in many ways, is far more complex. The glue of the Cold War has gone and old rivalries that date back before World War I have come back (not before World War II, but before World War I!). We're told that there is a New World Order, but nobody knows what that is. And in reality, it seems to mean what the wits have already dubbed as the "New World Disorder."

We now have a unipolar world with one ideology – capitalism, instead of two. Even China is moving in its own quite different way in the same direction. Management of the media with the use of buzz words like "market forces," "good government," and "human rights" is under way. Just as in the past, developing countries were being told there were only two approaches – communism or capitalism. Now we're all being told there is only capitalism. Everyone must conform.

The new order is now to be within the parameters set by only one superpower and its allies, even though such concepts as good government and human rights vary from society to society. People do have other ideas out there in the Third World and they make up more than half the world's population.

The danger now is that their voice is going to be heard even less than before and that the voice of the triumphant West will be increasingly dominant. The United Nations stands in grave danger of being hijacked by the developed world because of sheer economic might, even in its time of recession.

When the horror of Somalia was reported by some outstanding journalists, attention finally switched there, but Yugoslavia was far more important because of its wider political implications for peace in Europe. Turmoil in the horn of Africa threatened nobody except the lives of the people living there.

The danger that reporting from the West and our selection of news will become even more one-sided than much of it has been in the past seems, to me, to be very real. The end of the Cold War has opened up the opportunity for us to look at everything afresh. What has happened so far is not very encouraging.

The Western press has largely lost interest in the developing world and its problems. When President Kaunda was thrown out of power in Zambia, it was a good story for 24 hours because he had been a famous name in the headlines for 27 years. But how the new government has been shaping up, what its new policies are, who are the new personalities – no one is bothering to report. Yet, once upon a time, I remember when the Soviet ambassador in Lusaka was the key figure in directing the Soviet Cold War effort in Southern Africa, and a guerrilla war was being waged across the Zambezi, Zambia was of intense interest in the West, and every twist and turn of its policy was reported. Today, it's becoming as much a backwater as it had been in the days when it was a sleepy British colony called Northern Rhodesia. The struggles in Namibia and Angola promoted by the Cold War protagonists kept those countries constantly in the news. Today Namibia is independent and peaceful and an African success story, but very rarely reported.

Now, of course, as one who sat at the sharp end of Fleet Street newspaper editorial direction for quite a few years, I understand as well as all the journalists here today why this is so. The hard news is where the action is. This will always be the case. In the last two or three years, the action has been in Moscow, Berlin, and Belgrade. It's been in the Gulf. Not since 1945 has there been such a series of historical events. And there's much more to come, of course.

Yet we have seen how, especially in relation to the environment, the world is being increasingly forced to move towards Marshall McLuhan's global village. People are mixing up at an extraordinary rate. Their needs and aspirations are ours, too. We must understand them better and we must help our readers and listeners to understand them better.

A few weeks ago (September, 1992), the Non-aligned Movement held in Indonesia the first summit since the Cold War ended. I don't know how much coverage the event received in Canada, but in Britain it was almost nothing. The Western media has decided that this grouping of 108 countries – two-thirds of the world – is no longer of any importance. They never did think much of it, of course, preferring to see it as a group of rickety countries that always seemed to be anti-Western and pro-Communist, happy to turn a blind eye to the fact that as well as containing Castro and Khadaffy, it also had as members pro-Western, capitalist countries like Indonesia and Malaysia.

The historical verdict on the Non-aligned Movement, I suspect, is likely to prove more positive. For all its imperfections, it will be seen as having played a most important role in keeping the Cold War from becoming hot and this movement will act as a buffer between the superpowers.

Be that as it may, today the movement is generally seen as having no raison d'être and indeed the main theme in Jakarta was the identification of a new role. The verdict was that it has a very important role in the future as the voice of the so-called South, the voice of the underprivileged.

The prime minister of Malaysia, Mahathir Mohamad, made a striking speech in Jackstraw, which again, so far as I can see, was totally unreported in the West. In it, he pointed out that for the developing world, a unipolar world was every bit as threatening as a bipolar world. Without the option to defect to the other side, he said, developing countries could expect less wooing and more threats. The developing countries would therefore have to protect themselves.

A New World Order could not be determined by the few and forced on the many. What worked in one country or region might not work in another. He called for change in the composition of the U.N. Security Council – more permanent members with veto rights.

This issue is surely going to be one of the big diplomatic stories of the coming years. The British Foreign and Commonwealth Secretary, in a most significant speech the other day, said the U.N. should take on an "imperial role" (and *he* put it in quotes), in usurping national sovereignty and taking over as controlling power when governments collapse. If the U.N. is not reformed, however, one can see what Mahathir meant when he warned in his Jakarta speech against the revival of the old Western colonialism, and Washington and London are very reluctant to talk about Security Council reform.

So the disappearance of the Non-aligned Movement – which might now be well advised to change its name – would be disastrous, because not only, in most cases, are the poor of the world poorer, their voice is also weaker than it was in the 1960s and 1970s. The materialist reigns of Reagan and Thatcher saw to that. Since the 1981 meeting in Cancun, Mexico, there has been no real dialogue between the rich and the poor. The talk of a new world economic order was effectively squashed.

Now the talk is only of a new world order. It has always, of course, been simplistic to talk of rich and poor, but as journalists, we have to talk in shorthand in headlines and news labels. Some countries, mainly in Southeast Asia, are no longer poor and others are not as well off as they were. But the great divide between Fanon's *Wretched of the Earth* and those living in the suburbs of Sydney or London or Vancouver is as great as it ever was. And the progress in closing that divide that has been made in the last century in the countries of Europe and North America has to be replicated elsewhere.

It will not happen unless the poorer countries have a platform to ensure that they are not fobbed off with a single form of medicine for all their ills prescribed by a single power and its allies. The Non-aligned Movement can provide such a platform. The Commonwealth – and few of you here this morning would expect me not to mention the Commonwealth – could be crucially important in helping a new rich/poor dialogue because its membership covers the entire economic spectrum. Currently, it seems to me, Britain and Canada, among others, are choosing to ignore its value. A Ghanaian diplomat in London said to me the other day, "You don't seem to realize that now that the U.N. is being run by the U.S., the Commonwealth is all we've got left."

The media in the West should not allow itself to be news-managed by those who want a single order and a single focus that may all too easily be leading to a new form of colonialism. What the developing countries are saying, what is coming from outspoken leaders like Mahathir Mohamad from Malaysia, unpalatable as it might be to Western ears, needs to be reported and it is not.

Some will say that lack of coverage of events like the Non-aligned summit is in some respects due to economic constraints and the recession and the inability to send journalists into these distant and often expensive areas. This is an excuse. Local correspondents could be found to do all these things in fact, as I have long pointed out, should be used more anyway. Massive advances in cheap communications makes reporting so much easier.

There has to be a will and an interest. Many will say our readers and listeners are just not interested in these faraway places. I just don't believe this to be true. In my experience, many editors have usually underestimated their public.

The hugely competitive medium of television seems to me, to do rather better than print. In Britain, the best in depth international reporting is, most of the time, not in the newspapers but on television and radio. Television documentaries on overseas affairs are many and the high ratings indicate large followings.

The big danger in this post-Cold War world is that we're beginning to narrow our focus instead of widening it. In these next two days, I hope we can consider how this can be avoided and how we can not just change the glasses we've been wearing for the last 40 years, but make sure that the new pair has lenses with a wider angle.

(DEREK INGRAM is founder of Gemini News Service in London, England).

Information and the New World Order

Kuldip Nayar
Columnist and former Editor, United News India

The end of war, whether hot or cold, does not usher in a new order. It leaves only victors and the vanquished. The order that emerges is that of the victor.

The hot war of the 1940s witnessed the allies winning – the West and the Soviet Union. Only the West won the Cold War of the 1980s. The order from the 1950s to the 1980s was that of the West in certain parts of the world, and of the Soviet Union in some others. These orders clashed more in the realm of ideas than on one ground. These ideas influenced us, the Third World countries, the most because we were emerging from a long tunnel of slavery into the sunshine of freedom and opportunity.

How do we develop? Through the ballot box keeping the society open? Or through an authoritarian system – by removing the right to vote? These orders seemed to have different policies, but their methods were the same. They used money, power, deceit, espionage, and ambitious local rulers to have their say or influence. We slaves of yesterday were suspicious of both. We wanted to develop in our own way, to be left alone. We had problems that our rulers had left behind

– the problems of poverty and underdevelopment – the problems of backwardness. . . .

The West and the Communists were trying to get us in their orbit – military camps, barracks. In a way, it was a democratic world versus the communist world, but in real terms it was the capitalist society versus the communist society. We talked about egalitarianism; we were told that the development, if conducted in a particular way, would lead us to something which the other parts of the world had enjoyed. But we found from our experience that it was another kind of imperialism. Imperialism of the West, imperialism of the East. They wanted us to be pawns in their games. So, we were important because both sought us while expanding their area of operation. That was the time when Nehru, Sukarno, Nasser, Tito – got together and created what is called the Non-aligned Movement. This movement did have a positive influence on the side of peace, but we got together not only to save peace; we wanted to be left alone. Because we wanted to save our own heritage, our own culture, our own way of living, and even our own way of government.

The information order which was unveiled at UNESCO was not ideal, but it did favor a fairer coverage. We were all the time seeing through the West and were also governed by the Western media, Western correspondents. Their angle, though at times independent I must admit, was most of the time slanted, biased by preconceived notions. I remember I headed this United News of India (UNI), a news agency. We used to buy Associate Press (AP). We detected (we did a lot of studies) that seventy percent was propaganda. Not mere information on the West – I could understand that they were feeding the entire world and since most subscribers are affluent, they would naturally cover those things. But it was mere propaganda of America, of the American government.

Now that the hot war and the Cold War are over, you find a "New Order." I am, as a journalist, very allergic to the words "order," and "discipline," because these are all methods of controlling information. But let us presume there is something called, "New Order." In that order where is the East? Where are we people? We have tried our own Non-aligned News Pool, which I must admit was a cesspool because its members were mostly from countries ruled by dictators: military dictators or other dictators. So whatever was filtering through was dictated; it was not news. I recall that first in the UNI and then when I was at the *Statesman* as its editor in Delhi, then at the *Indian Express* as editor , we found that this Nonaligned pool was part of the Indian Foreign Office. So we failed there.

Now, another attempt is being made. All of the countries of SAARC – the South Asian Association for Regional Cooperation – have a news service which means that the news services of this area will combine and then we shall be disseminating information. Maybe that will work – I don't know. The countries are Bangladesh, Pakistan, India, Nepal, Sri Lanka and Bhutan. In some of these, even though they have a democratic system, the military is looking over their shoulders. My feeling is that in Third World countries where the military has come once, it has not gone back. It may have gone back to barracks, but it doesn't really go back. So we have a problem there. I don't know how this SAARC will work, but we are hoping that it will.

What happened at UNESCO? In talking of a new information order, we did not visualize that one day there would be a revolution as far as technology is concerned. We thought that we would like to save our culture, the way we live, the way we want to be. But we now realize that the skies do not belong to us, the air doesn't belong to us, and now what you have is CNN, and the BBC.

We would like to save our own things. CNN is a 24 hour service, a very good news service, a very good analysis, maybe as good as the BBC. But where do we come in? What I find in my country – and it must be happening to other developing countries – is that we have a system in which our culture, our own music, is being pushed to the background because people want to watch Hollywood movies and want to listen to Western music.

When we do not even have resources to feed our people, how do we save our culture? That's a very big question with us because, as I said, the satellites are all over. And the news agencies of the West still have the upper hand. They haven't improved in any way in the sense that they are not reporting us the way they should. In fact, we are the poor who should not be mentioned.

In the earlier order, when the Soviet Union was on the scene, maybe you can say that we played one against the other. But at least we had some say. Now we don't have any say because now the West has won. We don't have any balancing force – at least as far as I can see. Maybe some day there will be a dollar world, a yen world, a mark world or European currency world whatever it may be. But, in that world, how much will we count? Where will we come into the picture? I don't know.

But as far as our culture is concerned, we have the same problem within our own country as within all Third World countries. We have developed areas, we have underdeveloped areas. Though the Soviet Union or the Soviet Bloc is gone once and for all, there are some people who predict that someday the hard core in the Soviet Union is going to come back. I don't see that happening. But what I do see happening in this world is that if the kind of gap which prevails today continues – poor-rich and North-South – I'm more worried about the well-being of my people, and the well being of people living in the Third World countries.

I am more worried about how we can save what heritage we still have. You know, Mahatma Gandhi, father of our nation, was against the machine, not because he was against innovation, but because he was against the dehumanization of man. Nehru once said, "Even if India has developed, India has all the industries, the laboratories, the factories, but if in the process India has lost its soul, that achievement is not worth having." How do we help retain our value system? That is the big challenge before us – not only in India, but in Pakistan, Bangladesh, our whole Third World. I have a feeling that just as many thousands of years ago as it is written in the Bible, that the wise men came from the East, some day those people are going to come again from the East to save the soul of the West.

But in our country, which is also a subcontinent, we are facing similar problems as some of those Canada is facing – some states are pulling apart. We are still backward, uneducated, but still we have something good: we believe very strongly in the unity of the country.

Another problem before us is, and this I encountered when I was High Commissioner in London, Albert Victoria Museum has in its basement at least ninety percent of valuable relics of India, art pieces which, the museum director said, cannot be displayed even in the next hundred years because they have no money. They don't have the gallery space, so they will stay there. I tried my best during my short stay in England to see if we could receive some assistance so we could display our own heritage to our people in India.

But, I drew a blank – nothing doing. Britain, when it ruled lots of countries, acquired a lots of things. As the director put it, "We have purchased them." They had purchased them at that time before independence, when no one knew what "purchased" meant.

So can it be possible to get certain things back because this is our heritage? In the India library there, there are lots of manuscripts, there is much original material belonging to India. These kinds of things, we will never get again. I couldn't even get them in photostat copies because they said you will have to pay for it. The material stretches for 20 miles, so it is not possible. We can't even afford that much money. Maybe some day we will.

The point I'm trying to make is that information is, in its general sense, linked with this same kind of thing. I don't know whether we can reverse the process – the process that has the West in a superior position, where the West dominates information. The West dominates the media. Accepting that there is no going back, however much we may plead with our old masters, what can be done? That is the challenge before us.

I have no suggestion to make, but maybe we can regionally do something like Gemini News Service does globally, drawing on media people from different parts of the area. Can we do that?

The weaker countries are distant from each other. We in India know very little about Africa. We criticize the West because it doesn't give any coverage to us. But I find in India that's the same way for Africa. Maybe they'll cover some uprising or some famine. They will make news just like in the West in a similar way. Is it a question of attitude?

Now that I have retired more or less, and I'm on the other side of my life, I'm finding out that we journalists have many prejudices built-in. Don't we think that this is news? That this is what will sell? What the totalitarian countries do – selling only what they call the "positive side of the news" – is probably not correct. But we the journalists, we the media, can we not think somewhat differently and think of the people as ultimately one. It is a small world. Communication has brought it very close.

Can this world, instead of being divided into East or West, North or South, can something be worked out for the people? It is important that we tread a path which is moral in the general sense; which is noble, which is Christian, which belongs to what the forefathers of the West believed in. Because, after all, you in the West worked very hard. From the wilderness you have created something which is enviable. We come to the West because we praise it, we admire it. We may envy you, but that is another story. That envy is a good quality, it's not a bad quality. Jealousy is a bad quality.

Somebody told me yesterday, "The people here say, 'To hell with the Third World countries, why should we help them?'" and "This is an unending kind of poverty, unending kind of underdevelopment." But it's only a question of time. We are more than half the world already in numbers. The poor man refuses to be poor now – he's articulate – he tries to burn things – he tries to undo things through violence and anger. Is it possible, some day, that we might say that "We are poor because you made us poor? You exploited us. We were your colonies."

I've never forgotten this little story. When I went to London, I took along a servant. Early during our stay, I asked him, "So, how does London look to you?" He said, "The whole city they have built by looting us." This was an ordinary man, and he said, "The one thing, one thing we must do, when we return, we must take back the Kohinoor diamond." It is in the Tower of London. I must give credit to the man who showed it to me. He said, "I am very apologetic in showing it to you; after all, it's yours." But anyway, you can see, I was very much struck by his remark.

The point I am trying to make, ladies and gentlemen, is that it is time the West did some introspection, that yes, we are backward, we are poor, maybe we deserve our own ills, because of our own deficiencies, but we have been slaves for years. India was enslaved for 150 years. And there are lots of problems with us today. We may not hate the people – we don't hate people – but those are things that are very much there.

And also, please do not sell your outmoded weapons to us. You can blame us, "Why are you fighting among yourselves?" Yes, it's a tragedy. It's a tragedy that since partition, India and Pakistan have not been able to settle into some kind of friendly relationship. It's a tragedy that we have gone to war three times. It's a tragedy that the borders are still not open and that we still allow a Pakistani into our country to visit only three cities, and they do the same to us. A white man can come, any other man come from outside, and can go all over the country. But when it comes to a Pakistani or Indian, they are confined to only three cities.

What that information order is going to be – that is a challenge for us journalists sitting here. This cannot be an order where we would be destroying our own culture. This would not be an order where you would try to westernize us. This will be an order where we will live in our own way – open, democratic, secular, yes. But, if we want to differ from you, that's all right. Do not try to say that everything in the West is good whether it is the media, whether it is a policy. Maybe we're are not good in English – we don't know much English. Maybe in my country only five percent of people speak English. But that doesn't mean that the people who are expressing themselves in their own language are in any way inferior.

Some of the best literature in the world is in our languages. So can we get out a journal for this great literature in several languages? Can we put out a journal once a year where we read the best literature, the best news stories, the best features? Maybe in a different language? Maybe in Bengali, Punjabi, Urdu, Hindi, or some other language – whatever it may be – from Africa and others, but the best of it?

The point I started making and I am ending with is, it is up to you. Even though the Cold War is over (the hot war was over some years back), it seems to us that a new order, the order of the West's making, the order made by those who ruled us, is being introduced into our parts of the world. Maybe some rulers will help you, because those rulers are there because of the barrel not the ballot. And you have seen in the past how many reactionary rulers disappeared without a trace. Those who rule their people through military power, through the weapons supplied by the West, will also be destroyed by the people. In the same way, we will reject the information order which is imposed on us.

(KULDIP NAYAR was a founding contributor to Gemini News Service. He is one of the most widely read and wellknown journalists in India. He was editor of the United News of India, held many top editorial posts and has written many provocative books. He was incarcerated during the emergency when Mrs. Indira Gandhi was prime minister. He was also a diplomat and was Indian High Commissioner in London.

Open Discussion

Daniel Nelson (former Gemini Associate Editor):

Before we get into the fact that people don't want to read about the Third World, or there's no money, or there are dictatorships and journalists can't go there, I have come to believe over the years that the key reason for all of this is news management. And I think Western journalists don't realize how supine they've become in the way that they get briefings from their own governments and have accepted an ideology – they're very proud, in a sense, to be cynical. Their cynicism is now about the media and not very often about their own governments. They've taken on an ideology. I don't think they realize how much they are controlled. People have just picked up things without thinking about their origins.

Someone said at the beginning, "The world is a common property resource to all of us." The South doesn't feel like that. Journalists ought to know that. The very word "global," "common heritage of mankind," that's what the real battle is over when people say the "common heritage of mankind." To most people in developing countries, that means people in industrialized countries getting a hand on their resources. It's a rather spurious internationalism. We all use the language, and have forgotten to question what it means. I think, similarly, "freedom" came up a couple of times. "Freedom" is such a loaded term. It's like "free trade." Free trade, to me, is just whoever is top dog gets the benefit. "Fair trade," possibly. But I think journalists in the North have lost a lot of ability to question some of these concepts. In a country like Uganda, very often the journalists are very much more aware of the ideology that their own government is pushing on them and resist it better than we in the West do now.

If the world is heading for industrialization, and that is the unstated aim of international development, although no one quite says it, that's really what everybody seems to want. You're going to take on a value system. And I think that unless that is really brought into the open and people say, "Do we want it, and under what terms?" then what passes for international development is totally destructive. I've come, myself, to hate the whole concept of development, aid, and internationalism as it's used because of this. It is a loaded value system. It has to be, I think, differentiated.

Joe Thloloe (*The Sowetan*, Johannesburg) :

Aren't we making an assumption about the victory of the Western system over the Eastern system? Is it possible that this integration of the present order started in the East and is, in fact, spreading to the West? That the present recession might just be a symptom of a much deeper disease than we are looking at? Is it possible? Are we looking at this when we look at the disintegration of the Eastern bloc?

Kuldip Nayar:

If you are thinking that this Eastern world, or what was the Soviet Union once, will have any power to come back the way it did – while disintegrating itself, it would disintegrate our Western world – no, I don't agree with you there. I think that whatever was the Soviet Union is finished forever. I wish I could be proved wrong because at least there would be a balancing factor.

Derek Ingram:

It's quite ironic that at a time when the West has apparently won the Cold War, in fact, capitalism has never been in so much confusion as in the last three or four years, and it's getting worse.

Kuldip Nayar:

Even the disintegration of the West doesn't mean that the other power will ever get revived or have the same kind of power. It is possible that the world may get divided in some other blocs. But I don't see the ruble coming up again in that sense.

Mohamad Hamaludin (originally from Guyana, now editor, *Miami Times*):

My question is, isn't there a possibility we will have an acceleration of the exploitation of the resources of the Third World, rather than a diminution? If that is so, then how do you respond to it?

Kuldip Nayar:

I fully agree with you that maybe some other kind of imperialism will creep in. It is possible. How do we check it? I don't think we're in a position to check the Third World countries because we will be needing resources, and resources are very limited. We may go even to the extent of harming each other to get the resources.

Mohamad Hamaludin:

But isn't this the time, when the other system is also weak, for the Third World to come together and become stronger?

Kuldip Nayar:

I think that if the rulers in the Third World countries could at least end their mutual kind of hostility – they are hating each other and spending a lot of money in arming themselves – if we could really do something about that, maybe we should see some light at the end of the tunnel.

Derek Ingram:

It seems to me that the Non-aligned Movement does have an enormous opportunity to recast itself now and rename itself, which is good, but I'm not very confident. There's an incredible lack of leadership, at the moment, in the world. Most of the Western leaders are on their last legs. And there are no outstanding figures in the Third World either, at the moment, or very few. Not of the Tito-Nehru calibre. They don't seem to be there. They'll obviously come up again, but they're not there at the moment.

Wafula Oguttu (Editor, *The Monitor*, Uganda):

People are waking up politically and they are saying what they want to say without being labelled "pro-Soviet," "pro-Chinese," pro-whatever" etc. And I think the world is going to be different. I'd like to ask Mr. Nayar: you say that there will never be a system like the old Soviet Union – communism or socialism. How sure are you? Because at the same time in your speech, you have said that we are exploited, we are oppressed, we are asking the West to be understanding in morality, or understanding of capitalism becoming reformed. I appreciate the part that communism had a lot of influence over capitalism. And they married somewhere in the social and welfare society. Can this be spread over so that the South benefits from the welfare system of the North?

Kuldip Nayar:

Now, when I said never, I meant the Soviet Union as such. I didn't mean that some kind of ideology against exploitation or against capitalism wouldn't come up. I'm sure that if the exploitation continues and the backwardness and the poverty continues in that area, some other kind of ideology which will be asking for equalitarianism or something like that, would come up. But that will not be Soviet sponsored.

Wafula Oguttu:

My second question is: Usually when I talk with journalists or people from the North (Europe or America), I find that they are annoyingly ignorant of us in the South. They don't seem to appreciate how we live, what we like, as Mr. Nayar was saying. You find that a journalist from the *Globe and Mail* comes to Uganda with a lot of fixed ideas. We people who are supposed to cultivate and make the world understand, how can we solve the problem of their ignorance so that we can be informed informers?

Norman Webster (*Montreal Gazette*):

We certainly do bring our own prejudices and upbringing with us. I think you would find a surprising amount of willingness to see the real picture; to be fair to the people of countries, if not necessarily the governments of those countries who are doing some of the things which are, in fact, oppressing the people. Often the negative reports which appear in the Western press are of really rather nasty things being done to people in the Third World, and not necessarily trashing and spitting on the cultures and the aspirations of those people.

What is being done and what might be done in a sensible, straightforward way for the developing world to inform itself about its other members? Because, again although I don't entirely agree with some of the criticisms of Western agencies, the fact is that they are there to inform Western countries about the rest of the world; they're not there to inform the rest of the world about itself. In a genuine search for information, I ask, what is being done and what might be done in a practical, straightforward, and indeed, fairly inexpensive way similar to Gemini News Service?

Kuldip Nayar:

I think I mentioned a small experiment. I have initiated the idea with several of our countries with news agencies. So what I am trying to do is constitute a desk in Colombo to which people will be drawn from all over these seven countries. Expenses will be small because only those people have to be paid. They pick up the agency copy, rewrite or redraft it, and send it back to the same network. Maybe we could do the same kind of thing in other parts of Asia or other regions.

The only problem is that in quite a few countries, information is not free in the sense that you are thinking. If a news agency is not independent, then what we will get will be something slanted. That is the reason I thought if we could start with where democracy has more or less taken roots, let's do it that way. Bangladesh, Pakistan, Nepal – these were all countries which were under one kind of totalitarianism or other. Now they are relatively free. We can start with that. I thought that this way, if we can develop a news service which has credibility, then the West will be bound by it.

Anjum Niaz (*Daily Dawn*, Pakistan):

You mentioned that Indians strongly believe in the unity of the country, but at the moment, there is a resurgence going on in Kashmir, and they are asking for independence and Pakistan is, of course, supporting that. So my question is, why don't we set things right in our own house first, and why don't we as the journalists or the media in the subcontinent try to get to know each other better?

My second point is about the SAARC media news agency. Again for something like this, to really be practical or to really take off or become a reality, I feel that we have to settle our own differences. And the seven countries in the SAARC region are still not – well, we still do have our differences. And for instance, to give you an example of the Kohinoor Diamond which you mentioned, Mr. Nayar, we in Pakistan claim it to be ours! We think that it belongs to us, and not to India! So we have to resolve this between ourselves first, before we get on.

Kuldip Nayar:

I think that in my speech I said that we should be sorting out our affairs. And, I said I think it's a pity. And, as far as the Kohinoor Diamond is concerned, let it come to the subcontinent, and you can take it. But it should move from London, that's all. It should be nearer to us. That's the point I was trying to make.

Ngozi Anyaegbunam (*Daily Times*, Nigeria):

We all have agreed the world is getting smaller and smaller by the advantage of communication – by the advantage of industrialized communication. You can sit here in Canada and punch some buttons and a radio is sending messages to Nigeria. But we are becoming kind of laid back. We are relaxing. We are giving up our responsibilities as human beings who should be in control of the world and handing over all responsibilities to the buttons we are punching.

So, if we are talking about knowing about one another in the world, if we are talking about living together in one small global village, we have to think about educating ourselves, about knowing a lot more. A journalist should be more educated than before because the world is getting smaller and smaller. In Nigeria, for instance, what about books? We don't have books there. We sit there and watch CNN. Whatever we get from there is what we use. And, of course, we know that that's not the authentic version.

I would also like to talk about the question of dictatorship in the world today. I am coming from a country where the ruler, the President, is in uniform. We are hoping, very soon, to transcend into a democratically elected government, but that is not enough. Because in a world where people do not control their lives, they are still being dictated somehow. We know that today America is ruling the whole world, telling us how to live our lives. And, as far as I'm concerned, that is dictatorship in an ironical way. They are telling us how to live our lives in the same way they are telling their journalists what to say about us.

But we shouldn't stop at the Western journalists. Even we in the Third World are told what to say. And what we are told to say is not necessarily from our leaders. It still comes back from America, because America runs most of the things that we do. And, therefore, they tell our leaders what to do. The IMF (International Monetary Fund), for instance, the World Bank, they sit down and tell you that since they are giving you so much, you have to do this, you have to do that. And so the journalist has no choice but to say what his government has asked him to say, unless he has some kind of independent funding somewhere. In other words, if he has been trained and he is free-lancing, for instance, with a body or institution like Gemini News, in that case, the journalist can sit down and think for himself.

In fact, even if you are supposed to be independent, in my own country, (we have a lot of newspapers owned by individuals), from time to time, the government comes in and closes these institutions down. This is simply a case of governments that are desperate to dance to the tune of their masters somewhere. So most of the Third World countries are controlled, tele-guided, by some form of remote control. All I'm saying is that we are in a situation where somebody is somewhere pulling all the strings, and we have to think about that.

Kuldip:

I am always saying, "Let's have a system where people are the masters."

Clyde Sanger (North-South Institute, Ottawa):

I was in Africa for eight years, and it was a subject that haunted me in a way, because I was an outsider during that time. But I could accumulate knowledge of a country – of Uganda, or of Zimbabwe. One did rely on a sort of pyramid of stringers in each country. Nathan Shamayarira, for instance, was our stringer in Zimbabwe, and you couldn't have gotten more into the nationalist movement in the 1960s than that. Norman Webster, when he was the editor of the *Globe and Mail*, was responsible for about twelve foreign bureaus. And that did, indeed, bring back to Canadians, at least, a better view of Africa, Asia, Latin America than we had had before. The problem is that people do not stay long enough.

The other point I want to make is really about world view. We've talked about capitalism and communism and the two societies and whether the disintegration in the East is coming toward the West. I see it in a way in these huge trading blocks. The European community is struggling a bit, and we here in North America have our doubts about the North American Free Trade Agreement. I would like it to be "fair trade" area. But Chile is on the point of application to this free trade area, NAFTA. It's going to be a vertical North-South arrangement.

Similarly, Europe has tied in the Lome Convention countries, and there is growing up in the Pacific – the Asia-Pacific Economic Cooperation Group, in which Japan is the leading member. I don't quite know what part China is going to play. This leaves a lot of people out. So, I'm not sure that we haven't got this vertical disintegration of the world like that. There's also a disintegration in the government departments in a country like Canada. The concentration in CIDA (Canadian International Development Agency) is on international development, whatever bad vibes that phrase may bring up with various people.

But we've heard about the whole question of the arms race. CIDA does not concern itself with peace issues. It doesn't give money to peace movements. You have to cloak your proposals to CIDA in terms of international development. I think we have to be far less compartmentalized and far more broad-minded in Canadian policy making if we're going to deal with the world we're facing in the 1990s and the next century.

Luis Tricot (Free-lancer, Chile):

I may agree that the Cold War as we know it is over, but I think we are experiencing perhaps the coldest war ever in the history of mankind, and that's the war of market forces against basic human rights – a world where profit is the only thing that matters, irrespective of how we may attain it – a world where economic freedom is far, far more important than human freedom.

Economic freedom, of course, means basically the freedom of the rich to get richer. In the process, men, women, human beings, do not really matter. I mean, by the end of this year, a million people will have died in Somalia, and who cares? If a country like Burkina Faso in Africa disappears, no one will really notice. If a country like Bolivia or Guatemala in South America disappears, nobody will notice. If a country like Bangladesh disappears, nobody will really care – because they're not important economically or politically.

As for this so-called "New World Order" which was announced by President Bush after the Gulf War – after the United States, with the help of the United Nations and in the name of peace, in my name and in your name actually, dropped 80 000 tonnes of bombs on Iraqi people – I think that's terrible.

You talk about the Third World, the need to unite, the importance of unity to face the United States or unipolar capitalism, the importance of unity to counterbalance the power of the three main blocks after the end of the Cold War, but the Third World is now fighting for its own survival – and that is the problem. And in so doing, countries like Chile are going to unite with the United States. Mexico has already applied for the NAFTA Agreement with Canada and the United States. So, the Third World is obviously divided.

But you talk about the Third World as being one single world – but most of the dominant classes in the governments, the rulers there, are trying to accommodate their economies and their political systems to this New World Order. So the problem is not whether these governments will try to fight against this new imperialism, but what about the people there? I mean I don't really think the Third World governments will actually do anything except to accept the new rules, so I don't expect anything from them, from the governments. Have you got any hope that the people of those countries will do anything first against their governments, and then against this New World Order?

Kuldip Nayar:

That is a realistic remark you make.

Allan Thompson (1991 Gemini Fellow, International Development Research Centre, Canada):

I think McLuhan's global village sort of came and went before we realized. I think we've moved now from the global village to the global suburb where, with all these wonderful means of communications that we have, we're quite smug in thinking that that brings us the world, and that we are this big global village where everyone knows everything that they need to know.

I'm sure if you did a content analysis, you would probably find half the attention span for Somalia's situation that there was for Ethiopia. And yet, we're talking about this global village and the wonderful means of communication that we have – we just don't use them. It's like we're taking computers and using them as typewriters. So, when you're talking about preserving heritage, promoting culture, all of that could be done, yet there we are sitting – there with the clicker watching CNN bringing us the same tripe day after day. And we think that because it's live and because it's coming to us immediately that somehow this is reality. We make sort of assumptions like yes, the West has won the Cold War. I mean, who's saying that the West won anything?

Patrick Nagle (Southam News, Canada):

I just want to plead with everybody to forget about the idea that there's some massive conspiracy to make all of this happen one way or the other – particularly in the media. It's just not possible to organize a conspiracy unless it's a conspiracy of incompetence and stupidity. The way things happen has more chaotic appearances than coordinated experiences. The fact that after the event you can draw a conclusion from it in no way means that the event was influenced prior to its happening. I get very upset when people attribute events to conspiracies, particularly within journalism.

Kuldip Nayar:

I don't know who used the term "conspiracy" but my point is that there does have to be some kind of maybe ignorance or guided information. Take, for example now, this Gulf War. Now we are getting to know lots of things which we did not know when we were covering it. If we had known at that time, maybe our reaction would have been different. Maybe certain things were saved from us by the Americans or whoever was responsible. So they did not tell us the full story at that time. So this is happening in every country. But we, the journalists seemed to lap up, at that time, what was told to us. And we seem to rationalize and justify it.

Patrick Nagle:

The notion that we can know things in advance of their happening is entirely foreign to my experience. As far as the Gulf is concerned, within days of the U.N. declaration, there was tons of information available about what was going to happen and what was intended to happen. There were immense amounts of really profound information available about how the coalition was forming and what the problems were with the makeup of the coalition. The event itself – the Gulf War lasted exactly four days.

Kuldip Nayar:

I'm talking about the operation. Those four days. We did not know how America destroyed, the amount of bombs they threw. We didn't know that type of thing.

Patrick Nagle:

Well, I'm afraid we did, sir. Anybody who'd read anything about Vietnam knew exactly what carpet bombing was. The question of the information being available is not the same as the information being used. The information was there. The fact that there were 400 000 U.S. military people in the Gulf is enough to inform any sensible person that there's a loud noise about to occur. And it did.

Two years previously, the United States was financing Saddam against the Ayatollah. The massive shift in the United States foreign policy, which was joined by the other major powers was all visible in front of us.

Derek Ingram:

We are talking about such things as the precision of the bombing which we were told about on the first day of the Gulf War and the second day. And everybody was led to think that buildings were being picked out and everything was one hundred percent accurate. We now know this was not at all the case. The impression went on for quite a while that there had been this incredible precision – and there was not that precision.

Bill Cunningham (University of Regina 1991-92 Max Bell Fellow and Canadian television journalist):

A conspiracy wasn't really what triggered the thing. But, once the shooting started, there was a tremendous conspiracy involved in suppressing the information.

William Saidi (editor, *Sunday Times*, Zimbabwe):

We had a debate in Zimbabwe recently about the virtues of ownership of the press by private citizens and by the government. The argument in favour of ownership of the press by the government went something like this: the people will be told what their government is doing for them. The people will be told what the opposition says it will do for them but cannot do because it has neither the resources nor the power to do so; neither has it got the popularity to even take over from the government. What the government tells the people is what is happening – the "truth" in other words.

The ownership of the press by private citizens was characterized from the government's side as based strictly on greed. Whoever owned the newspaper wanted to make money regardless of what the people were told.

The independent press put forward the argument that the morality of the government owning not just newspapers but television and radio was highly questionable When you consider that the government would like to remain in power for all time, and will use these media to perpetuate its rule. I know people could be locked up and have been locked up, or worse.

So, I think that as long as we believe that our own press, our own situation in Africa for instance, is satisfactory, with military dictatorships, and other dictatorships, we have a very, very narrow view of what constitutes freedom of the press. I think we should look at our situation first because the dictatorships that have sprung up in Africa have been helped by the absence of a critical press.

Jill Forrester (Former Gemini Scholar):

Kuldip Nayar made a point regarding the need for introspection in the West and how the East might one day save the whole of the West. I think we in the industrialized nations have to look at what we've lost as people and what the developing world has that we have lost. When I was in Asia, people looked up so much to the fact that I was educated and that I had shoes and all these things, and I kept wanting them to realize that they had something that we didn't, but the point just didn't seem to get across. As for human values winning out over market forces, is there any hope? In Saskatchewan here, there are a lot of people starting to learn about spiritual values from native people. Elderly people and young people are all going out to learn about what aboriginal people in Canada have that we have lost. So, maybe there is some hope.

Notes

[1]ASEAN: Association of South East Asian Nations.

[2]CARICOM: Caribbean Community.

[3]SADCC: Southern African Developments Co-ordination Conference.

[4]ECOWAS: Economic Community of West African States.

3

Africa: Beyond Famine and Civil War

Opening Remarks

William Saidi
Editor, *Sunday Times* (Zimbabwe)

The end of the Cold War presents a challenge for all African journalists because at the height of the Cold War, the African countries were divided. There were those who followed the path set out not only by Marx, but by Lenin and Mao, and also by people like Che Guevara and Castro. And then there were others who thought they would play it by ear, which meant that they just wanted to find out which system would benefit them the most. This system tended to support the Western philosophy of "live and let live." So, there were two camps during the Cold War. Also, there were countries which felt obligated to follow certain paths because, in their struggle for independence, they relied for support on the countries of the East: the Soviet Union, and the People's Republic of China. Most of the countries in Eastern Europe supported the independence struggles of most of the countries in Southern Africa except for Botswana and Malawi. So these countries followed the policy of Marxism and Leninism at the beginning, and some of them are only now adapting to the profound changes in world politics.

Ngozi Anyaegbunam,

Daily Times (Nigeria)

It's as if something massive is carrying all of us along in a very turbulent current. And you just have to follow the current: you can't swim against it.

We know that what is happening in the world today is not just communication. It's not just economics, it's not just politics. Everything is involved. I think the world has received a massive jolt lately. And, therefore, we are all reacting to that jolt. We are in a vigorous state of flux at this stage, and I think that's what all of us are here for: to try to grapple with what is happening.

The Cold War took place and it's like we were observers. Some of us belonged to the Non-aligned nations in those days, but it's ended, and the consequences, unfortunately, are affecting everybody, even though we were not participants. Almost every country now is restless; some are threatening to break up, some are trying one thing or the other, but all of them are very fundamental experiments that are affecting the countries structurally.

In my own country, I will start with the Structural Adjustment Program (SAP). It's a kind of economic reform that is taking place which we inherited from the International Monetary Fund, the World Bank, those financial big names in the world that tell us what to do with our lives. I don't know how we fell into the trap of receiving a loan from them, but you know what it means to get a loan from these people. It snowballs. With time, you can't control it any more, and then you end up in a beggarly situation where they tell you how to live your life. And that is what we have now.

But, having said that, I believe there is something essentially good about the SAP in my country. It makes us look inwards, what we call the backward integration. In other words, we don't go out any more to import all the time. We try to help ourselves. We try to be self-reliant. We try not to dissipate the little foreign exchange we have importing unnecessary goods. To that extent, I think that SAP is okay.

SAP has also devalued our currency very much. At this stage in fact, we can't control it any more. There was a time when one naira was one and a half dollars (U.S. dollars). Now at the time I left my country, you could get twenty four Naira for one dollar. It's become that bad. So you find that the devaluation is more than 2 000 percent over a few years now. A lot of these things have happened. Sometimes you feel like you've gone through several generations in one lifetime. A lot of people are suffering because we inherited SAP and are swallowing it without adaptation. The people who gave us SAP did not study our situation. That is the problem we are talking about: communication, empathy, understanding other people's culture before you introduce some kind of system.

We inherited SAP but we did not adapt it to suit us, and therefore the majority of the people are suffering. But, I think that with time, if we are resilient enough to survive it, there's going to be something good coming out of it.

The New World Order is such that the people who dictate to us how to manage our economy are not interested anymore, really, in what is happening. It's as if something massive is carrying all of us along in a very turbulent current. And, you just have to follow the current: you can't swim against it. And that is actually the attitude of the United States, I'm afraid to say. They are not interested. There is this kind of very frightening arrogance in their posture; you just have to follow us or you get left behind. They don't even stop any more to look and wonder what is happening to somebody, for example, my patient on whom I have administered this drug.

Then there is the transitional program which is taking place right now. We are hoping that by 1993, we'll have a duly constitutionally elected government.

Right now we have the military in power. That would have earned us a lot of applause during the Cold War because in those days it used to be fashionable.

Right now, we have never worked as hard as we are working to get into democracy. But nobody is noticing any more. What they are reporting about us instead is something to do with riots, famine, and the unrest which, I think, is universal. You can find riots, you can find floods, you can find the cyclone wind in the U.S. also. Just as you have the pestilence, you also have the progress going on. But they are more interested in reporting those aspects of ours that portray us in a negative light. They don't think about those things we are doing to improve our lives. To them it doesn't matter.

You will ask what are we doing to portray ourselves? If somebody is not portraying us – what are you doing? I will say that you know as well as I do that communication is a very expensive business. And to that extent, we are handicapped as journalists from the Third World, from Nigeria. We cannot pitch against journalists of the developed world. We cannot compete with them in terms of reaching out to the world to say that this is what we are doing. So we are merely saying that if they have to report us, let them try and be balanced about it. Just as you report about our famine and our riots, about our unrest, you should also report that we are doing something constructive.

This is the global village we are in. We all belong to it whether we like it or not. It is one big family. We must be made to feel that we are relevant in some way. We must be made to feel that we relate to the rest of the world in some way that is positive also. Because you know that when you say somebody is no good all the time it affects the person in a psychological way.

The third thing coming from Nigeria now is the reparation movement. It was started by an individual, actually, Chief M.K.O. Abiola. He is also a newspaper publisher. He is very rich, but he is one of those few unique rich ones who are also still in touch with humanity, so he has been empathetic enough to start the reparation movement to insist that, just like Germany got reparation from the West, Africa ought to get some kind of reparation for the long years of slavery.

That movement is on now but, of course, nobody is talking about it except us in Nigeria and some other countries in Africa. But it's big and should be mentioned. And, for whatever it is worth, whether we get reparations or not, it's worth talking about. Even if we don't get it in terms of money, it's worth some degree of introspection. The West needs to spend some time reflecting. Somehow, the Third World cannot be blamed for all the problems it has today.

Joe Thloloe

Managing Editor of *Sowetan*, Johannesburg, South Africa

(Joe Thloloe expands on this oral presentation in the written paper he submitted, which is included on pages 59-63)

It is a story that has not been told, because we as journalists don't have the imagination or the patience to tell it as it should be told.

I've been a journalist since 1961. I've worked on the *World*, the *Rand Daily Mail*, *Drum*, *Golden City Post.* I've been around for a while. We journalists love shorthand; we love the headlines. And I believe that's one of the problems that we face in South Africa today. The shorthand, the headlines, have made us gloss over the real story. I believe this is increasingly going to be a problem with journalism around the world.

What is the story in South Africa today after the Cold War? I believe the story is about the "stagger" – that we're staggering away from apartheid and hopefully moving toward a democracy. It's a painful stagger, and I think that summarizes the story. It is a story of the millions of people – very anxious men and women who lived through apartheid and who are now scared of violent deaths and of the future generally.

Now let me go back to the shorthand we use. South Africa has been very fortunate in that it is well-covered around the world. Well-covered in the sense that everybody you meet knows what apartheid is. But, unfortunately, the media used shorthand. We have defined apartheid very superficially. People think of apartheid as a vertical line separating blacks from whites. White toilets/black toilets, white beaches/black beaches. That's why, when the government said that we are doing away with the Separate Amenities Act, the world believed apartheid had come to an end. And it's far from ending.

Apartheid is a horizontal separation of society according to race. If you take any figures that measure power, that measure wealth, that measure privilege, you will find that the top layer in society is white. The second layer is so-called "Indians," people from Asia, from India, from the East essentially. The Third layer is "coloreds" – that's people of mixed race, black and white. And at the bottom of the pile you find indigenous Africans. That is a stratification of society. It is a self-sustaining system. I get a bad education, so there is no way I can get a good job. And because I cannot get a good job, there is no way that my child is going to get a better education. Now we're caught in that very vicious cycle.

Now we've not been able to explain this to the world as the media. And that is why people around the world are now pushing apartheid – are pushing South

Africa – to the backburner. The problems there are being solved or have been solved.

But, as I say, it is a story of the ordinary man and woman. The hungry faces in the queue for a job. The small child who wrestles with a crust of dried porridge. It is a story that has not been told because we as journalists don't have the imagination or the patience to tell it as it should be told. We prefer the broad canvass – the broad brush. I can interview a de Klerk, I can interview a Mandela. I can talk about the A.N.C, but that man down there who really suffers under apartheid doesn't have a voice.

I know I'm going to cross swords with some people, but let me talk about foreign correspondents who come into the country. They come in. They have read about South Africa. They know the names. They know the issues. They come in with a shopping list. I must talk to Mandela. I must talk to Tutu. I must talk to de Klerk. And they fall into the same groove that everybody has trodden before. They will stay in the top hotels in Johannesburg, and yet the story is in the burning townships, and that story never gets told.

Let me change that slightly. Some journalists do tell it beautifully. I remember that the BBC once did a piece on my country. I know South Africa, but I was almost in tears at the end of watching that documentary. I think in 1989 the *Philadelphia Enquirer* won a Pulitzer Prize. The correspondent there went off the beaten track and interviewed the ordinary men and women in the townships. And from that series they won a Pulitzer Prize. As I say, some people have the imagination and they have the patience to tell the story.

Either the foreign correspondent comes in or the newspaper will appoint a South African correspondent. But he's usually a white correspondent. He is somebody who knows the burning townships just slightly better than the correspondent who comes from abroad. He doesn't live in the townships, he doesn't know what's happening there. He just goes in on occasional forays. The problem is, again, the ordinary man and woman don't have a voice.

But at the end of it, what is the story? As I said, the story is this violent transition. The violence continues, ten people die each day. Everybody I meet wants to know why it is happening. The first reason is that there is this rivalry between black political organizations that is responsible for some of the violence. But then there is terror, sheer terror – terrorism I should perhaps call it – where armed men walk into a train full of passengers and open fire. This has nothing to do with political differences. They don't know who the passengers are, they don't know what their political affiliations are. It's just sheer terror.

My hypothesis is that there's a flying squad that generates this type of terror. They will walk into a township, open fire on the residents there, and the residents will then believe they were being attacked by men from the "hostels." And they will go out attacking the "hostels." My belief is that, at this point, the flying squad just pulls out and the fighting is left to flare on its own.

There is a very strange randomness in this violence. But there seems to be some pattern behind it. On the eve of major political events, it flares up. It moves from one township to another. As I say, there's a pattern to this randomness that suggests a guiding hand. But, I'm ashamed to say, the media have not investigated this. Both local media as well as foreign correspondents.

We have excuses: we don't have the manpower to do it, we don't have the resources, we have deadlines to meet, we can't afford to let people out to do that job for long stretches of time. Just excuses. And yet, the media have more credibility than the police. Witnesses would much more easily talk to the media than the police.

The major handicap is that we are commercial publications. Our owners expect us to make a profit, and they're not prepared to invest in this type of work. And I still believe that it is our job as journalists (a) to define the story, and (b) to go out digging for the truth and then allowing the ordinary man and woman to have a say in the running of his or her life.

Wafulu Oguttu

Editor, *Monitor,* Uganda

> It is very interesting for those of us who lived under the Cold War and worked as journalists because the West (capitalism) used us to grow.

My paper is titled, "The Fall of Berlin Unveils New Africa To The West." I chose that title because I think the West has changed a lot since 1989, vis-a-vis, how they look at Africa. I think the fall of that Wall liberated us in Africa.

From 1985 up to July of this year, I was editing a newspaper called the *Weekly Topic.* The paper is owned by three gentlemen who, when they started, were just ordinary people – okay, politicians, but not in the government. Then in 1986, they joined the government. And now the three of them serve in the government as cabinet ministers.

We have had three years of struggling to maintain the paper as an independent paper. But because they are now part of the government, it has been difficult to maintain this paper as an independent paper. So, we reached a crisis because they have this corruption. Corruption is also in America. It's also in Canada, but there's a lot of corruption in Africa, particularly because in Africa poor politicians use politics to make money. So our government talks about corruption too. And particularly the President. Recently, the President, upon retuning from Rio, chose to condemn corruption.

And so I got disgusted and I wrote an editorial. I said, Why do you go crying about corruption? You must act. You know those who are corrupt. And that wasn't very palatable to the President and the owners of the paper, the ministers.

So they kicked me upstairs. They said I should now be in charge of the group; I was made a manager instead of being editor. Well, I quit after a week.

And I'm saying the fall of the Berlin Wall and therefore the end of the Cold War liberated us because what I did is, I quit, and my assistants, also editors (six of them) also quit with me, and we started a newspaper of our own, The *Monitor*. And so far, the paper has the second largest circulation in the country. It is only two months old, but it has picked up precisely because people were disgusted with the way I was treated, that I was sort of being gagged. So, down there in Africa, or in Uganda, people are beginning to say that they also want to have a voice. And I got so many letters supporting us and I got so much good will, that the paper has kept on increasing circulation.

Now, I'm saying we're liberated. Why? If this had happened in 1987 or 1988 or 1989, maybe someone would have said, "No. Look. These are communists." Because if you are in Canada here, you don't know how we have suffered under the Cold War because during the Cold War essentially the battlefield was in the Third World. We didn't have the freedom to think. If you expressed something which was pleasing to government or pleasing to somebody in government, or pleasing to an ambassador or a high commissioner from Canada, or America, or whatever, then they labelled you something. If they invited you to a party at their embassies and if you said something, or you talked of something, or you wrote something which didn't please them, they labelled you a "communist" or "Moscow-leaning" or "Peking," or they labelled Uganda pro-Libyan – that sort of nonsense.

During the Cold War, the West and some journalists from the West were very dishonest. In a manner they talk of democracy – you come from democracies: American, Canada, Britain. But then, for instance, in my own country, Britain and Israel engineered a coup against an elected government and put in place a man called Idi Amin. Amin wasn't put in power by us, but by the British and the Israelis. And you know, Uganda is associated with the name Idi Amin. Even here, when I said Uganda, I'm sure many of you thought, "Oh, Idi Amin." Right?

This man was praised as a giant – a humble giant – which is nonsense. But the man had shot himself into power. Now, I'm saying you are dishonest that way. You have been dishonest in that what was good for the goose wasn't good for the gander in our case. It is that if a regime didn't please the West, then the West could remove it in a coup. We know it happened in 1964 – Sylvanus Olympio of Togo was removed just like that, was ejected. And Nkrumah was removed. Lumumba of Zaire was removed. They were just removed. And no protests – only Western praise. No protests against the violation of human rights or democracy. No. It was okay.

But now! Now they are saying that "Africa also needs a democracy. Africa now should have this." No, these are double standards. I am saying that there's been some element of dishonesty here.

There was something good about the Cold War, though, for governments – particularly in Africa. They had room to maneuver. At least you can play the Americans against the Russians – one camp against the other. But in the world we are dealing with today, we are being ruled by the West through the IMF and World Bank.

During that time of the Cold War, there was a way of saying, "Fine, if the Americans are being harsh, then let's call the Soviet Ambassador." And then the Americans would pay attention to our concerns and vice versa. Or the Americans might provide money to topple the government. This was common. That's why I'm saying the Cold War battlefields were in Africa. We suffered in that war.

African societies are the least understood in the world. There are a lot of assumptions about us. It is as if we don't have anything of our own. That's why we are always pro-something, we are always an appendage of something else. As annoying as it is, unfortunately it is true.

Sometimes when I'm in Uganda I am amused because we have a radio station – one radio station – owned by the government. And you know, there is something interesting about radio stations in Africa. If three gentlemen (or five, or ten) sit in a tank or a personnel carrier with a few guns and announce, "From today I am your leader," that is the end. That man is a government from that day. It is politicized radio. It's one radio station, and you grab it, and you are in the business of government. But that radio station of Uganda is not heard beyond fifty miles from the capital.

My newspaper is circulating around Kampala. We can't go very far out into the villages. The radio doesn't go. The newspapers also do not go. So, the people remain uninformed. Those who can afford it listen to international radio.

The radio which is heard beyond fifty miles of the capital are the BBC, the Voice of America, Radio France International, even Radio Canada International. So even our own people hear about events happening in our capital, Kampala, from international radio stations rather than from the Uganda radio station. The news comes from Kampala to London. It's treated. Then it is sent back through the BBC. The BBC a very popular radio stationthroughout the world. It is very, very popular. Everybody in Africa listens to the BBC. So the BBC rules the world in a manner.

I think the time is coming when we should have broadcasting pluralism in Africa, when we should liberate the radio from the governments. So far, some people in Burkina Faso and Mali are forming their own private radio stations. In an illiterate society, radio is more useful. People will listen. The television might be better, but it is more expensive to set up. So we need to liberate radios and radio stations from government, and reach more and more people. And perhaps organizations in the North which are for human rights should be helping journalists down there in Africa to set up radio stations. I say this to the people of the North: helping us build radio stations perhaps is better than sending us your old clothes.

There is a tribe in my country: the starving. The aid that came from America was oil, "butter oil" they call it. These people don't eat butter oil. They don't need it. But maybe instead people need to be given seeds, or some communication equipment so they are told if you do ABC, you will not have famine in the following year. There is a saying that if somebody has famine, don't give him fish all the time; give him a hook so that he can hook the fish himself – that is better.

Before the end of the Cold War, we used to be told, and even Western journalists used to write, that Kenya and Ivory Coast were the democracies of Africa. These were democracies of Africa. These were the economic miracles of Africa. And Mobutu was a nice man, a nice guy, even when he was taking money away. He took four billion dollars from Zaire to Switzerland, and the country had a debt of three billion dollars. But this man was always glorified as a good man because he was supporting the West in the Cold War. So Kenya and the Ivory Coast, and even Malawi, these were countries that were seen as stable democracies, as economic miracles.

Then the Berlin Wall fell and the real stories, the reality about those countries, came out. So it is very interesting for those of us who lived under the Cold War and worked as journalists. Now, because the West used us (or capitalism has used us), we'll have to ask a lot of questions.

Even Savimbi, in Angola, was seen as a good man; he was for democracy, he was given a lot of money, a lot of weapons. The legitimate government of Angola was considered a dictatorship, because its leaders were friends with the Soviet Union.

After the Soviet Union fell, after the Kremlin was taken over by George Bush, we began to see that Savimbi even killed his own deputies – he subjected them to torture. This was never told before.

In the New World Order, we are told we need two political parties or political pluralism. We are told we need a good government, we need human rights. But nobody is addressing the question, "What are human rights?" Is it only being taken to jail or shot on the streets of South Africa? Is there nothing else? Because, to me, if I don't have food and clothing – even if I live in the tropics on the equator, I still need to cover myself, even if just for decency, and if I don't have medical treatment, if I don't have a house – then my basic human rights are being violated. Nobody's addressing these issues. Nobody questions these issues. Look at Ethiopia. Look at Somalia. Why?

I always see my mother in the village – she works a lot. She keeps on working and working and they tell her to just work and grow more coffee. In Regina, a cup of coffee remains the same price for maybe three years or five years, or even six. But in Uganda, a kilogram of coffee has fallen from four dollars a kilogram to eight-six and now eighty American cents. So, this mother of mine must work many times harder to earn the four dollars. But she has a life.

We are told that black people who were sold were taken out of the continent and sold in the Americas. And the imperialists also took out vast resources from Africa – gold, diamonds, uranium worth $130 trillion. Whoever says that? Now that there's no Cold War, we should talk because now we aren't going to be called communists or socialists or whatever. We shall be talking about what affects humanity.

We have no news agency on the continent. We had a New International Order created by UNESCO which was well-meaning. In Africa, some governments set up an agency called the PanAfrican News Agency (PANA). But we don't have any viable news agency on the continent. Only private individuals on the continent could do this if they came together – not governments. Governments would want to use a news agency for propaganda and some of those governments are not very good.

We are so dominated from outside, from without. Because our budget is seventy-five percent borrowed money, the government can't say anything. Everything is dictated by the Americans, by the IMF, by the World Bank. Do this, do that. You can't develop if you are so dominated, if you can't be yourself. And this, to me, maybe not only in Uganda, but in the whole of Africa, is the issue: foreign domination.

Then there is the problem of our environment. Okay, you have no trees here on the prairies. We have a lot of trees. My country is on the equator. But we are cutting the trees to cook food. We don't heat houses. If we were heating houses like you do it would be more serious. But we have the problem of environmental degradation. We need a lot of publicity on these issues. We definitely need support.

These are the issues which are very serious in Africa and in my country which journalists should begin raising in the aftermath of the Cold War.

Open Discussion

William Saidi:

Wafulu mentioned the coverage of the African scene by foreign correspondents. In many countries, the question of African dignity was at the crux of coverage because most African countries felt that they were not being covered with dignity at all. And this went back to the days of the colonial governments.

In my country for, instance, after independence, the government took over the press that used to be owned by the colonialists. And one of the first things they emphasized was that they wanted the African to be given back his dignity. And that was because during the colonial days, the African was covered in the newspapers only to the extent that he was in court for raping some white woman or because he had stolen something from some white person's house or he had murdered someone on some farm somewhere. And, even then he wasn't treated with any dignity – what was given was just his first name. He was just called the African; Jack killed mister so and so. There was no question of identifying him in full or anything like that.

So when the papers were taken over by the government initially, you would then find that, in fact, an African farmer in the remotest part of the area was being reported as Mister Zachariah so and so, the owner of a farm. His picture was there because, in fact, you never saw pictures of Africans in the papers during the early days. There was his picture there with his family, even if he had twenty children and five wives, that was okay. Nobody complained about that. This was the important thing: to give ourselves the dignity that we had been deprived of by the colonial government.

I wanted to mention the role Gemini has played in trying to give back to the Africans the dignity that, I'm afraid, most of the famous Western news agencies have not bothered to give them at all. And that means not to depict Africans to be people who are only interested in coups and corruption and all these things but who actually develop their countries: they can build dams, they're as conscious of developing their countries as everybody else in the world even if they haven't got the means. And I think that's what Gemini has done; it's made Africans walk tall and know that they are people who can actually think for themselves and do things for themselves, that would be accepted as development in any context whatsoever – not just in the context of the IMF or the World Bank.

Ngozi Anyaegbunam:

We [Nigeria] have a lot of newspapers now, privately owned. To that extent, the government of Nigeria is liberal. It allows a lot of people to start newspapers, magazines and so on. And the curious aspect of it is that really, these newspapers don't make money at this time. They are so highly subsidized that you begin to wonder what these people want in starting all these newspapers. But I know what they want – they want power, not money. Because a lot of them have money, those who start these newspapers.

The latest is that the government is handing out licenses to individuals, to start television houses, radios. And you'd be surprised. A lot of them have free expression. They have free expression. I'm happy to say that. Lately, for quite some time now, nobody has been thrown into detention. Nobody has been harassed for delivering the news.

I work for the *Daily Times,* 60% owned by government. But, from time to time, I do write editorials, or in my column I do say things that make me hold my breath for 24 hours after publication and nobody calls me up on the phone for a chat or invites me over – then I breathe easy again. So, to that extent, I must say that it's part of the gradual easing of the military and the gradual march into the transitional program and then finally democracy.

Patrick Nagle:

I'd just like to point out that while the Cold War may be dead, the dialectic is not. Poverty and ignorance are the root cause of all of the miseries that the world faces, and that addressing those by reporting is a continuing job and should not be, under any circumstances, rejected. And it should not be thought that it is ever forgotten.

The question of ownership is what I think should be addressed. Governments in Africa control the media two ways: by the outright ownership of broadcast outlets, they can control in countries like Zimbabwe, they can control a newspaper just by the amount of newsprint allocation the newspaper gets, either in terms of product from the government mill or else a foreign exchange allocation to purchase paper offshore.

The ownership of the *Sowetan* has been a longtime problem. The owners of the Sowetan are a major multinational corporation and could, quite conceivably, change their minds about the value of that newspaper the way they changed their minds about the value of the *Rand Daily Mail.*

I'm glad once again that Wafula raised the question of PANA. That, from a Western correspondent's point of view, was an unmitigated disaster of an experiment, and was less than worthless from the point of view of getting the point of view of Africa anywhere into the Western world.

Rajah Munamava (Namibia):

I would like to say that I am for the bashing of the Western media – not because I'm being spiteful; not because I hate them; but I think they deserve some bashing because of their selective morality, their selective perception when it comes to Third World countries and the First World.

Murray Burt(retired Canadian editor):

I haven't heard a major fact here today expressed that I haven't known about from reading my local paper, or watching the broadcast media.

Ngozi Anyaegbunam:

You've been reading about Nigeria and the Structural Adjustment Program?

Murray Burt:

Yes, Ma'am.

Ngozi Anyaegbunam:

And you've been reading about the Transitional Program to the South Republic in Nigeria?

Murray Burt:

No, Ma'am . . .

Ngozi Anyaegbunam:

Well, you see the problem is this. For instance, there was a time when we rioted in Nigeria. Those riots were not just riots in themselves. They were consequences of decisions by the IMF, the Structural Adjustment Program. When it started biting on the populace, people started rioting. But you see, they reported this in isolation. They showed people rioting, giving the impression that Nigerians very irrational and killing themselves in bloodbaths all written in red on CNN. That was painful. They should have gone to the genesis of it to say how it started. They did not care.

Joe Thloloe:

The very simple story that I have been picking up from the *New York Times* and the *Washington Post* is that de Klerk happens to be a hero of the Western world. And it is only recently that *Time Magazine* came out criticizing him. When the A.N.C. broke off talks with the government, the A.N.C. was depicted as the villain in the piece, and everybody has been trying to pressure them to go back to negotiations. Again, without trying to understand why there was this break in relations. As I say, it's the perspective from which it's written that worries me.

Wafulu Oguttu:

I also read the [*Globe and Mail, Newsweek, Time Magazine, New York Times, Washington Post*], and the stories I hear today about Uganda is that it is an economic miracle! Why? Maybe you in Canada do not understand what this Structural Adjustment Programme(SAP) is. There are things which are ordered by the IMF and the World Bank that we follow. And, even if it were becoming poorer and poorer in the villages, they [western reporters] say they have merchandise in shops which we can't buy. The western reporters also say that we are doing very well. This is the sort of thing you read about in the your papers. But, in reality, people have become poorer. Like, the example I gave of my mother and the coffee growing.

Written Submissions

Reporting After the End of Cold War

William Saidi, Managing Editor, *Sunday Times* Zimbabwe

The biggest stories in Zimbabwe are the drought and the economy. The two are so inter-related it is difficult to focus on one without relating it to the other.

Zimbabwe is going through its worst drought in recorded history. Some economists have said that it is also the victim of the worst economic bungling, if not in living memory, then certainly in many decades. The Structural Adjustment Program backed by the IMF and the World Bank is having a most undesirable effect on the standard of living. The standard of living of ordinary people has plummeted to dangerous, almost starvation levels. Crimes of violence, usually associated with robbery, are on the increase. White collar crime, involving public servants as well as middle-rank and top-rank personnel in the private sector is also rising. There is even talk of leaders profiting illicitly from international drought relief. For the white community, things may be tough, but there has been no noticeable change in their lifestyle. There is an easy explanation for this: what is scarce today and what has been disastrously affected by the drought is maize meal. This is the staple food of nearly ninety percent of all Zimbabweans. Nearly seventy percent of them live in the rural areas and it is there that the food shortage is most acute. So, perhaps it is easy to understand why international press coverage of this situation is hardly worth commenting on, except for the occasional piece when the British, American, Canadian, French, Russian, Belgian or UNDP envoy hands over a sizeable food donation to starving people in some remote corner of the country.

The relationship between the Western Press and the developing countries, even with the end of the Cold War, is still cool. Only when it directly involves their home-country, do foreign journalists in developing countries show enthusiasm for a story. They are also ecstatic when there is a political scandal, a cabinet reshuffle or the removal from office of some arrogant, press-baiting official. Exceptions are the feature services, such as Gemini, IPS and Panos, whose criteria for coverage seems, by comparison, to be almost altruistic.

The end of the Cold War has not improved things to any great extent. An American news agency journalist in Harare told me recently that it was becoming almost impossible for him to "sell" an ordinary story about Zimbabwe to his editors in New York. There is "compassion fatigue" among many developed countries towards Africa. I am told that in the United States, whenever pictures of starving African children in Somalia, Ethiopia or Mozambique are flashed on the television screens, the tendency among ordinary Americans is to switch off their sets. It would seem that editors are switching off their "compassion ears" whenever their journalist in developing countries suggest stories about the devastating effects of the drought in most of Africa.

Is it because, in a number of cases, the African countries have not acted with self-reliance to avert the full-scale effects of drought? Certainly, in Zimbabwe the bungling that preceded the declaration of a national disaster early this year was quite remarkable. For one thing, maize was sold to another country at a time when it was known that the prospects of a bumper harvest were dim. For another thing, international food agencies had warned the government that the country would face a serious food deficit in 1992/93. That these warnings were ignored cannot be blamed on anyone except a government reluctant to act because it generally hates bad news. Although most African governments hate bad news and sometimes want to shoot the messenger, they are especially hostile when the bearer is a foreigner.

Zimbabwe's struggle for independence was aided by the communists of China, the Soviet Union and Eastern Europe. After independence, Zimbabwe was firmly anchored in the Socialist camp. At the end of the Cold War, in spite of all the evidence that "Communism Was Dead," the government continued its flirtation with Marxism. In tandem with that it continued its lukewarm attitude towards the western press. An atmosphere of mutual suspicion existed between the two: the government, for its part, still felt that the Western journalist was out to discredit its policies only because they were not Western: the Western journalist was mistrustful of the ruling party's declarations that it was pursuing a mixed economy policy or political pluralism. These suspicions were, unfortunately, shared by some industrialists who were, and still are, an important source of "inside" information for the foreign Western journalist in Zimbabwe.

The attitude of the government towards the foreign press has to be viewed in relation to the government's attitude towards the press in general. This attitude, unfortunately, is still one of "If you are not with us, then you are against us." The government, through the Zimbabwe Mass Media Trust, is the owner of a chain of newspapers including the largest-selling daily, the *Herald.* Apart from the occasional (and sometimes quite risky) venture into the unfamiliar territory of objective reporting or editorializing, most of the five newspapers follow the straight-and-narrow path of toeing the government line.

The emergence of an indigenous independent press has not been entirely welcomed by the government. Top-ranking officials have described the non-government press as "The yell" or "The Opposition Press." The *Herald* has recently used "gutter press" to describe the independent press.

In Zimbabwe today, another story not being pursued vigorously by the international press is the emergence of opposition parties. Perhaps some of them lack credibility. Perhaps some have tended to belong, almost, to the "lunatic fringe" of Zimbabwean politics. The law legalizing the funding of political parties by the Treasury has not been properly covered or even commented on by a foreign press preoccupied with Bosnia-Herzogovina, the Maastricht Treaty and the US presidential election. That piece of legislation means, in essence, that the ruling party, which todays holds a staggering majority in Parliament (there are only three opposition MPs in a one hundred and fifty person legislature) can use the taxpayer's money to fund its operations. The Ministry of Political Affairs, under which this was done for many years, was abolished under pressure, not only from ordinary taxpayers, but also from some Members of Parliament of the ruling party. So there is the threat to Zimbabwe's burgeoning democracy to report on. It is also one story which illustrates the government's longing for the good old days of the Cold War.

The truth is that it will be some time before the countries of the region regard the foreign press with equanimity. Angola, Mozambique, Zimbabwe, Namibia, Zambia and, finally South Africa are not going to be weaned off their socialist breast overnight. At the height of the Cold War, the Soviets, the Chinese and East European countries helped many Africans to achieve their independence from the West. In return, they expected these countries to follow the Marxist-Leninist ideology of an almost closed society and a controlled press.

Malawi and Botswana were exceptions, with the former turning, shortly after independence in 1964, into a police state, a one-party, one-leader country. Botswana, on the other hand, developed into a unique experiment in democracy. Today, all the countries of the region are headed for the same destination – a democratic experience such as only a few of them have experienced since independence.

The end of a two-superpower ideological scenario has created problems. In Zimbabwe, there was open regret that the Soviet Union had ceased to be the socialist standard-bearer. In fact, one cabinet minister described the whole Gorbachev era of perestroika and glasnost as "an aberration" which he hoped would soon blow itself out. This regret was reflected in the news columns of the government press which continued to promote the idea that socialism was not dead and would live forever.

Grudgingly, the government has had to accept that the one-superpower situation in world politics is here to stay. Once in a while, the official press takes a swipe at that one superpower, especially on two fronts – South Africa and Palestine.

In general, however, the government seems to be gradually settling down to a world in which its former guiding light – Marxism-Leninism – stands thoroughly discredited and the philosophy of its erstwhile enemy – capitalism – is in the ascendancy. It seems to want to compensate for this with an inordinate faith in the power of the Non-aligned Movement.

What is truly sad, not only for Zimbabwe, but also for many other developing countries, is that the real story in the region is not being given its proper place in the Western press. This is the story of the people's right to food, shelter and free speech, even in Zimbabwe which, unlike Angola, Mozambique, Malawi or even Zambia, has enjoyed a relatively free and independent press.

The hunger, poverty and general poor health of the people, despite the strenuous efforts of the governments, can at times be ascribed to the governments rather than to the North-South divide. The story of the ordinary people's plight in Southern Africa is not being told to the world as well as it should. Now that the cold war is over, the Western press should focus attention on how ordinary people's lives are being affected by their government's policies. There is, of course, a global dimension to the suffering of poor people. However, some of it could be alleviated if governments were made to devote more resources to their plight than to armaments, prestigious projects and political repression. That is going to be the big story in Southern Africa for decades to come.

Reporting Africa After the End of the Cold War

A Nigerian Perspective

Ngozi Anyaegbunam, *Daily Times* of Nigeria

The end of the Cold War was not a surprise to the developing and non-allied nations of the world. Many people in these countries saw the end of the cold war with the advent of "Glasnost." Many experienced observers of Soviet affairs in the developing world were convinced that "Glasnost" was a pre-revolutionary situation that could set off domestic, nationalist and international conflicts of unprecedented dimensions throughout the region. Its domino effect throughout the region was unrivaled in the history of communism. Eventually, when the end came, everyone was relieved on the one hand and very apprehensive on the other because of the obvious vacuum created by the collapse of socialist ideology.

There was a stampede among allied nations of the West to provide relief to a defeated "ideological enemy." Aid poured in from all the western-controlled agencies of the world. Many of us in the developing world were concerned that, with all the attention given to Eastern Europe and the former Soviet Union, Africa and other parts of the developing world would now be perpetually relegated to the background.

It then became obvious that no matter how persuasive the argument for Africa and the developing world, the new alignments and interest bonds would no longer find Africa a viable preoccupation. The United States and its Western allies may spend less on arms now, but they are certainly not willing to spend more to commiserate with the never-ending poverty of Africa and the developing world. They would rather deal with Eastern Europe, Latin America and Asia – regions which possess the required basic potential for economic development, and more importantly, which possess the ethnic alignment.

Consequently, Africa and the rest of the developing world have been forced to face the new realities of a New World Order with one super-power whose geopolitical and strategic interest may not be compatible with that of the developing world.

The lot of Africa and the developing nations was not any better in the pre-cold war era despite all the concerns and worry expressed by the developing world via the debate on the New World Information and Communication Order.

The pre-occupation of the western press with adverse news items – coups, earthquakes, hunger, famine, inept political leadership of the developing world – continues. The one-sided flow of information from the West continues. The obsessions with news about Africa and the developing world that amuse and win ratings-wars continues. It may be suitable for the western palate, but it certainly is detrimental to morale in developing countries.

The neglect of meaningful and development-oriented news continues. Members of the western press, not surprisingly has towed the line of their respective governments in concentrating attention on the constituents of the form Soviet Bloc. Not even the unprecedented developments in the fight to dismantle apartheid in South Africa have received adequate coverage. The release of Nelson Mandela, for instance, could not compete with the collapse of the Berlin Wall for attention. The unprecedented advances towards democracy in Nigeria, Sudan and Kenya could not command the same level of importance with fights for independence and sovereignty by former states within the Soviet Union. The attention of the western press simply shifted to areas of the world where more American aid flowed – the former Soviet Union and its bloc of nations.

Nigeria, and indeed the entire African continent are at the crossroads. The wind of political and economic change is blowing fiercely across the entire African continent. From Lagos to Nairobi to Accra, the story is the same. The days of sit-tight leaders are gone. The urge to embrace the multi-party democratic idea seems unstoppable.

The most populous black nation in the world currently under a military dictatorship, Nigeria since 1986 has embraced a twin program of Economic Structural Adjustment and the idea of a transition to a democratically elected civilian government. These two events are by far the most important issues on the nation's agenda.

In the pre-Cold War era, these two major stories would have received tremendous media play in the West, especially in Britain and America. Nigeria would have been held up as an example to other African nations that must toe the democracy line in order to qualify for American aid. It would have been very important to hold Nigeria up to her neighbors, especially those who were friends and allies of the then Soviet bloc such as Ethiopia in East Africa. However, under the post-cold war era, movement towards democracy in Nigeria had received little or no attention in mainstream media. This may have been informed by the fact that the collapse of the Soviet empire, establishes the superiority of capitalist ideology, that developing nations whether encouraged by western aid or not must allow democracy to reign if they want to survive. In other words, a developing nation should no longer expect to be congratulated for embracing democracy. It is after all, the only way to go.

The Structural Adjustment Program (SAP)

This is the boldest economic step ever embarked upon by a Nigerian leader. The World Bank and its subsidiary, the IMF, approved SAP as a means of de-regulating the Nigerian economy and gearing it towards a market–driven phenomenon. This adjustment program is essentially laudable. Yet it has brought untold hardship on millions of Nigerians. This is mainly because it was not modified to suit Nigerians' peculiar purposes. The nation's currency has been de-valued by over 1000 percent. The inflation rate in about the same. The government has tried to cushion the severe effects of SAP through various relief measures for the working class.

This program may be painful, but it has forced Nigerians to look inward for their economic survival. The backward integration process that resulted may be slow, but it is also sure. Small and medium-scale cottage industries have sprung up here and there, all in an effort to produce enough goods and services for the nation's teeming population. SAP has the nation cutting its coat to the right size. The dependence on foreign-imported goods has been drastically reduced. Industries are now bent on sourcing most of their raw materials locally in an effort to reduce prices of finished goods.

The story of SAP and the bravery of the Nigerian people in embracing it is yet to be told by the western press. No media of the West has taken the pains to understand what SAP has done to or for Nigeria. The attention of the western press has rather arbitrarily been focused on one or two riots that have accompanied SAP. The real story has been ignored because the western media are more inclined to report and x-ray the economic problems of the newly independent soviet states.

Western Media Approaches

After over a decade of debate on the New World Information and Communication Order, one would have expected the western media by now to show greater understanding and appreciation of issues and problems of the developing world. Unfortunately, in the prevailing post-cold war era, one senses a greater degree of self-inflicted ignorance rather than understanding. The story lines are still the same for the western media. These stories still portray African and the rest of the developing world as dark and hopeless centres of the globe where virtually nothing works.

Often western journalists who write these stories are not familiar with the real story of development in the Third World. The current movement for reparations for the colonization of Africa is a good example. This is one major story that is yet to receive adequate attention in the west. The media in the West have simply refused to understand the underlying philosophy of reparations. In short they seem to have closed their minds to any problems emanating from Africa.

The Electronic Media

Allow me now to make a few observations concerning this vital organ of the mass media. Television, as we all know, remains the most explosive and influential element of the media. The emergence of new technologies has truly made the world, one controllable village linked up via satellite.

There is no part of the world today that CNN has not reached and made an impact.

More than ever before, the proliferation of western television programs remains the most potent weapon of cultural imperialism. Indeed, the developing world seems to have resigned itself to fate in this regard. While most of the countries of the developing world can physically defend their boarders, they have no defence against the technological invasion known as "Satellite." The result is that in most homes in Nigeria today, CNN, MTV, SKY ONE, etc., are the favorite channels rather than the local station. Even on some of the local stations, foreign, syndicated programs still dominate air time. Unfortunately, the expectation and taste of the local audience keeps growing in sophistication because of exposure to western programs which improve by the day in quality of production, content and universal topicality. Clearly, the local producers in Nigeria, starved of resources and training, are at a great disadvantage.

The influence of western programs can be countered, but only minimally, by providing training and resources for the local producers and by an outright ban on foreign programs or limiting the percentage of foreign programs aired on local stations.

In the pre-cold war era, most governments in the developing world, saw radio and television as the exclusive preserve of government. They were simply too scared to allow privatization of the electronic media. Broadcasting then was simply an instrument of state propaganda, via "development education."

However, in the post-cold war Third World, the hold of governments on the electronic media is loosening a great deal. It does portend positively for the electronic media. In Nigeria, for example, the government has kept to its word to privatize the broadcasting medium. It is indeed an exciting era for broadcasters who will now have a wider showcase for their talents and creativity. Already, Nigerian investors are raring to go for private radio/television licenses. When these stations become fully operational, the traditional government monopoly on the electronic media would have been broken for good.

Conclusion

The post-cold war era poses a tremendous challenge to the attitudes of the western media. It calls for empathy on the part of western media. The developing world should not be assumed to remain static. We might not be moving as fast as the rest of the world, but we are an equally dynamic region of the globe where political and economic changes are rapidly taking place. Western media should commit greater resources to the reporting of the developing world.

South Africa and the Media After the Cold War

Joe Thloloe Managing Editor, *Sowetan,* Johannesburg, South Africa

The South African story today is tailor-made for us journalists, who love the superficial. Blood is flowing – 10 people a day die in the political violence sweeping the black townships. That provides good copy. Two or three political leaders and organizations have already been identified as the major players and that is an adequate number of characters for us to handle. We prefer the vast canvas with two or three major figures and argue that readers want only the broad picture and skip over the details.

South Africa since the end of the Cold War has been staggering painfully away from apartheid, and hopefully towards a democracy. It is a story that can be told from the vantage point of National Party leader and State President F.W. De Klerk, African National Congress president Nelson Mandela and Inkatha Freedom Party president Mangosuthu Buthelezi. It can be told from the angle of their parties. In fact, it is almost always written and photographed from these heights.

I want to argue that that is only part of the story. The real story is that of the millions of anxious men, women and children who have lived through apartheid and are now scared of violent death and of the future generally.

The word apartheid, from the Afrikaans, the language of a section of the ruling group in South Africa, is now well-known around the world, thanks to the media.

The irony is that it did not get notorious because of what it is but because of the resistance to it. It became a household name when television screens around the world showed the violence perpetrated by the South African police against the people who resisted it. There was the massacre of 69 people in the small township of Sharpeville, south of Johannesburg, on March 21, 1960.

There was the shooting of unarmed schoolchildren on June 16, 1976; there were the street battles between young activists and the police between 1984 and 1986; there was the brutal killing of Steve Biko in police custody on September

12, 1977. We could go on and on. It was police activity that outraged the civilized world. The media glossed over what apartheid really was. We conveyed the impression that it was the legal, vertical separation of black from white, through measures such as the separate Amenities Act which prescribed racially separate public facilities like beaches and swimming pools and the Immorality Act which forbade marriage across the colour line.

The media, both South African and international, projected this meaning of apartheid. The media are largely responsible for the confusion today among the friends of the disenfranchised. As far as they are concerned, apartheid is gone or is about to go, so the story of South Africa is pushed to the back.

Apartheid is in fact a horizontal separation of people by "race," with whites in the top layer, Indians in the second layer, "coloureds" in the third layer and the indigenous Africans at the bottom of the heap.

If we take any statistics that measure wealth and power this stratification becomes very obvious. Take, for example, what the Government spends on the education of each child: In the financial year 1989/90, the Government spent R3 739 on a white child; R2 659 on an Indian child; R1 983 on a coloured child; and R930 on an indigenous African child. Thus the expenditure on the white child was four times what was spent on the indigenous African child.

If we turn to the average annual salaries and wages per worker in the manufacturing industry in 1989 we find the same hierarchy: Whites, R21 404; Indians, R8 820; coloured, R6 570; and indigenous African, R6 270.

This shows us apartheid is a self-perpetuating system: one cannot hope to get a decent job when one has had inferior education; one cannot hope to pay for better education for one's children to get out of the pit when one is earning so little.

This is the real story of apartheid.

And it is this system that South Africans committed to democracy are trying to dismantle.

It is a story best captured by the hungry faces in the queue to get temporary work from passing white motorists. It is the story of the little baby with mucous running down her upper lip as she wrestles with a crust of dried porridge.

It is the story of the man who will agree to go on a killing rampage for a fee that will feed his family.

It is a story that has not been adequately told simply because very few journalists have had the imagination or the patience to tell it.

The foreign correspondent comes to South Africa: He's read about the country and its leaders. He will come here with a shopping list of the people he must interview and the organizations he must see. He is thus bound to go over the same ground as his predecessors. He will talk to Mandela, De Klerk, Tutu, Chikane, Bennie Alexander, Buthelezi.

Our man will live in the top hotels in Johannesburg and Cape Town and will go on occasional forays into the burning townships, where he should be getting his story.

The alternative, for example, is for foreign media to get stringers in the country. The irony is that very few, almost none, of the stringers are from the black townships. They will almost always be people who know the ghettos only slightly better than the foreign correspondents posted to South Africa. If we argue that the white journalists are hired because they are better, we are in fact reinforcing the apartheid I spoke about earlier.

I will not bore you with the story of the Soviets helping find a settlement for Namibia and Angola as the Cold War was winding down. The South African diplomats involved in the negotiations gained enough confidence to start talking of a deal for all in our country. They also saw this as the only way they could pull South Africa back from economic disaster – apartheid is very costly. We all know about the palace coup that saw the exit of the arrogant, finger-pointing P.W. Botha and the entry of De Klerk as president of South Africa.

Initially, hope swept throughout the country in 1990 as political organizations like the ANC, the South African Communist Party and the Pan-Africanist Congress were unbanned. High profile political prisoners were released. We appeared to be marching to *uhuru.* Mandela was shaking hands with De klerk and calling him a man of integrity. Then the jockeying for power started along with the hard bargaining at the negotiating table. There was unease among the whites who saw themselves losing their privileged status.

Anger also rose from the ground – from that ordinary man and woman I mentioned earlier – as they saw apartheid laws being repealed without affecting their daily lives.

The Land Acts, which barred blacks from owning land in "white areas" and allocated more than 80 percent of the land to whites, were repealed. Blacks can now buy land wherever they wish. Catch 22 is that they do not have the money and the land remains in white hands.

Influx control laws that barred indigenous Africans from being in urban areas unless they had a special permit were repealed.Africans rushed to the cities and towns, only to find that there was no accommodation or employment for them.

"Why is Mandela talking to these people when our lives are not changing," is the complaint from the ground.

De Klerk stopped being a man of integrity as gloves were torn off.

At another level there is the traditional rivalry between the black political parties. And this is the gap that appears to have been taken by people determined to block the transition. They exploit social differences, cultural differences and residential differences to fan the violence.

My hypothesis is that there is a flying squad that goes into an area and attacks one faction. That faction will believe, without investigating, that the attack came from its rivals and will go out to "revenge." By that time the squad has left the scene.

Every time we interview the people involved in the violence, they tell us they were attacked first and took up arms to defend themselves. There is very little evidence to support the story that their rivals attacked first. There is a patter to the violence: It flares up on the eve of important political events. It rotates in a planned randomness – flares up here while it quiets down there and then when an area believes it has found peace at last, it explodes again.

The Government, so efficient when it fought the liberation movements, is surprisingly helpless in the face of this violence. Peace Accords, peace Committees, judicial commissions of inquiry have not helped.

What are we in the media doing to find the culprits? Very little. We are happy to give the gory details of the last attack. We are happy to churn out the statistics. We are chasing the sensational and being superficial. We give the usual excuses that we do not have the manpower to investigate. The daily deadline has to be met.

Is it not time that we went back to our primary calling: that of digging up the truth, however unpleasant, and publishing it to allow the man in the street to make decisions about his life? After all, the media in South Africa has more credibility than the policy. Witnesses are more likely to talk to us than to the police. We need to invest in this type of investigation if we are to play an effective role in the new South Africa free of apartheid.

Fall of Berlin Wall Unveils 'New' Africa To the West

Wafulu Oguttu Editor-in-Chief, *The Monitor*, Kampala, Uganda

I hope we all still remember the Berlin Wall. To some people it was a great wall. To others it was a torturous and infamous wall, while to some it was absolutely necessary for their survival.

The Berlin Wall was perhaps the most significant thing that symbolized the non-peaceful co-existence nature of Capitalism versus Socialism. The conflict between the two systems was at first seen as that of Western Europe against Eastern Europe. Later the description did not make much sense any longer. So it was baptized "The Cold War." It was cold in Europe but hot in the Third World.

In Europe, the East-West front-line was clearly defined on the map. The rules of the game were mutually acknowledged. But elsewhere, especially in the Third World, which provided the actual battle fields for the Cold War, the front lines kept on moving. In the process this constantly caused instability and confusion in those parts of the world. Their politics and international relations were characterized mainly by deceit, threats and all sorts of manipulations which helped to keep dictatorships in power.

Then, major players like the USA, USSR, Britain and France greatly interfered with and influenced the politics and economy of Third World countries. Then, it was common for any of these big four to plot and by force remove from power an 'unfriendly' regime in any Third World State and instal a puppet one instead. If a coup d'état was not necessary then the 'unfriendly' leader was simply bought with a few millions of dollars for his secret account in Swiss banks.

Now the Berlin Wall is no more. Thanks to the non-dynamic nature of politics in the then Eastern block, the work of western intelligence agencies and the support capitalism received from the sophisticated mass media.

In many respects, the fall of the Berlin Wall which signalled the end of the Cold War was a good thing. For us in Africa we have gained a lot although at the same time we have lost something. Our governments have lost the ability to play the big powers against each other to their advantage.

We have also lost even the little economic independence we had during the Cold War. As colonies of some European powers, we were supported in the 60s by the East and to a certain extent by the USA in our independence struggle. After winning independence, the East bloc countries offered to the Third World alternative trading partners and sources of loans. Then there was room to manoeuvre against the harsh conditions imposed by the International Monetary Funds (IMF) and the World Bank.

The most important point to note here, however, is that whether under the Cold War or after, lots of major events in Africa are still influenced from outside the continent. African societies are the least understood by other communities elsewhere. The little that is known about Africa outside the continent is what has been selectively taken out through foreign eyes and ears. Many foreign journalists and academic researchers have come to Africa with wrong fixations and outright subjectivism. While in Africa, these townships have looked at our societies using only their own values.

Naturally such people have come out with wrong conclusions in most cases. When they return home these western journalists are transformed into instant experts on Africa and present to the world their warped image of our continent.

For lack of resources or an enabling environment African countries can not project themselves to the rest of the world. Africa's radio and TV stations hardly go beyond the individual countries where they are situated, let alone reaching any part outside the continent. In fact Western Radio stations like BBC, VOA, Radio France International etc., reach more Africa audiences than the national stations.

African newspapers and magazines also rarely go beyond the capital cities where they are printed. There is no serious local news agency on the continent. In essence, Africa still remains a "dark continent" that is unknown to the peoples of the north who hardly listen, view nor read anything positive and objective prepared by Africans themselves.

Outside the continent, the Africans are voiceless. For a long time Western interest have determined how African communities and states were to be portrayed internationally or even at home.

Countries like Kenya and Malawi in eastern Africa (where I happen to come from), Zaire in Central Africa and Ivory Coast and Togo in West Africa were always described by the Western press and governments as "economic miracles and stable democracies."

Dictatorial governments in these countries received massive financial support from the West just because they were openly on the side of the West in the Cold War. In Africa, we knew all along these governments were corrupt and repressive, but we were voiceless. We knew, for example, that Jonas Savimbi and his rebel force UNITA were constantly violating the human rights of those under their controlled territory. But this did not stop the USA from giving them more and more weapons and millions of dollars.

To Washington and the American press it was UNITA which represented democracy in Angola which the MPLA of President Eduardo Dos Santos stood for a dictatorship and violation of human rights. The logic here was simple, UNITA was an ally, while MPLA was under the influence of USSR. But once Washington took control of the Kremlin then Savimbi was suddenly discovered to have been violating human rights in his controlled territory!

Through coup d'états Western government put puppet regimes in power. Even Idi Amin in Uganda was installed by Britain and Israel through a bloody coup.

What is now coming out after the Cold War shows us one thing – that the West, including some sections of their press – has all along been dishonest, selfish, and hypocritical in their relationships with Africa.

To them, it needed the smashing down of the Berlin Wall, before they could see that Africa also needed democracy and human rights. The Wall had to come down before the West could see that even Zaire, Kenya, Malawi, Togo, Ivory Coast, for example, were not democracies after all.

The Wall had to come down before the West determined that, in order to qualify for further foreign loans African countries now had to fulfill some new conditionalities other than of 'friendship and cooperation'. Immediately after the Wall went down there was a wave of "political pluralism" in Eastern Europe which was also extended to Africa. Now the West wanted pluralism everywhere.

Political pluralism in Africa however, whether in the past or now has not been understood in the West. Perhaps this is because of western arrogance. There is a lot of pontification here.

Since early 1990, Western leaders and their press have constantly sang the song of multipartyism as the continent's only salvation, Why so belatedly? Why then did the West, for example, sponsor gunmen to topple the elected Togo government of Silvanos Olympio, Nkrumah in Ghana and Patrice Lumumba in Congo Kinshasa? This was in the 60s and was the beginning of confusion in Africa. This was hardly ten years after the first African country got her independence from colonial Britain. Besides, leaders of most political parties in Africa use tribalism and religion to manipulate their followers.

Another conditionality which the West has now discovered as being necessary for Africa is "good government." This has been discovered by Britain: the same Britain which put Idi Amin in power in my country and which before 1990 had supported several repressive regimes elsewhere in Africa.

The West which for centuries plundered Africa, sold its people as slaves, caused economic stagnation, poverty and disease in their various "spheres of influence," has now discovered the need for human rights in Africa as well. It is estimated that before independence alone, Africa had lost to the West resources equivalent to $130 trillion. No one ever wants to talk about this. To the West, human rights are only political not economic.

Which human right is more fundamental than the right to life? Human rights violations are not only being imprisoned and tortured. Denial of basics like food, shelter clothing and medical care is perhaps more serious. This is rarely raised by the Western press. Because these things are no longer issues to the majority in the West, the press there easily takes them for granted even in Africa. It is important to understand why Africans are so deprived despite long hours of laboring.

To try to solve the economic problems on the continent, the West has now discovered "privatization" based on the advice of the International Monetary Fund (IMF) and the World Bank. These two are purely traders in big money, in finance capital. In their present endeavour the two institutions have identified, Ghana and Uganda as their "success stories" in Africa. This propaganda has been amplified by the Western press.

I happen to come from Uganda and I am sorry to say that there is no economic 'success story' there. The majority of Ugandans especially those in the rural areas have become poorer. More so after the collapse of the coffee and cotton prices. Yet now we are being forced to pay heavier taxes for the up keep of the parasitic state bureaucracy.

The success story is perhaps in the total capture and impoverishment of Ugandans, not economic prosperity ushered in by IMF-inspired policies. Sooner or later the situation of Africa is bound to blow up when people can not tighten their belts any longer. If the IMF and the World Bank do not moderate their policies in Africa, we are bound to have violent uprisings on the continent. We should be allowed to look for our own solutions to our problems.

Most African governments have now lost automatic external support and become weaker, and we have less freedom in terms of economic relations than we had under the Cold War.

The US as the single super power would today like to rule the world or at least be present in every country in a big way to protect its interests. The new policy in Washington is now that of armed intervention especially in Third World countries. However, because of a declining economy at home as evidenced by the rapidly falling dollar, they would like to dominate Africa militarily without financial support. While President George Bush and Bill Clinton are both advocating armed intervention to "protect USA economic interests," Africa is totally off the chessboards of their presidential campaigns.

According to Mr. Hellinger, Director of the USA based thinktank, Development Group for Alternative Policies, American leaders are taking this position partly because of racism and partly because Washington's main regard in the so-called aid programmes is "to serve US foreign economic policy not Africa development."

It is good that after the destruction of the Berlin Wall, some western journalists and their media, including news agencies, now have been liberated from the Cold War narrow mindedness and are starting to look at Africa with clearer eyes. Of course there are some who remain as mechanical as ever mostly because of racism or sheer prejudice or being in the service of the establishments in their countries.

This latter group is the type who would rather fill their newspaper columns or air time with frivolous stories from Eastern Europe because these are 'their people' (similar race) than bother themselves with Africa. This is the type that used to look at African states, organizations or mass media institutions as "Moscow-leaning," "Pro-Peking," "with close links with Libya," etc. It was as if Africa had no interests or anything of its own.

Actually, some Western journalists still write quite amusing stuff on Africa. They will highlight and praise backward and retrogressive cultural practices. When they write political comments or reports, they will always make sure that they point out the tribal leanings of the governments, party or leader even if these are non-existent.

Now a new type of the more influential medium, television has also arrived in Africa. The US-based CNN and the BBC-TV are already having significant impact on Africa's decision makers, the middle class.

For years, Africa has lacked broadcasting pluralism. The TV and radio were a preserve of the governments, "in the interest of state security, law and order." This I think was understandable if looked at from the side of government. Since 1964 the continent has had about 70 successful coup d'etats whose conspiratorial leaders needed only a few weapons to capture the only national radio station and announce that they were now in charge. Radio and TV stations therefore were frequently used as instruments of grabbing political power through the gun. This made it difficult for them (governments) to authorize the existence of private stations. That indeed would cause "insecurity" to them. Then, Western governments did not talk about freedom of the press in Africa. Perhaps they also believed that such freedom would in fact destabilize governments of their close allies.

This policy partly denied most Africans broadcasting service. The situation is alarming. Only about 90 million people have access to radio, and much fewer to television. The great majority, about 400 million, live in total darkness. Either the broadcasting waves do not reach them or they do not have the receivers or if they do, cannot afford batteries for them. There is very little electricity in rural Africa.

But now broadcasting pluralism is beginning to take shape. Mali and Burkina Faso in Western Africa are leading with several private radio stations already. In Uganda, the Editors Association, UNEPA is already pressuring government to change the regulations and permit private stations to be set up.

What remains as the bigger problem for the African media, apart from economic hardships is effective news gathering and dissemination. And what appears to be almost an impossible task is for African media to reach and have some influence in the West and even in the East.

Pan-African News Agency (PANA) which was set up by African governments in the then spirit of the New Information Order was a stillborn child. It was an agency meant to do propaganda for African governments and so its demise was guaranteed. Such an agency could not simply compete with the well established western agencies. These, namely Reuters, AFP, AP UPI and now to an extent Xinhua News Agency(New China Agency) dominate our foreign news pages in Africa. PANA is nowhere.

This is a problem we cannot easily deal with. We have no better choice presently. But with increasing freedom of the press. I believe more African business people are going to invest in the media industry. First, we need to develop privately owned news and features syndicates to replace the existing state controlled-news agencies which are useless and moribund. Such syndicates could then strive to market their stories outside the continent, even if only on a small scale.

Already there is an emerging fine crop of private independent newspapers. Some big international agencies have also started to use local stringers. This shows some improvement. At least there will be some local input in the stories which come out of Africa even if they are distorted at thee editing stage. We need local news, syndicates and local stringers for international agencies because the locals at least understand the important issues which should be covered in Africa today. Foreign domination, building democratic societies and self-sustaining economies, the AIDS problem and environmental degradation are at the top on our agenda.

We in Africa need to answer the whys and hows on these issues ourselves. Some European governments, the USA, the IMF and the World Bank and some journalists would like the world to believe that they understand Africa's problems better than Africans themselves. They are always forcing their solutions down our throats. Naturally we get choked. Africa should be given a chance.

Perhaps the best thing to do is for the West to let African governments be on their own without any financial support for a while. That would help Africans to discover themselves better in the 'new' Africa which as we said earlier was unveiled to the West by the fall of the Berlin Wall in December 1989.

Africa Denied a Fair Hearing

Rajah Munamava and **Williams B. Nkuruh**

New Era Newspaper, Windhoek, Namibia

> Africa – Sub-Saharan Africa at least, has begun to look like an immense illustration of chaos theory, although some hope is forming on the margins. Much of the continent has turned into a battleground of contending dooms: AIDS and overpopulation, poverty, starvation, illiteracy, corruption, social breakdown, vanishing resources, overcrowded cities, drought, war and the homelessness of refugees. Africa has become the basket case of the planet. (*Time Magazine*)

It is not the intention of this paper to use *Time Magazine* as a yardstick for measuring media coverage of African events or those in our country and region. However, there is no wishing away the fact that the *Time* quotation above crystallizes, the most of us, not just the image of Africa projected to the world but the kind of stories that are told about Africa.

Much of Africa shares similar historical, economic and political experiences. Similarly, the tragedies that beset the peoples of Africa are rarely peculiar to any particular country. Differences exist but these are only in terms of degree.

For this reason, while the question above is country and region specific, this paper will seek to address issues generally, without pegging them to any particular region or country in Africa, though the same issues invariably apply in both Namibia and Southern Africa.

For much of the international media, and to some extent, the local media where freedom of the press is permitted, Africa is ironically seen as a continent in paralysis and chaos.

In paralysis because it has failed to develop, and chaotic because it has for long been the theatre of wars and civil strife. And given that the media is an agenda-setter, that it helps in forming opinions and shaping perceptions, this image of Africa, by extension becomes the image held by many in the world.

The principle of selective attention and perception advanced by communications theorists becomes invalid in the case of the western audience trying to view Africa through the eyes of the western press. The audience, to a great extent, cannot exercise their selective perception because they are victims of a dangerous form of selective exposure. The image they get of Africa is negative. Unfortunately, they have limited options.

Where, in African countries, press freedom does not exist, where press censorship legislations or mediocre communication infrastructure have limited free flow of information, the image of Africa does not even exist. What people were fed with, especially during the past era of dictatorships, were grandiose images of leaders who were larger than life, some kind of semi-gods.

Yet, the blood-curdling stories of dictatorships, of chaos, wars and disease are not the complete tale of the African character and experience. For if it were so, its people would have been completely decimated, their memory a mere statistic.

Despite the heavy odds against the continent and its people, life goes on, populations grow. Amidst its tears, songs of courage and fortitude emerge. New hopes and dreams rise amidst the grief. New sources of energy are discovered in the wells of despair and general fragility. All these indicate that somewhere out there lies another story, another image of Africa, of people in Southern Africa and Namibia that is not being told.

There are innumerable examples of such untold stories that point to the positive image of Africa and of Southern Africa. For illustration, this paper will look at a few such stories.

The Peace Process

For the last 100 years or more, Africa has known little peace. First, it was colonialism and slave trade. Then liberation wars came and tore African societies apart as families and whole societies disintegrated in their battle for independence. The euphoria of independence, when it finally came, was for many short lived. Dictatorships set in. Agony continued.

In Southern Africa, the wars of decolonisation lasted longer than elsewhere on the continent. Even where independence was granted as in Mozambique (1974) land Angola (1975) peace remained elusive, as civil wars took centre stage. Economies were destroyed, so were people's lives.

Now a wind of change, a wind of peace is blowing over the region. But how is the story of the peace process being told? In our estimation it is a tale that suffers from a serious case of omission. In much of the media, both local and international, the coverage of the peace and democratization process highlights mainly areas of potential conflict, or those aspects that might derail the process. Focus is specifically put on the whims of major political actors, the big politicians.

Most media continue to use the element of prominence as a yardstick for measuring newsworthiness. Almost all of them ignore the massive emotions and yearning of the common man for the period of peace. For the majority of the people in the region, the concept of a democratic government is a new phenomenon, yet the media makes little effort to portray the peoples' eagerness to embrace an alien phenomenon, to define for them what their role in such democracies will be; to bring to light their sense of relief engendered by the precious commodity of peace and their hopes for the future in the absence of wars. If the media does not tell these stories, who will?

People Rebuilding Their Lives

With the emergence of peace, people in Southern Africa are eager to rebuild their lives shattered by decades of wars. In Angola, Mozambique, South Africa, families were separated, others broken up altogether by wars. Young children went into exile leaving their families. On their return, the families were nowhere – all dead. How do these people react to these shocks? How do they reconcile themselves to this loss? How do they march forward as a people without roots?

Few of these stories interest the media. Instead, its preoccupation remains one of political tension, fragile peace initiatives, big finance and the marketplace, violence and death.

Rediscovering Cultural Identity

Through decades of colonialism, slavery, civil strife and chaos, the cultures of peoples' in Southern Africa, like elsewhere on the continent, were affected just as their lives were. Then came Christianity and its claims to be a civilizing culture that would bring light to the primitive cultures of the dark continent. This alienated people from their indigenous cultures.

Later, people were uprooted from their cultural milieu and thrown into the mines to toil for a little cash or the bush to fight for liberation. Their cultural identities were in several ways twisted out of shape as a result of their new roles and their struggles for survival under difficult circumstances.

As peace sets in, most of the people in the region are trying to rediscover their cultural identities, to discover who they were and to assess what it is about their indigenous cultures they should retrieve and carry along into the future.

Several cultural groups are to be seen working in different countries in Southern Africa. But does this struggle of a people to redefine their cultural identity attract any significant media attention? It does not. It is not important. Who is interested in tales of Himba's attachment to the sacred fire or the burning energy that builds out of a Zulu traditional dance?

These are, in most cases, consigned to the colourful pages of tourist brochures which does not only reduce a people's culture to a mere commercial-cum-tourist commodity but also limits access to knowledge of such culture by restricting it to those few Europeans and others with a sense of adventure and, of course, the money to pay for the adventure.

Battling Against the AIDS Scourge

For Africa and southern Africa, the tale of AIDS is one of horror. Statistics show that two out of every 40 people in Sub-Saharan Africa have been hit by the HIV virus. The media have been at the forefront in exposing this scourge in Africa, including suggestions, which experts have dismissed, that the disease originated on the continent.

Little has been said, however, of the role of the people, particularly of how the extended families and individuals, have helped to contain the psychological effects of the disease both on AIDS' patients and their families.

Faced with this nightmare, the Africans' fortitude has come to the fore. The reality that one of their family is destined to the grave has not caused in them alienation, but compassion and care. Few of these stories of fortitude and compassion amid adversity are ever told. Yet they ought to be told, for in them lies a lesson of courage.

They ought to be told, for they have the potential of encouraging others to care, particularly given that in the battle against a scourge that has defeated modern medicine and science, discipline, compassion and care remain humanity's only weapons. And perhaps, more significantly, they deserve to be told because this tale of humanity adds a positive element to a dented African image which for long has been portrayed by the media as one of brutality and chaos, of corruption and decay, of irresponsibility and bad governance.

Education

Like much else in Africa, the educational system is in a state of crisis. Population explosion in much of the continent has meant additional pressure for the expansion of the educational infrastructure which impoverished governments can ill-afford. Many children have no access to schools. Where such access exists, schools suffer from serious lack of teaching materials. Cases exist where one text book is shared by 10 and more children. Some of Africa's children have tree-shades for classrooms. Most teachers are under-qualified. Illiteracy is rampant. In countries like Mozambique, illiteracy stands at about 90 per cent.

Yet amid these difficulties, does education stop? No. It goes on. For many critical media practitioners, the state of education in Africa is a symbol of mismanagement. And perhaps, they are right. Yet there is another story that is not told. How do African children studying under these circumstance manage to outgrow such adversities and rise to graduate as doctors, engineers and so on? Many of them work in the West and have demonstrated professional competence. How do teachers, themselves under-trained, manage to guide the education process? Why don't they just hang up their boots? In answer to these questions lies a tall tale not only of refusal to surrender under adversity but of commendable achievement. Yet these stories are not told. And they should be told.

Plight of Women

Just how often do we tell stories of the African woman as she struggles to redefine her identity in a society that grudgingly acknowledges her humanity? Not very often. Perhaps, this is rooted in the fact that much of the local and international media are predominantly male. Or perhaps, because the women's story loses in the competition for space. Yet, no matter what defence we give, there is no wishing away the fact that the "mothers" of Africa have not been given a fair hearing.

Foreign Debts

Southern Africa and the whole continent are suffering from debilitating external debts. Africa currently owes more than one trillion American dollars. These debts have received great attention especially in the western media. This is understandable. After all, it is a reflection of Africa's bad governance.

These debts however, have pushed the continent into deeper levels of destitution as African governments labour to pay debts with resources they do not have as they enter into IMF/World Bank recommended structural adjustment programmes and accompanying cuts in public spending and other subsidies that hurt the common man. The indebtedness and the hurt it causes for millions of African men women and children is highlighted. And this is good. What is disturbing, however, is that the media fail to focus on the disinterest of the West in helping the continent to tame the impact of these debts, a disinterest that allows the perpetuation of a great human tragedy.

The Other Side of Africa

True, African governments may have been bad. Some continue along this twisted path of chaos that has caused immeasurable suffering to their peoples. But who said Africans must be judged by the character of their leadership? Who has decreed that the humanity of millions of Africans must be sacrificed for the brutality of a few dictators who caused them untold pain?

There is a better side of Africa, one that is not of chaos or alleged mystical resilience, but are of real heroic efforts in a dangerous game of survival. But we rarely focus on this heroism. Yet we should, for the world needs to know.

Governments may fail to exploit gold deposits. But do the African people stand back and let it go to waste? They do not. They dig it out with their hoes; sift the gold grains from the sand using rudimentary tools. This is not seen as imagination. It is not treated as a serious effort by the people fending for themselves. Instead it is projected to the world as a reflection of bad governance, of economies mismanaged, of societies dying.

The other side of Africa and of the African has already been seen by many in the international NGO movement. Some have initiated people to people developments projects. Why? Because they are convinced the African is not as bad or as corrupt as his/her past leadership may have been.

Unfortunately, the media have been slow in recognizing this. Yet, if the media is to function as an effective agent of change, in particular, to help the Africans rise from the quagmire they find themselves caught in, it will need to support them in evolving their other image which has for long been kept in the dark – that of good men and women who have through history, struggled against adversity not only to survive but also to assert their humanity.

The media can do this. But it will not be able to perform this service unless it redefines its values and bends its traditional yardsticks in measuring what is newsworthy.

Why the Omissions

Presently, the international, and to some extent, the media in Africa is still caged in by traditional news values such prominence, the bizare, wars, chaos, the extra-ordinary. Besides, the western media focus on that which will appeal to their western audience.

It would appear that for most western media practitioners, coups, bloodshed on African streets or concertina-chested famished Africans, among other horrors, constitute the images that tickle the western mind. African media practitioners, many of them beneficiaries of western media, training tend to replicate the attitude of Western media networks in their coverage of African events and experience.

And both the international and local media suffer from problems of manpower. Where the African journalists lack proper training, their western counterparts lack a deeper understanding of the African environment in which they operate. Besides, Western media agencies have not been able to deploy enough journalists to reach into the heart of Africa and still shy away from employing locals.

In the end, it is Africa that suffers as most media activity remains limited in and around the continent's capitals where coups, power struggles and often bloodshed, begin and end. If the media are to be of any help to Africa and its people as it trudges along the new path of rediscovery, democratization and reconstruction, a different approach to coverage will be necessary.

While tales of corruption and bad governance will inevitably be told, people must also be told of better methods of farming, their trials and achievements, too, must be brought to light. Most importantly, both the local and international media must realize that the story of Africa is not only of corruption and bad governance. The story of Africa is, in the main, of the African people, those simple men and women in the villages who wage battles against great adversity, always refusing to surrender, quite often achieving.

Glasnost Glosses Over Africa

The Ex-Soviet Media and Africa After The Cold War

Charles Quist-Adade, School of Journalism, University of Windsor

When the doors of Victor Vorster prison creaked open for Nelson Mandela to walk out to freedom in February 1990, the media in the western and the developing world virtually exploded with the news. Television and radio gave the story top billing and print media ran full-page spreads on the man who had not been seen outside the prison walls for nearly three decades.

Such was not the case in the then President Mikahail Gorbachev's Soviet Union. Central Television allotted less than 30 seconds at the tail end of its main evening news programme, *Vremya.*[1] The sports news of the day was rated higher.

The following day, *Pravda,* the main mouthpiece of the now disbanded Communist Party of the Soviet Union, buried the story (a short, unremarkable biographical sketch of Mandela) under a commentary on Soviet-US relations on page five. *Izvestia,* the organ of the Supreme Soviet carried nothing on Mandela's release. Instead, it published a report by its Southern African correspondent on threats by white South African nationalists to kill Mandela if he was freed.

The minimal coverage given to Mandela's release was not a slip of journalistic memory. Neither was it an isolated case. It was the trend in glasnost-style and post Cold War era journalism in the former Soviet Union, now the Commonwealth of Independent States (C.I.S.).

A recent survey[2] I made of a number leading ex-Soviet publications showed that marginalization of Africa over the past seven years has reached grotesque proportions. Perestroika and glasnost, the main planks of the Gorbachev reforms, went only as far as Europe, North America and some parts of Asia.

To Russian journalists, Africa still lies in the darkness of the pre-glasnost, (*Zastoi*) stagnation years of the seventies. That perhaps explains why hardly any report about Africa is complete without their favorite qualification "chërny" *kontinent* (the dark continent). The survey further revealed that contrary to popular belief, the ex-Soviet press built on the principles of Marxist-Leninism of proletarian internationalism, and "natural solidarity with the oppressed peoples of the developing world," falls far behind western publications in depth,

Charles Quist Adade is a Ghanaian journalist who lived in the former Soviet Union for nine-and-a-half years. While there, he studied for his M.A. and Ph.D. in Journalism and Sociology respectively. He was the correspondent for GEMINI NEWS SERVICE and a stringer for the London-based African magazines – *West Africa, New African, African Concord* etc. He is currently a visiting scholar at the University of Windsor, Canada.

frequency and "objectivity," even given the latter's extremely miserly and sensationalised coverage of Africa.

For November and December 1987, *Pravda* (Truth), *Izvestia* (News) and *Novoe Vremya* (New Times) published among them 107 journalistic pieces about 23 African countries as against 213 items about 22 African countries by the *Daily Telegraph, New York Times* and *Newsweek.*

Less than half (45.8 per cent of these stories in the Soviet press) were devoted to positive occurrences in Africa. By "positive" I mean stories that did not fall within the so-called "coup-famine syndrome" but instead covered topics like the economy, agriculture, diplomacy, African unity etc. The remaining 54.2 per cent were about the seamy side of African reality, i.e. about civil wars, border clashes, famine, disease etc.

More than 70 per cent were newsbriefs of between 30 to 60 words, mostly culled from the main western wire-services – the Associated Press, Reuter, Agence France Press and the United Press International. Twenty-five percent of the articles were banal, officious information or "diplomatic news" mostly about the arrivals and departures of Soviet delegations from this or that African country or the arrival of African delegates in the Soviet Union. This type of news, apparently meant to demonstrate to Soviet reader the generosity and friendliness of the Kremlin's Africa policy, was often accompanied by pictures.

The Soviet media remained silent on a number of issues reported by the western media, including a French literary award to a Moroccan writer and the demonstration of African students in China against racial discrimination.

In contrast, while the western publications also had about half their stories reflecting the brighter side of African life, more than four out of five were analytical and comprehensive. In some cases, notably with the *Daily Telegraph* and *New York Times*, the whole foreign page was devoted to African news and news analyses.

The fact that the three western publications carried twice as many articles as their Soviet counterparts during the period under review cannot be explained by their sizes or news holes for international news. The news hole for foreign news is about the same in all the publications. While the Western publications carry advertisements, *Pravda, Izvestia* and *Novoe Vremya* did not carry commercial advertisements until 1990.

In the western media, news originating from Africa was rated equal to news originating from other parts of the world when selected for placement by gatekeepers. If they were sensational or monumental enough they were put on the front pages. For example, the release of African National Congress activist Govan Mbeki from apartheid gaol captured the front pages of the *London Times,* while the *New York Times* and *Newsweek* ran several column-inch features on the event.

On the contrary, the Soviet press treated news coming from Africa as second rate. African news hardly ever attracted front-page treatment, not to mention editorial comment. For the period under review, only a telegram sent on board a plane by the former Ethiopian dictator, Mengistu Haile Mariam to Gorbachev appeared on the front page of *Pravda.*

Analytical articles remained largely moralizing and paternalistic. Journalists who tended to sympathize with Africa consistently leaned towards writing sob stories about famine, African AIDS, "the debt trap," crocodiles in the Nile river, and Egyptian mummies.

Some wrote with racist undertones. For example, one time prominent *Izvestia* columnist, Alexander Bovin (now Russia's ambassador to Israel) noted with "concern" that the continent could have a population explosion by the turn of the century unless the spread of AIDS was not checked. To him AIDS is playing a positive role in Africa by keeping the population down.

Later surveys of the Soviet press showed that marginalization of Africa advanced with the pace of glasnost. Terms like "solidarity," "disinterested aid," "proletarian internationalism," "socialist fraternity" etc, still employed in 1987 to describe Soviet-African relations, understandably, disappeared in later years. Coverage of Africa now does no more than catalogue the familiar disadvantages and woes of the continent – the world's highest infant mortality and adult morbidity rates, the lowest life expectancy, the threats of population explosion, AIDS famine *ad infinitum.*

While in the past such reports would surely have been spiced with accusations of "western complicity" or "international finance capital pillage," recent reports do not look for external culprits.

Most articles now put the blame on Africans themselves. For instance, *a Pravda* article captioned "*We are Africans in a European Home*",[5] that Africans wasted the "solid" amounts of western credits through bad management and corruption, and that tiny Belgium produces more goods than the whole of Africa taken together. Characteristically, other objective factors like the lopsided international economic order which is so skewed against most developing countries or the fact that the Belgian farmer receives subsidies more than the African farmer for the same amount of work, are glossed over.

The economic crisis and political uproar in the disintegrated Soviet Union may partly explain the "*glosovernost*" of the ex-Soviet "glasnost" media of Africa. In fact, the standard reply often heard in the C.I.S. when the question of Africa's marginalization by the new democratic media is raised is that domestic problems have taken media focus from the continent of Africa.

But my study of the "glasnost" press showed that coverage of foreign news did not fall during the Gorbachev years. On the contrary more countries and regions left out of the orbit of Soviet press coverage suddenly came to be covered regularly. Coverage of the countries of South Asia, the so-called tigers, has more than trebled. The study also showed that while *Newsweek's*[6] coverage of Africa and Latin America remained more or less stable in 1985 and 1990, *Novoe Vremya's* coverage of the two continents was halved twice for the same period. Thus, the "domestic crises" argument does not adequately reply to the question mentioned above.

The real reason, however, may be found in the boomerang effect of decades of paternalistic communist propaganda, which portrayed the ex-USSR as a big-hearted "Big Brother" lavishing free, and disinterested assistance in line with Marxist-Leninist humanitarianism on "poor and defenseless peoples of the developing world struggling against capitalist subjugation and neocolonialist blackmail.[7]

Historically, the Soviet media has painted a rather simplistic, idealistic and exotic picture of Africa. A well-known poster, popular among Soviets before perestroika summarizes it all: a muscular African man inside a map of Africa breaks a hefty chain from around his hand and feet.

The media then wrote that Africans would be better by breaking off the chains of colonial subjugation and dependence. And they would be far better off if they chose the Soviet road to socialism. This aspiration was taken as reality and media propaganda told Russians that with "disinterested" Soviet assistance it would not be long before Africans would break the fetters of imperialist domination and capitalist exploitation.

However, it was not the destinies of the "exploited" and "subjugated" in Africa but the scoring of ideological points in the Cold War that was the primary concern of the Kremlin's propaganda planners. The net effect of this propaganda has been the locating of Africans as part of the problem in Russia and other member states of the C.I.S. today. It is easy to understand why, now that the C.I.S. find itself in economic turmoil, Africa has become the convenient scape-goat.

But the new marginalization (Africa has always been marginalised by the Soviet media) has also something to do with the new eurocentrism engendered by Gorbachev's so-called new thinking.

"New thinking" which claims to have its roots in "universal human values"[8] has turned out to be eurocentrism and even racism for the political bureaucracy and the new media. For journalists and politicians, "new thinking" does not extend beyond the "Common European Home."

This explains why the "democrats" who took over from the communists after last year's failed coup, have used the mass media to launch anti-African, hysteria and rabble-rousing.

Democrats, from Boris Yeltsin, who said during a television interview after the coup last year that socialism should have been experimented in a small

African country and not in the huge Soviet Union – as though Africans are guinea pigs – to the founder of the Democratic Party of Russia, Nikolai Travkin, who accused the former communist leader of "wasting precious resources on people who have just begun to call themselves a people, and who have only descended from palm trees"[9] have employed the media in a hate campaign in order to marginalise the continent.

In fact, the Russian media have been used by fascists to sell their hate campaigns. In April this year, a television programme had fascists openly expressing their resentment of Africans and blacks in general.[10]

The country excluded from the *glosovernost11* phenomenon is South Africa.[11] It is now referred to as a land of "external spring" and is reported liberally and described in glowing terms. The ANC has been referred to as the "richest" liberation movement in the world and calls to cut aid to it have been made in the mainstream media including *Pravda* and *Izvestia.* The injustices of the apartheid system, the pet topic for Soviet journalists during the Cold War era, are hardly mentioned in recent reports.

Notes

[1]The main news program was discontinued almost immediately after the August 1991 putsch.

[2]The survey forms part of my Ph.D. dissertation, which compared the former Soviet and the western press on the portrayal of specific images of Africans.

[3]This period is also variously called the Brezhnev era, the neo-stalinist period and the period of "advanced socialism"

[4]In Russian, the word "*cherny*" means black. In the context used here it also means dark.

[5]*Pravda.* October 12, 1991 p.5

[6]*Newsweek* covered Africa 21 times in 1985 and 1990 while *Novoe Vremya (New Times* coverage dropped by more than 50 per cent (32:13)

[7]See A. Vasilyev's article in *Izvestia* of March 20, 1990 p. 6

[8]See Mikhail Gorbachev, *Perstroika and New Thinking for Our Country and World.* Progress Publishers, Moscow, 1985

[9]See *Literator.* (St Petersburg) December, 1990

[10]Several participants in the popular Russian TV programme, *Tema* (Theme) did not shy away from their racist emotion. One said in reply to a question, that he would emigrate to South Africa should the future president of Russia be a black man. According to hem it is easier to fight blacks in South Africa. Russians, he claimed, ar too soft.

[11]Even before the end of Cold War, South Africa was reported or in the Soviet press mor frequently than other African countries. In fact coverage of South Africa alone was twice the coverage of all African countries taken together.

Fundamental Misperceptions: The Media and the Islamic Revival

Allan Thompson, Gemini Fellow

The Islamic political revival in much of the developing world is arguably one of the most important elements of our post-Cold War era – and one most misunderstood by the Western news media.

That misunderstanding which often finds expression through the use of stereotypes, violent images and threatening headlines, is making its way into the belief system of many in the Western world - a development potentially more dangerous than the Islamic resurgence itself.

"Islamic fundamentalism has replaced communism as the West's bugbear," Islamabad-based journalist Mushahid Hussain argued in a recent article in the Far Eastern Economic Review. "the basis for a new Cold War between the West and Islam is being laid."[1]

Western decision-makers and ordinary citizens alike are fearful of what they are told is a resurgent Islam.

In Algeria, an Islamic political party swept local elections in 1990 and very nearly took power nationally at the end of 1991 before the military stepped into annul the vote that would have given Islamists majority control of parliament.

But those who breathed a sigh of relief that the generals had saved the world from yet another Islamic regime, should thing again. The "Muslim masses" aren't' rallying blindly to Islam. Rather, they are grasping for some chance to turn out corrupt, non-representative regimes. Many in the Arab world look to Islam not just out of religious zealotry and fanaticism, but often because of economic desperation and political repression and a desire to return to traditional, homegrown values.

Yet the political turbulence in Algeria and other parts of the Arab world has made so-called "Islamic fundamentalism" the flavor of the month in much of the Western media. And the tenor of many of those reports had been decidedly threatening.

Is it any wonder that some old cold warriors meeting at a key security policy conference of the North Atlantic Treaty Organization in Munich this past February wondered aloud if their new enemy was a resurgent Islam?

Reuters news agency reported at the time of how warnings of a growing threat from Muslim countries along the southern flank of the Atlantic alliance echoed through speeches at a high-level defence conference in Munich.[2]

Gerhard Stoltenberg, then Germany's defence minister, set the tone in his opening remarks: "A multitude of problems are combining into potential crises and conflicts in regions crucial to Europe," Reuters quoted him as saying. He continued, "Especially on the Islamic arc of tension stretching from Pakistan to Algeria, there is a zone of potential upheavals that reach into the direct vicinity of Europe. "There are risks that could seriously affect us."

For his part, Britain's chief of defence staff, Field Marshal Sir Richard Vincent, stressed that even moderate Muslims could present problems, noting that Riyadh's rockets could be a threat if they were moved west along the North African coast. "Saudi Arabia has Chinese-made weapons that could hit London or here tomorrow," Vincent said.

Later, NATO secretary-general Manfred Woerner warned during a visit to Moscow that "Islamic fundamentalists are increasingly strong in Central Asia," a development that "does not meet the interests of NATO."[3]

Are we harkening back to the Crusades, that historic clash between the Western world and Islam that seems to have left is mark on the collective psyche of both worlds? Those who are fearful of the Islamic revival have learned almost everything they know about this 20th century phenomenon from the news media. Most frequently, they have been told of a new wave of Islamic fervor that is often violent and inherently anti-democratic, a movement of religious "fanatics" and "extremists" that poses a real threat to the West and Western interests.

There is little attempt to explain the concept of Islamic Shari's law, beyond passing references to the veiling of women, hand-chopping for thieves and stoning for adulterers. There is seemingly no room for the intellectual debates going on in the Muslim world, many outside organized political movements, about the role of Islamic values in 20th century society.

We view the desire for a return to more traditional values as somehow alien, even though Christian "fundamentalist" movements in our own backyards have exerted considerable influence in the policy-making bodies of mainstream political parties.

The Republican Party of United States President George Bush was committed in the 1992 election campaign to a conservative manifesto crafted in part by religious "fundamentalists." "What is new this year is moralistic baggage, and the way that the Republicans are mythologizing the election as a moral crusade of good conservatism against liberal wickedness," Martin Walker reported in the *Guardian Weekly* newspaper.[4] The Christian Coalition run by television evangelist Pat Robertson controlled 32 of 107 seats on the committee drafting the Republican Party platform. As the *Guardian* pointed out, every sixth delegate to the Republican party's convention in Houston was a formal member of the Christian Coalition.

So what's so alien about "fundamentalism?"

In a Western world now several generations detached from a time when a majority of the population considered religion an important aspect of their daily lives, there is a failure to understand a culture that still attaches significantly more importance to religious values. We can't understand how someone can consider religion to be an integral part of daily life without being a religious fanatic or how Islam is an inherently political religion. Nor do we seem to comprehend a rejection of political models seen as Western and a desire to return to what are though of as more traditional Muslim or Arab values and customs, after decades of western cultural domination.

It is worth noting that the favorite media label of "Islamic fundamentalist," popularized in the flurry of news coverage of the 1979 Iranian revolution, is one that few Islamic activists would apply to themselves. After a decade's use, its connotations are entirely negative and its all-encompassing simplicity confusing.

According to Islamic specialist John Esposito, "Western analysts have often assumed the monolithic nature of Islam and of "Islamic fundamentalism" thereby obscuring the diversity of ideological interpretations and the even greater diversity of actual practise in Muslim societies."

So even the words we use to describe the many-facetted Islamic revival are loaded with connotations we no longer notice. But the images conjured up in our heads by the words "Islamic fundamentalist" are unmistakable.

An otherwise reasonably balanced *New York Times* magazine article published this year on the topic had as its main illustration a picture more than a page wide showing a band of turban-wearing horsemen, advancing in a cloud of dust, swords waving wildly about their heads.[5]

News media accounts are replete with references to fanatics, religious zealots, violent activists — as if that's all there is to the ground-swell of Islamic political thinking in the Muslim world.

Of course, there are reactionary and often violent political forces at work in many Muslim countries, right-wing religious parties harkening back to another age. But that's not all there is to it. Others are grappling with the issue of how to accommodate Islamic political forces, to carry out a dialogue with them and accommodate them within the society. If more reactionary forces are constantly harangued by the Western media, and repressed by governments in their own countries, they will be even ore likely to turn to violence some intellectuals fear. We don't hear from those people very often.

The media must try harder to unravel the complexities of one of the most important developments of our time, rather than resorting to sword-wielding stereotypes. For there can be no underestimating the media's role in shaping the Western world's opinions of Islamic movements.

The seeming remoteness of international affairs from our daily lives causes us to be even ore reliant on the media for the substance of our mental pictures of the world. As Jack Shaheen suggests in a study of Western media coverage of the Arab world: "the greater the distance we are from any group . . . the greater the reliance upon preconceived images about that group."[6]

In forming our images and beliefs about the world of international affairs, a world that is for most, outside of our direct experience, our reliance on the media is exacerbated. In *The Press and Foreign Policy,* Bernard Cohen argues that policy makers get more information from the press than they get from diplomatic sources, and generally they get it more quickly.[7]

It is ironic that media reports, often criticized for being government-oriented, shallow and lacking in analysis, become the basis of our opinions. We take those media accounts and made them part of the belief system that will shape our judgment of future events. In the case of Islamic politics, those judgments are often tainted by the predominant media theme of a new wave of Islamic fervor that is violent, anti-democratic and threatening. But in fundamental ways, such themes are misleading.

The Islamic revival - intensified in recent years - is far from new. It began in the latter part of the last century, with Islam a banner and rallying cry in anti-imperialist battles in Sudan and North Africa. The Muslim Brotherhood was founded by Hasan al-Banna in Egypt in 1928 and has had an active role in the Arab world in one way or another ever since.

Islamic forces participated in the Algerian struggle for independence from France that ended in 1962 and were caught up in countless other political balancing acts between autocratic post-independence leaders like tunisia's Habib Bourguiba and leftist political forces.

And looking back even further, scholars like Akbar Ahmed suggest the tensions we are witnessing now are rooted in the two other great historical encounters between Islam and the West. The first began with the 7th century rise of Islam, the conquest of Spain and the arrival of Islamic armies in France and Sicily. that encounter reached a dramatic climax during the Crusades of the Middle Ages and ended in the seventeenth century when the Ottomans were halted at Vienna.

The second encounter occurred during the period of European colonialism when the entire Muslim world was placed under European rule. The third and present encounter, punctuated by such violent confrontations as the Arab-Israeli wars and the Gulf War, is described by Akbar Ahmed as "perhaps the most complex and bitter of all. The weapons are culture and media propaganda."[8]

That "media propaganda" is fixated upon the extremists fringe of Islamic politics at the expense of all other aspects and are stuck on the idea that Islamic political movements are all inherently anti-democratic, a notion that often confuses anti-Western sentiment for an all-out rejection of democratic ideals.

While there are valid concerns about what type of "democracy" the Islamic Salvation front would have fostered in Algeria had it been allowed to attain power, little consideration was given the possibility that the Islamists would have been willing to compromise in the interests of re-election.

"Some leaders of Islamic movements have spoken out against Western-style democracy and a parliamentary system of government," Esposito argues. "Their negative reaction has often been part of the general rejection of European colonial influence, a defence of Islam against further dependence on the West rather than a wholesale rejection of democracy."

Surely, in the case of Algeria, there was some chance of compromise. The Islamic party leadership was split over whether to rush headlong into re-introducing Islamic law or to offer Algerians a more moderate program. It's a good bet that pragmatic politics would have prevailed. there were already hints that President Chadli Benjedid - who under the Algerian constitution would still have held the reigns of power - was, in the end, willing to compromise and work with an Islamist parliament. That most certainly brought about his downfall. The military forced his resignation and cancelled the decisive second round of elections to create the power vacuum it was so eager to fill.

The Algerian elections were a landmark because they were the furthest any Islamic party had every gone in a free vote. contrary to the prevailing media wisdom, Islamic politics is not necessarily antithetical to democratic institutions.

Admittedly, Iran's Islamic republic came about by revolution, Sudan's by military coup. But even Iran's leadership now seems much more willing to establish good relations with the West, rhetoric notwithstanding. And in Egypt, Jordan and Yemen, Islamic parties have participated in some way in parliament — hardly an anti-democratic way to act.

When the Iranian-backed Hizbollah or Party of God took part in Lebanon's recent elections — the first in 22 years — media reports noted fearfully what was astounding was the fact that Hizbollah had opted to contest the election at all, rather than continue its struggle to establish an Islamic republic instaunchyly secular Lebanon from without. but all these and other such fundamental misconceptions of Islamic politics have already had a lasting impact.

With the collapse of communism new enemies are being found, and new friends being made. Michael Collins Dunn argues, for example, that U.S. policy-makers have already mistakenly equated Islamic movements in the newly independent republics of Central Asia with the Iranian model. Dun criticizes the U.S. for embracing "neocommunists" in Uzbekistan, Tajikistan and Turkmenistan as a best alternative to the imagined fundamentalist threat from Iran.

"The dynamic of Islamic revival in Central Asia is, as it has been for centuries, primarily Sufi . . . This approach to Islam is totallyalien to the 'fundamentalism' encountered in Algeria and elsewhere. Yet it is being equated, in U.S. policy-making, with the Iranian mode . . ."[9]

So, we can see that important world decisions are being made on the basis of misconceptions. Sadly, there will be more in the new Cold War.

Notes

[1]Mushahid Hussain, "Islamic fundamentalism is the West's new enemy." Originally published in the *Far Eastern Economic Review* and reprinted in the *Toronto Star*, July 8, 1992.

[2]From a Reuters news agency report, moved on the wire service February 20, 1992.

3This was referred to in the Hussain article mentioned in note 1.

[4]Martin Walker, "Bush claims God as a Republican." *Guardian Weekly*, August 30, 1992, p. 8.

[5]Judith Miller, "The Islamic Wave." *New York Times Magazine*, May 31, 1992, p. 23.

[6]Jack Shaheen, "Media Coverage of the Middle East: Perception and Foreign Policy," *Annals of the American Academy of Political and Social Sciences*, 482, November 1984, p. 171.

[7]Bernard C. Cohn, *The Press and Foreign Policy* (Princeton: University Press, 1963), p. 13.

[8]Akbar Ahmed, "Islam: The Roots of Misperception." *History Today* 41: pp. 29-31, April 1991. This reference from p. 29.

[9]Michael Collins Dunn, "Revivalist Islam and Democracy: Thinking About the Algerian Quandary." *Middle East Policy*, Vol. 1 No. 2, pp. 16-22, this reference from p. 21.

4

The Caribbean and Latin America

Escaping Cultural Imperialism

Opening Remarks

Rex Nettleford
University of the West Indies

I first of all would like to welcome our Canadian friends back on track. Why? Because I wouldn't for one moment have mistaken you as members of the Western Media (capital "W," capital "M"). I've always identified with Canada as brothers in a colonial setting. Subject to cultural penetration and all that. And certainly, as a Caribbean person, there is a longstanding relationship with Canada that I grew up with. We kept their fisherman in Newfoundland and Nova Scotia alive for many years. And they in turn, in fact, were always in conspiracy with us in the Caribbean in all defiance of imperial authority. So I want to put their hearts at rest. And please identify with us on this particular score.

The topic of this session also suggests something of a shift in emphasis and a change in the quality of perception as to what this thing about our own position in the world at large after the Cold War is supposed to be.

In fact we, from the Caribbean, have a sense of continuity in our existence and in the human condition which has not changed since the fall of the Berlin Wall. But now at least stand up – stand up for your rights and help take that wall down! So we are part and parcel of that, but nevertheless, life goes on as, in fact, it has gone on for 500 years.

You hear all this talk about democracy which these fellows are talking about, and we in the Caribbean have, incidentally – and lest you forget – the oldest elected legislature in the entire Americas.

I'll start from my left – things are reversed these days, you know – and then go to the right. That too, is a bit of an inversion, because for somebody from the Caribbean to be on the right is almost a contradiction in terms. But then these designations are becoming increasingly irrelevant anyway. One last thing I should say about this panel which is peculiar, and again, this is Derek Ingram's idea of a joke, that the fellow on the far right resides in Miami, which in fact we in Jamaica refer to as Kingstown 19. It constitutes a demographic space occupied by people from the Caribbean including, indeed, the people from Cuba. Cuba is a Caribbean country. And it's interesting, Derek, that you should include in Latin America and the Caribbean, a piece of the United States of America.

I'm going to ask Mr. Tricot ... again all this mix up – French pronunciation from Spanish – anyway Luis Tricot from Chile will lead off.

Luis Tricot

Freelance Journalist, Santiago, Chile

> But now, on the whole, the media in Latin America: newspapers, television, radio are really just reproducing the myth of democracy.

I'm a freelance journalist and a sociologist and, above all, I'm a social fighter – or at least I try to be. It's not easy, especially these days.

I just would like to say a few things about the collapse of the socialist camp. I think people tend to talk about the triumph or the victory of new liberalism or capitalism. I don't see it that way. I don't think that the collapse of the socialist camp is synonymous with a victory of capitalism for the simple reason that capitalism has not resolved mankind's problems, and it will never do so. So we cannot talk about a triumph.

What we can talk about, though, is the unipolar domination, or unchallenged domination of the capitalist countries nowadays. That's a reality. That's a fact that we cannot ignore. So, in a sense we have gone back to the pre-Russian Revolution period. And, I say "in a sense" because as you all know, history never repeats itself. And, as someone pointed out correctly, dialectics go on. Social and historical government goes on.

I think it's important to say that today the market economy is a dominant economic system. And that's the system of capitalism. But also a new liberalism is an ideology. And that's very important to remember. This, in spite of what Mr. Fukuyama, and I don't know any Japanese so I can't pronounce that name either, in spite of Mr. Francis Fukuyama's efforts to try to convince us of the end of ideology, of the end of history, and of the death of ideologies. I mean, simply stating that is making an ideological statement.

This ideological statement is that there is only one system now: capitalism, and only one value system, which are capitalist values, the values of democracy and freedom, liberty, individual rights, the free function in an economy, a non-interventionist state in the economy. But these are all values that have been appropriated by the dominant classes throughout the years. Because there's nothing like a harmonious and humanitarian world. It has never been so, and it will never be so under the rule of capital.

I think that this is very important to remember because they're trying to tell us that we're entering the era of a classless, harmonious, non-confrontational society. It's only a question of looking at the map and seeing that that's not quite true. Look at Yugoslavia, look at Iraq, Panama, and a bit farther back, Grenada, and so on and so forth. But we are concerned with Latin America now, so I won't talk about that anymore.

Capitalism always tried to convince us that its values were the best values and anything or anybody who opposed those values was an enemy of the system. He was a communist or a Marxist or whatever, or subversive, and he had to be fought.

So now we have a very peculiar transitional process going on in Latin America where we have democratically-elected governments but nothing has happened to the military. As someone said to me the other day, "The military are out of power, but someone forgot to tell them." And that's quite right, too. And the best example of that is Chile. We have still General Pinochet as the commander-in-chief of the army still today.

The best example of that is that torturers, criminals, all those who violated human rights walk freely in the streets while there are still political prisoners in Chilean jails, for instance. So it's a very peculiar transition to democracy.

The media in Latin America played a very important role in the anti-totalitarian struggle. If it hadn't been for the media, perhaps it would have taken longer to get rid of the military. But now, on the whole, the media in Latin America, newspapers, television, radio and so on, are really just reproducing the myth of democracy. Because democracy in Latin America, it is only a formality. We have elections. Yes, that's true, we have elections. We have the right to elect our representatives every five or six years . . . whatever. But the military are still there. It's a form of democracy. It's a democracy in inverted corners. Just like the Greek democracy. It was never the government of the people. Women were excluded from Greek democracy. Slaves were excluded. Foreigners were excluded. So it was only a very tiny and small minority who ruled Athens at the time.

Well it is the same in Latin America now. A capitalist class, a political class, a privileged elite are governing in the name of democracy. And the media are simply helping by not saying this, by keeping quiet about it. Little has changed in Latin America. The economic model applied by the military dictatorships is exactly the same – it has not been changed. Their oppression continues, although obviously not on the scale that it used to be, but it's still repression. Violation of human rights continues just as one of our African friends said before. Human rights are not only the question of physical freedom, but it has to deal with the right to live, to get a new vocation, to get a house, etc. In Latin America, there are 200 million poor people. Not a thousand, two thousand, or a hundred thousand; two hundred million people living in poverty. Eighty-eight million of them are destitute – completely destitute. In Brazil alone you have thirty million people who are illiterate. Seven million people in Brazil live in the streets. Just to mention a few cold statistics and facts.

And corruption, of course, is rampant in Latin America. Not only in Mexico where it's sort of a national passtime really, but in other countries: Chile, Argentina, Brazil. Ecological devastation in Latin America continues: deforestation, air contamination, soil contamination. So little has changed.

But the problem is that the media are contributing to creating a feeling of normality and stability. Because people are tired of dictatorship. People fear the military. They don't want them to come back, so they prefer, as one shanty-town dweller said to me once, "Yes, we know that little has changed, but we'd rather be poor under a democratic government than be poor under a dictatorial government." And that summarizes the feelings of our people.

Just one more thing: the media is playing a very fundamental role in Latin America in trying to erase the past from the memories – from the collective memory of our peoples, which I think is terrible. They're asking us to forget and forgive. So they want us to forget about the past, about the dictatorship, about the past, about violations of human rights – all in the name of national reconciliation and harmony. The same way they want us to forget about the invasion of America 500 years ago by the Spaniards and the Portuguese. Seventy million indigenous people lost their lives; they were killed. Seventy million of them! And they want us to forget and forgive in the name of progress, national harmony, and so on.

Very few people know that on October 9 this year, in a few more days, a nationalist strike will take place in Latin America. A strike as a symbol of resistance against the invasion of America 500 years ago. Very few people know about it. All of the Latin American governments, with the sole exception of Cuba, are celebrating 1492. They are celebrating the destruction of whole cultures, of the economic and social organizations of our indigenous peoples. They are celebrating this – all again in the name of national/international peace, harmony, and reconciliation.

Sharon Marshall

Caribbean Journalists Association, Barbados

Being within the footprint of most U.S. domestic satellites means we are inundated with American programming.

I'm news coordinator with the Caribbean Broadcasting Union which is one of seven regional broadcasting unions that exist around the world, more or less modelled on the European Broadcasting Union.

The Caribbean is one of the areas in the world where the Cold War isn't quite over yet. And that's because Cuba is part of the Caribbean. It is a fact which many people don't recognize, and particularly people from the anglophone Caribbean. I am concerned about Cuba, not only as a journalist, but I should hasten to add that I have four generations of relatives in Cuba (that's where my mother was born) and on the day of the attempted coup in the Soviet Union, she and I left Havana on an air flight for Kingston by way of Managua. Those of you who have been following the progress of the Torricelli Bill in the US legislature know that the United States is hellbent on tightening the embargo against Cuba which has existed for more than thirty years; the Republicans and the Democrats seem to find common ground in this one area.

Fidel Castro is not Cuba, even though for some people they are synonymous. There are millions of Cubans who have been suffering because of the embargo and Cuba, as the site of the missile crisis, as the site of the Bay of Pigs invasion, is well-known to most people, and it is a country whose economy depended very heavily on the Soviet Union. Now that the Soviet Union no longer exists, the opportunities for, as *Newsweek* put it recently, squeezing Fidel seemed to have improved.

It's not only economic measures that this aspect of the Cold War has used, but broadcasting has also been called into service through TV Marti which is beamed at Havana. Recently, a US government committee which looks at its international broadcasting policy recommended that TV Marti be closed, primarily, they said, because in the aftermath of the Cold War, it no longer makes sense. The other reason is that the government would save $18 million.

Cuba and the rest of the Caribbean are within the shadow of the United States. And I know this is a situation with which most Canadians can identify. Our television programming is largely American. There is some British programming, and recently, there has been an effort to increase the amount of local and regional programming. But, being within the footprint of most US domestic satellites means we are inundated with American programming.

For several years, the Caribbean Broadcasting Union has existed as an association of the radio and television stations in the Caribbean, both publicly and privately owned. And in the last five years or so, a concerted effort has been made to produce more programming for regional consumption. I am part of that process.

Our main tools for countering some of this cultural imperialism have been through the establishment of a regional news exchange, via satellite. It is a daily exchange where countries in the region can learn more about each other. Jamaicans send news items to Trinidad and to Barbados via satellite, and in turn we send material to Jamaica – it's all shared. In that way, we learn a lot more about each other because the situation which existed prior to the establishment of Caribvision was that we would know what was happening in the furthest corners of Eastern Europe, but we didn't know what was happening with our neighbours next door. And there has been a tremendous improvement in that regard. There is a lot more that needs to be done, but in the words of a famous Chinese gentleman, "The longest journey begins with a small, short step."

The news exchange has also developed into Caribscope which has become extremely popular. Caribscope is a weekly magazine program with longer features about various aspects of the Caribbean. People have been educated in an entertaining way about various aspects of our cultural heritage, for example, about festivals in St. Lucia, which is 35 minutes away by plane. Before, we never knew anything about in Barbados. The Caribbean is much as a melting pot as anywhere else. East Indians, Africans, Syrians have all settled there, and we're learning a lot more about each other's cultures and in the same process are helping to preserve those cultural traditions.

The situation now in the Caribbean is one of great economic upheaval. When I heard Ngozi speak of the situation in Nigeria, it was almost a parallel of what is happening in Barbados and several other Caribbean countries. We are for the larger territories, now into 25-30 years of independence, largely from Britain and other European powers. And, in the heady days of independence, we thought, "Well, now we are in charge of our own destiny." And we are beginning to see that there's a new colonialism. The centre of power is moving from Britain to Washington, and the IMF and the World Bank are very much a part of our vocabulary. Structural Adjustment Programs are very much a part of the debate about the future of the Caribbean. We accept the notion that we can only make progress if we do it together because individually we are so small and uninfluential.

That has been one of the tasks of the West Indian Commission which was established by regional governments to talk to the people of the Caribbean, not only in the region, but what we call the diaspora, in metropolitan centres here, in Canada, and Britain and the United States about how they see the future. That will be the subject of a very important debate, a meeting of Caribbean leaders at the end of this month. The West Indian Commission sees an extremely important role for the media in helping to forge that future.

Rex Nettleford

In the English-speaking Caribbean, and that has spread to the other parts of the Caribbean too, the people themselves have certain alternatives to cultural imperialism and depend on the media for support. So one is likely to hear more Reggae in the eastern Caribbean on a daily basis than in Jamaica. And one is likely to hear more Soka in Jamaica than in the eastern Caribbean. Now those of you who don't know what this is all about – it has to do with popular music, which has taken the world by storm, including Japan. So there are things going on there which I've often asked my own students in the School of Communications at the University of the West Indies to pay special attention to. The sort of things that affect the people themselves, particularly those who don't read the editorials of the leading newspapers, but listen a great deal to what the radio says.

Mohammad Hamaludin,

Editor, *Miami Times*

> For cultural imperialism is not an isolated disease. It is part of a diseased body. It is directly linked to economic and political imperialism and journalist vaccination must be intended to cure the whole patient.

I was born in Guyana. I was a school teacher. I became a journalist. I emigrated to the United States in 1984. I am the editor of the largest black newspaper in the Southern United States, and one of the largest five in the country. It's seventy years old.

On the subject of escaping cultural imperialism and the role of the media, I must confess that my thoughts have evolved rather profoundly since I emigrated to the United States eight years ago. At that time, I believed all the slogans about a nebulous thing called "cultural imperialism" which was responsible for much of the ills of the Caribbean, Latin America, and the rest of the Third World. Now I'm not quite so sure.

One of the responses to cultural imperrialism has been to import expensive equipment such as broadcast production hardware or to invest in expensive printing presses and machinery and hope that the presence of technological marvels will somehow erect defences to cultural imperialism. But there is a story about a young woman student driver who rushed up to her driving instructor one day and breathlessly proclaimed, "I did it. I did it. I saw a sign that said 'Parking – 60 minutes' and I did it in 30 minutes." If you feel offended that the story is about a young woman, please feel free to substitute 'young man' instead.

I am also reminded about a story of the two hillbillies. One was visiting his friend one day at the same time that the man was putting the final pieces of a jigsaw puzzle in place.

Friend: So you finished it.

Puzzle player: Yup.

Friend: How long did it take?

Puzzle player: About two weeks.

Friend: Two weeks! That's a long time to complete a jigsaw puzzle.

Puzzle player: Nope. Say's right here on the box, '2 to 5 years.'

Sometimes we in the media think we have made such marvellous progress in our zeal to accomplish some defined goal that we don't even realize that we are aiming at the wrong target. Of course, sometimes we know the goal, but we misjudge the effects of what we do. The *New York Times* once ran a sample of professor jokes. One goes like this: A scientist put a frog on the floor and told it to jump. The frog jumped. The scientist measured and wrote in his log, "Frog jumped twelve feet with both legs." The scientist cut off one of the frog's legs and told it to jump. It did. The scientist measured and wrote, "Frog jumped six feet with one leg." Then he cut off the frog's other leg and told the frog to jump. This time it did not, even after five minutes of encouragement. The scientist finally gave up and wrote in his log, "Frog can't hear when both legs are cut off."

I have come around to believing that too much emphasis is being put on this thing called "cultural imperialism" without knowing what it is and what it does. To me, cultural imperialism is largely irrelevant to the argument that there are millions of peasants, 200 million plus, and other very poor people, very oppressed people, in the Caribbean, Latin America, and the rest of the Third World. They do not suffer from cultural imperialism as it is defined. They suffer from imperialism period. They suffer from systems that are designed to enrich a very small, elite group in their countries who are the surrogates for masters from abroad. These poor people cannot afford to buy television sets, much less satellite dishes, so as to be able to become victims of brainwashing through cultural imperialism. Nor can they afford radio. And many cannot even read a newspaper. The cultural imperialism they suffer from is one that their own leaders have embraced from abroad and imposed on them. Their rulers find it necessary to adapt to and adopt a culture of the foreign patrons and insulate themselves from the clamour of the masses through an alien culture.

The role of the media. If our domestic media in the Third World is to import expensive hardware without the capability to produce the massive amount of software, the domestic programs that are needed, then the media is just a part of cultural imperialism because it will simply be a conduit for foreign programs and brainwashing. If it is to import expensive presses and simply use news sources and canned material from abroad, that too is contributing to cultural imperialism.

Journalists and media must come down absolutely on the side of their people as the surest way of helping their countries escape from cultural imperialism. The problem is that it requires a frontal assault, not only on the system that allows a handful of privileged people to impose alien trends on their people, but also on the media itself. That is so, because the media, as a rule, is part and parcel of the system. Its fortunes are inextricably linked to those of the exploiters and their surrogates. It is doubtful that the established media will even be able to break out of this mold.

So one way to escape from cultural imperialism is to create and develop new media organizations. This new media generation should not only bring indigenous cultural influences to the fore, the hopes and aspirations of the people, and their joys and sorrows, but also sternly question sternly the undemocratic manner in which the Western democracies rule the world; to question what the West and the former Soviet bloc as to why they were able to consume so much of the world's resources for an ideological confrontation. And now the winners are left so depleted that the consumption will only rise. And it must question the fundamental bases of their societies when these bases are false. The Brazilian media, for example, must question the absence of Afro-Brazilians from the so-called mainstream. After all, Brazil has the largest population of people of African descent outside of Nigeria in the world, but they are an invisible people in the Brazilian mainstream.

None of this has to do with the Cold War or the absence thereof. It just has to do with national will. The imperative is to challenge and seek escape from not merely cultural imperialism. For cultural imperialism is not an isolated disease. It is part of a diseased body. It is directly linked to economic and political imperialism and journalist vaccination must be intended to cure the whole patient. Unless journalists and the media are willing to embark on such a dangerous mission and accept it as dangerous, we would merely be perpetrating what I call, "superficial journalism." We would, in fact, continue to be part of the cultural imperialism ourselves. We would be fooling ourselves into believing that we have made major accomplishments when we take only 30 minutes to park in a 60 minute zone; or when we can complete a jigsaw puzzle in 2 weeks whereas the box said 2 to 5 years.

In the final analysis, we would be no different from the scientist who came to the conclusion that if you cut off a frog's legs and it refuses your order to jump, it's not because it has no legs, but because you have deprived it of hearing.

Open Discussion

(Unidentified questioner):

My question is to Mr. Tricot. What is your comment on the role of the Brazilian press given what has recently happened to President Collor? You mentioned that perhaps people in Latin America prefer to be poor in a democracy rather than poor under dictatorship.

Luis Tricot:

I think there is a maxim in journalism that if something that happens is not reported, it just doesn't happen. It's as if it never existed. So it was very important, the role played by the newspapers, television, and so on, in Brazil.

It's a very special case because Collor was being questioned by everyone – almost everyone from right to left. That's not the case in other Latin American countries. So, in that sense, I don't think that you would get the media in Chile and Argentina to question their Presidents as they did in Brazil.

As to what's going to happen, it's hard to tell. In the elections a few years ago, in 1989, Luis Ignacio Da Silva (known as "Lula") was the losing candidate, receiving about 30 million votes. He represents the Worker's Party in Brazil, which is sort of a new experiment there, really. It has no organization as such; it has very little finance and funding, and comes from the grassroots communities. It is the first time that something like this has happened in Latin America.

Now, whether they will benefit from this crisis or not, I don't really know simply because Brazil is a microcosm of what happens in Latin America as a whole. It was there that we had the first military dictatorship in 1964. It was also the first country that began to take steps towards the partial democratization of society. So what happens there is very important. It's very important for all of Latin America, but the world has changed so much, it's very difficult to tell what's going to happen there now.

Clyde Sanger:

It's a question to Sharon Marshall. I'm really impressed by your paper and the way that you brought out what Caribvision is doing. I want to tie it up with the failure of the Pan-African News Agency. I think one of the factors that led to failure of the Pan-African News Agency hasn't been mentioned, which was that the different news agencies were expected to exchange their news on a sort of barter system. And, of course, it came at the very bottom of their priorities.

I remember being in the Zimbabwe News Agency, and they just didn't have time, or it certainly was their lowest priority, and so there was less news passing between Zimbabwe and Zambia than there was during the Central African Federation in the 50s. But you seem to have succeeded in this way. I just wonder if there are lessons here from the Caribbean that African countries can pick up and have a second go with.

Sharon Marshall:

Caribvision is a television news exchange, and in 1990 I was invited to Dakar, where the African countries were just about to set up their own satellite TV news exchange, Afrovision, which still exists. It's struggling, but it got off the ground and worked in an environment where there was a great deal of skepticism.

The Caribbean also has a regional news agency, CANA, which is one of the success stories. I don't know what the secret is. But, it's worked.

Even though Caribvision has been in existence as a structured news exchange for five years or more now, there are many, many frustrations. There is a growing development that the newsrooms want to offer positive news stories, or let me restate that, they don't want to offer what are perceived as negative stories about their countries because the Caribbean largely depends on tourism for foreign exchange.

And the perception is that if reports about violence in Kingston or violence in Barbados is picked up by CNN which monitors the exchange, then it will be detrimental to the tourist trade. And largely because the news organizations are state-wned or state-run, there is this concern about the national image of the country. That's one of the frustrations.

Clyde Sanger:

Is this service available outside the region?

Sharon Marshall:

Yes, it is available outside. We did have an agreement with the E.B.U. (European Broadcasting Union) through their New York office, but our domestic news or regional news doesn't generate the same kind of excitement. Well, when Mandela was in Kingston, there was a lot of interest. So I think there has to be some catalyst for generating the kind of interest in our exchange.

Clyde Sanger:

Could you not sell it at least in Toronto?

Sharon Marshall:

Well, we do have a contract with Channel 47, the multicultural channel, and they take the Caribscope program which has less dated features.

The Caribbean News Agency would be a more appropriate counterpart to PANA. And I think the difference is in the structure because CANA is set up as a professional news agency – it doesn't exist out of the foreign offices of individual countries. I think that is its strength, and it is a very well-respected news agency.

Mohamad Hamaludin:

Let me take it a bit farther because I was associated with CANA. I was a correspondent for many years.

When we're knocking the governments, let us at least give some of them credit. CANA would not have been founded if it had not been for a policy decision by the heads of government of the Caribbean Community that they no longer wanted Reuter to feed information to the Caribbean, where the situation existed that the story that a Trinidad newspaper (an hour's flight away) wanted, had to be fed into London, and somebody used the word, "treated," sent back to the Barbados desk of Reuter, and then filed back into Trinidad. But, to their credit, they did not impose it. They said that this was what they wanted as a policy and they set the ball rolling.

It is going because it's the only thing of any consequence in the Caribbean that brings news out into the world. And it has had some credibility because CANA entered into an exchange arrangement with Reuter and they pay for that arrangement. So they use – at one time they had a Reuter/CANA and a CANA/Reuter byline on their stories. I think they have dropped that now. So, sometimes you have the good. Sometimes you have the bad. Sometimes you have the indifferent.

Gerry Sperling

I teach at the School of Journalism and Communications here. I have a question for Mohamad Hamaludin. You were suggesting that journalists should be engaged in the struggle to end exploitation. I was wondering if you were just speaking to journalists in the Third World, first of all; and secondly, do you do that at the *Miami Times?* And, since we all want to learn from our Third World brothers and sisters, are there any lessons?

We have some editors here from western newspapers and reporters – it seems to be an interesting idea, journalists engaged in a struggle to make change as opposed to simply reporting other people's struggles to make change.

Mohamad Hamaludin:

Yes, we do that at the *Miami Times*. It's both an advocate newspaper – it's a black, an African-American newspaper, and they're in a perpetual state of struggle, and it's difficult to isolate yourself from that – but we also produce a very professional newspaper. We try to separate what we call "struggles" in the editorial and oped pages from the reporting of the news.

On journalists engaging in the struggle: the situation in the Third World, I think, is so serious that whether you regard yourself as being engaged or not, you are engaged. It depends where you are engaged. What I am saying is this is a point in time when new definitions are coming about. People are getting new code words and new buzz words. Everything is being thrown topsy-turvy. It would be stupid and puerile of people to think that they can sit down and continue to do what they have been doing in the past and everything is going to be okay.

And the second thing is that the tie-in between media and business (business being the ruling class in capitalism) is not peculiar to the Third World. There was an interesting article in either *Mother Jones* or *Harpers* about two months ago, where the connection between the corporate media and the corporate world and, for instance, the Republican party is spelled out in very great detail. If you are a journalist who is paid a million dollars and given shares as your ratings go up, you have a problem, I think. And this has happened with some people – how do they separate their corporate interests from the news?

To answer your question more directly, I think it's a matter of conscience for the journalist – if the journalist feels comfortable doing what he is doing and thinks that that's a profession, fine. If he isn't and he feels that as a citizen of the Third World he wants to bring about changes, then I don't know if he should engage in a struggle to the extent of picking up a weapon, but he can go and do what our friend from Uganda did, start his own newspaper. It's going to be a very poor – and in his case, he's doing okay, he says – but in many cases, you are going to be poor. You might die in poverty, but you will have provided an alternative means of communicating and being communicated to.

Rex Nettleford:

In fact, it's not simply who owns the media. It's really how you own it and how you behave. In the English-speaking Caribbean, whether by good luck or otherwise, there are some things which have emerged. Governments sometimes see themselves as facilitators and regulators rather than as prison wardens and we have certainly been encouraging that. Also, there are traditions which have developed where we will take governments' money and still vote against them. We, of course, do that on the international scene. So that is expected.

There is an animal who has emerged throughout the Caribbean, the talk show host, who of course, was or still is, a print journalist. And that character rivals politicians in his populist attraction. So there are all sorts of checks and balances which are developing outside of the formal constitutional provisions. It was the governments who appointed the West Indian Commission as an independent commission, really to criticize the government.

Thanks to Canadians, CIDA helped in funding that West Indian Commission. Not a penny came from any government of the Caribbean. And the media have been very important in this; they speak very freely, as you know, even when they're employed by the government.

So there is that contextual factor and, however fragile it is, it exists. And it is unlike what happens in many Third World countries that I know. So that has to be taken into account; you are really dealing in a different ambience altogether when you talk about "freedom" and "democracy." But we ourselves have serious reservations about those buzz words which have assaulted us over the past half a century.

Bernard Proulx:

I'm from Radio Quebec. I was very interested in Sharon Marshall's depiction of how various islands in the Caribbean are trying to give one another more information using your television, of course. It brings me to wonder, one year now after the coup in Haiti, what kind of coverage is being given on your TV and possibly Professor Nettleford could comment on this.

Sharon Marshall:

Haiti and Cuba are, in many respects, the two strange animals in the Caribbean. I think there is a lot of respect for Haiti as the oldest independent country in the region, but we don't know a great deal about it. The images that have come to us have been largely from sources outside of the region. The coverage immediately after the coup was largely through Aristide because after he went to Venezuela, he went to a lot of the Caribbean countries, and it was his perspective that was told. We don't know a great deal about the government which has installed itself there.

Rex Nettleford:

They would not like you to know because we have decided not to recognize, not to treat them, and naturally they would treat us in a like manner. The Oval Office (in Washington), of course, is critical in this. I happen to know that it is the view of many of the Caribbean governments that they are not quite sure what Washington is doing. They see a certain ambivalence in Washington's position. And they arc being very careful.

Incidentally, we have learned how to survive over the past four hundred years. So we are not going to allow ourselves to become scapegoats. You see, Washington is prepared for the Caribbean to take on the responsibility when it suits Washington. That's part of the cultural imperialism.

On the thing of cultural imperialism, I agree with you, it's imperialism; but in fact by "cultural" one is not meaning a little bit of dance or a little bit of music, not at all. We are all exposed to jazz and whatever else comes from the United States of America. It goes much deeper than that. There is a thing called the Declaration of Santa Fé which is very clearly an effort to establish hegemonic control over the region. All the scholarships will be given for the people from the Caribbean to study in the United States of America – not in the University of the West Indies or the other universities there. We are aching for funds to help our people – but they must go to the United States to be conditioned. That's very, very clear.

The thing with Haiti, of course, is that the US government is willing to use us as a kind of intermediary as long as it enhances the American geopolitical position. Unfortunately, we really haven't had an opportunity to have a real influence since the fall of Aristide. Before that, we had something of an influence. Not enough. Probably because if we had that much influence, Aristide might still be there.

Mohamad Hamaludin:

But I still think that this business of cultural imperialism has to be defined because I don't think Bush is asking Michael Manley to intervene in Haiti. It has much to do with cultural imperialism. It has to do with the impression that Washington has of some of our leaders. Remember six or eight or ten governments, probably six, joined the Americans to overthrow the Grenadian government. And if you keep doing that, Washington will believe they can use you when they want to use you – it suits them. My position is that you can stop that by refusing, by saying, "No." If Manley is doing that, more power to him.

Rex Nettleford:

And remember, in the Cold War situation, there were people who were against communism because it had been thrown down their throats. All the people who are from colonial countries here will understand this. We have this strange situation where, in fact, all this politbureau and Marxism-Leninism nonsense went on while the Queen remained the Head of State.

Bill Cunningham:

I was going to ask the Caribbean people to speak about Grenada. I think the so-called Western media misreported what happened there. And I wondered how accurately the Caribbean journals, newspapers, broadcasting, portrayed events in Grenada. Because, in my view, from what I know about this story, the whole invasion thing was totally misrepresented.

Norman Webster:

I just wanted to follow up on this debate about the relationship between imperialism and cultural imperialism and, I think, ideology is a big part of what we are talking about.

I remember during the Gulf War, there was very little focus on the big picture, on the analysis of what was actually going on, the analysis of strategic interests in that area in terms of oil, the analysis of setting the agenda for the New World Order and the appropriate role that the United States had in mind for the United Nations which was as a bird, with clipped wings. Now some of us managed to get that analysis and that information through the alternative press. It didn't come to us, obviously, through the mainstream media.

I do remember though, at the time, that a lot of the professional journalistic community in Canada was quite enamoured with the rhetoric of the war that was coming out of the Pentagon, the rhetoric of collateral casualties and the sort of Pentagon-speak that was coming out to cover the reality of what was really going on. I raise this because I think, as a metaphor for what I think we are getting a lot of right now which is fiscal double speak, the rhetoric of deficit hysteria for example, the sort of rhetoric we get from the World Bank and the International Monetary Fund, through Structural Adjustment Programs, that there is no other alternative, that there is only one way to solve our problems.

I think that a lot of the professional media have become captives of that rhetoric, that ideological rhetoric of the dominant classes as you are arguing, and I'm wondering, in the light of the continental economic integration of the Americas now, what sort of advice you could give to our media workers in Canada about how to deal with that sort of language and move beyond it? I have a friend, a companero, from Guatemala who once said to me that imperialism worked through guns, but that became less advantageous to the Americans at some point and, instead of carrying guns, the imperialists carry briefcases, and in their briefcases they carry trade agreements. So I'd like you to demystify a little bit for our mystified community here about that.

Luis Tricot:

I don't know whether that last statement is quite true or not. I mean the Americans did not take their briefcases to Iraq, you know, plenty of weapons there and they did the same thing in Panama recently, Nicaragua, El Salvador, etc., etc., etc. I mean I do agree with you that they have changed their methods, because they know it is very profitable from an image point of view to work in the cultural ideological political fields.

I don't think there is such a thing as free trade, myself. I mean, we're talking about the emergence of three main blocs as you know. Europe, headed by Germany; Japan and its allies; and then the United States and Canada and Mexico. Those are three blocs – three closed blocs – which want to implement very protectionist policies in order to make the best use of what they call comparative advantages. So it wouldn't be surprising with this free trade agreement with Mexico and Canada, that's materialized that Canada would disappear and so eventually would Mexico. I mean, there is no counterbalance, there is nothing to challenge the United States.

On the other hand, you have Japan. I think Japan will be the most powerful economy – it will be more powerful than the United States by the end of this century or the beginning of the next century. And Japan is investing a lot in Latin America as well. It's the principal investor now.

I think what we have to try to do is determine the agenda ourselves; I mean the news agenda. The newspapers and television and so on are just saying and reproducing what the dominant classes are saying and dictating. Reporting the developing world after the Cold War to me means reporting increasing poverty, a widening of the gap between the rich countries and the poor countries, continuous ecological devastation, militarization of international politics. Those are the issues that we should try to raise constantly.

Rex Nettleford:

Just as a footnote to what he said. I was at a meeting recently with the IDB (International Development Bank) in Washington. The spokesperson for Mr. Bush told us all the plans for NAFTA and then announced in the presence of a highly praised member of the Canadian foreign service responsible for Latin America and the Caribbean that Chile – that talks with Chile were about to be started with respect to their sharing in the deal. That Canadian foreign ministry officer knew nothing about it. It gives you an idea of where the future lies with NAFTA. Would you like to add anything?

Luis Tricot:

You hinted that the Cold War in your region is not over because of the struggle between the Americans and Cuba. Now, I would like to know the role of the media vis-a-vis that struggle – especially the local media – and the source of information, the local media.

Sharon Marshall:

I don't know the status of bilateral relations between the Cuban media and other Caribbean countries, but I can tell you that they have applied for associate membership in the CBU, and we already have a form of cooperation with them; they contribute to Caribscope and we get features produced in Cuba about the situation there which are distributed through our normal programming channels throughout the region.

Rex Nettleford:

Between Jamaica and Cuba the connections are very close. In fact, there are lots of Canadians, Mexicans and Jamaicans there, where the people really stuck to their guns there, despite the Oval Office. You now have Jamaican hotel owners investing in the tourist industry in Cuba. And entrepreneurs who are great market forces advocates in Jamaica are now discovering (went to the right schools, you know Harvard and elsewhere) the great potential of Cuba. So despite the Oval Office and despite the threats which hang over us, there is a persistence in maintaining the relationship. And the media have really been very, very good in this and have been part and parcel of this.

Sharon Marshall:

I think that generally, the tone of editorials on the situation has been quite good. But don't forget that someone mentioned earlier today the shift in the US perception of Iraq. There was a time when Iraq and the US were friends. And their image was quite different from the image that we have today. Japan's image has been rehabilitated since World War II. Germany's image. And I think there is a degree of consciousness on the part of journalists and editors about how the image of Cuba has been manipulated by Washington and because of the historical connections, people are travelling there far more frequently than they have been in the past and they are seeing for themselves.

(Unidentified questioner):

I have a question I would like to direct to Luis Tricot. I had the privilege to work in Ecuador for six months about a year and one-half ago. I lived in a small rural village and it was quite economically poor. What I keep hearing over and over again in this conference are the words "New World Order" and the "end of the Cold War." But, as we all know here, the vast majority of the world's population are poor, (I happened to be in Ecuador when the Gulf War was occurring) and I kept hearing through ABC News, George Bush announcing on the television screen about the New World Order. I would love to take a film crew down to the village where I lived or any village in any Third World nation and talk to rural villagers and see how it was a new world for them, because I didn't see it, and I don't think they saw it either.

My question is about Latin America. When I left after six months of working there, I didn't have a feeling at all that things were going to get better in Ecuador – especially in rural parts of the country. The economic chains that are on Third World nations have not been loosened as far as I can see. I see the debt continuing to grow – that old story of continued underdevelopment and continued reliance on First World nations.

How much prominence is this given in Chile in the media? How are we going to make this go away or how are we going to manage this so as to allow countries in the world to develop programs for their citizens that will alleviate or end the situation of three different worlds in one planet?

Luis Tricot:

You're right. Latin America's external debt amounts to $426 billion, so it's absolutely impossible to pay it. We'll never repay it. The same thing applies to Chile. The amount of investment last year in Latin America was more or less $40 billion. But the annual interest owing is $40 billion. So it's impossible to develop.

President Menem of Argentina was very happy only last week because parliament at last approved a law that enables him to sell the state oil enterprise. And he was very happy and he said so because these $8,000 million that he will get for the state enterprise will enable him to pay the interest of the country's $55 billion external debt. It's impossible. So that's why I am saying that little has changed in Latin America because the economic model is exactly the same as before, during the military dictatorship.

Rex Nettleford:

Your question – underneath, there was, I think, what was the media doing to inform the ordinary people whose lives are not at all affected one way or the other by this – and probably were not even conscious of the gravity of the debt which hangs over them?

I want to ask the same question about the ordinary American people and for that matter, Canada. We hear that the United States is the greatest indebted nation in the world – that it is deeply in debt.

It's amazing how universal these questions really are in this global village. I'm not sure whether this division into the developed and the developing world is an appropriate one in the present circumstances for certain things. And the journalists have a real responsibility.

Mohamad Hamaludin:

The comparison between the Third World debt, of course, is an interesting one. To use Ross Perot's term, I find it "fascinating." And, in fact, Ross Perot is the reason why I am talking. Because what you probably need in the Third World is a Ross Perot. What he is trying to do, in fact, is impose IMF rules on America. They don't realize that. Because they are so badly in debt all over, if they were a Third World country, you would have riots in the streets. But the comparison ends there because – yes, we had the riot in L.A., but you don't relate the riot in L.A. to the fact that the national debt is so big. But the IMF is directly responsible for every riot in the Third World.

The comparison ends there because, qualitatively, the United States still has the capacity and the economy that can eventually pay the debt. The Third World has absolutely no such capability. And that is where I think the problem arises because the person at the lower level – the peasants – are impacted because the money borrowed to help them did not go to them.

Daniel Nelson:

I just want to say something about PANA, because PANA was hopeless, there's no doubt about it. But I personally feel that it's harder to overthrow imperialism than it is to overthrow a dictatorship. PANA was there, it was African at least, and Africans could get their hands on it. They can't get their hands on the big international western-owned agencies. And I think it's sometimes important. A lot of people in the West dismissed the whole thing saying, "Keep off PANA, you don't know what you're doing. Stick with the western agencies." In fact, at least it brings it within potential control. That's a different battle, but if it's within their grasp – even if it's hopeless, undemocratic, editorially useless – a battle can be fought over it, it's within your reach. I think tactically it might be better to say, "We'll wait until there are a few rich papers in Nigeria and South Africa and Uganda, and we'll form our own thing." That's a decision to be made, but I wouldn't sometimes write off hopeless organizations if they are within reach while the international ones aren't.

But what I really wanted to say is that I think one of the reasons for the difficulty of coverage of economic issues in the North is jargon. Northern journalists are brought to think there is no ideology – there is a sort of free market – it's not regarded as an ideology. And you can report it. And we have words for it. But a lot of people in developing countries who are at the receiving end of the economic system express it in a very different way.

Actually, we haven't found a way of delivering that message yet. I think that's one of the problems – of the frustration. If we try to report it in your words, it's dismissed. I become sort of a loony, lefty journalist, not in the mainstream. We don't even much like talking about capitalism and words like that because that somehow is ideological and we are supposed to be free of it. I think we have to somehow find a way of expressing those concerns in a way that's acceptable to our editors.

Luis Tricot:

One of the things I want to suggest is that you diversify your own culture. Diversify your own community or country or society or city – your own province. If you can make it multicultural and make it diverse, if you can be broad enough to move away from your centred view of yourself in the world and bring in more reporting, more reporters, more journalists who are Afro-Canadian, who are native Indians. How many of the national or provincial newspapers have native Indians working with them or Afro-Canadians? If you start to create a plurality within your own country and your own province and your own city, you can then start to build a constituency which will be interested in those issues in which you think that people are not interested.

Ngozi Anyaegbunam:

Earlier in the day two students of journalism at the University of Regina came to me and they wanted to know how they would go about it, getting work in Nigeria. We would be very happy to welcome them to work even in *Daily Times,* I can guarantee that.

But then there's a problem. The problem is how to pay them. Like I said earlier on, 1 dollar in Nigeria is 24 naira now. If you pay me, say 2 000 naira, I'm a Nigerian and I know how to live on 2 000 naira. Don't bother to convert it to dollars, because if you do, you will wonder if I'm still alive.

So I made it clear that if they want to come to work in Nigeria, we wouldn't be the ones to pay them. Yes, we have some people like that, but there are not many of them. They are either sent by UNESCO, UNICEF, the UN, and so on. So they are there and, of course, if you come to Nigeria and you are paid in dollars, you live like a lord. The point is there will be this illusion that if they come there and it has to be *Daily Times,* I will pay them in naira. So all I'm trying to say – we've been talking about PANA and so on and so forth, and encouraging some journalists to come.

I am saying that Africa, the way we are now, the way IMF has kept us, the way the World Bank has kept us, is becoming a very closed continent.

Rex Nettleford:

I was really very serious in inviting my Canadian colleagues to put their hearts at rest – don't think they are part of the West that is being bashed. One of the marvellous things about Canada is that up to now, it has not betrayed any imperialist ambitions.

I was a founding governor of the International Development Research Centre. I still think it is one of the great innovations of the 20th century, and could only have come out of Canada to show that kind of altruism. It was an excellent, excellent innovation on the part of Canadian leaders, where they voted their money and allowed foreigners to come in and administer it. I mean, this is unheard of. Its aim was to build up the research capabilities within developing countries where, in fact, important and appropriate knowledge bases that depend on development could be generated. This, of course, is something that no other, no other technical assistance agency in any other country in the North Atlantic has done. The Swedes tried to emulate it, but it's not quite the same thing. And I want to pay tribute to Canada for that.

It has also committed itself to something like the Commonwealth of Learning, another mechanism which is intended not to bring the Third World into some mainstream, but to have the Third World help determine the main stream. And I think this is very important. So my Canadian friends, I want to thank you all, and please do not take the bashing as being directed at you. I would hate to feel that you really feel yourselves to be part of the developed world.

Written Submissions

Reporting in the Caribbean after the Cold War

Sharon Marshall, Caribbean Broadcasting Union, Barbados

The Cold War era was a period in which the terms East and West were much more than mere geographical designations. It was a time when the world was neatly divided by an "Iron Curtain" into two camps – adherents of Communism and followers of democratic capitalism.

The two superpowers – the Soviet Union and the United States – were at the head of these camps. The other industrialized nations aligned themselves with one or the other superpower because of shared economic interests or political philosophy. The countries of what came to be known as the Third World – mainly newly-independent former colonies of European powers – were courted by the superpowers, and they signed on based on genuine ideological commitment or economic self-interest. But the attempt at world domination by these two superpowers also gave rise to the Non-aligned Movement, which sought to take an independent line.

For people of my generation it seemed like a situation which had always been and one which would last forever. A different configuration of the world was difficult – if not impossible – to imagine. But that was before the 90s.

The dismantling of the Berlin Wall and the break-up of the Soviet Union are two events which for many signal the end of the Cold War, but the Caribbean is one of the areas of the world where the Cold War isn't over yet. The largest island in the Caribbean archipelago – the site of the 1961 Bay of Pigs invasion attempt, and the source of the 1962 missile crisis – still has an Iron Curtain of sorts at Guantanamo Bay. Just ninety miles off the coast of Florida, Cuba is still a potent reminder of the Cold War era and the reason it's not quite over in the Caribbean. The demise of Communism in Europe and the disintegration of the Soviet Union have had dire consequences for Cuba's economy, but Cuban leader Fidel Castro has become even more adamant that the country will remain communist.

The September 14th, 1992 issue of *Newsweek* magazine contains an article entitled "Putting the Squeeze on Fidel" which examines the arguments for and against tightening the economic embargo which the United States imposed against Cuba more than thirty years ago. The author of that article writes of President Castro: "Despite the end of Soviet subsidies, the fall of communism and desperate food and oil shortages, the old man totters on, scrounging sustenance wherever he can."

In its editorial of July 20th the *Barbados Advocate* picked up on the theme that, for the United States, the problem appears to be not so much Cuba, but Castro.

> The United States, when first imposing the trade embargo on Cuba, had stated that if the communist government in Cuba wanted better relations, the Castro regime would have to ensure that Cuba desisted from spreading and supporting terrorism or revolution in Latin America and must withdraw its forces from Angola where a civil war was then raging, with Cuban surrogates backing the communist elements in the strife in exchange for Russian financial support.
>
> The Soviet Union has since broken up and Cuba no longer enjoys the preferential trade relations it had with the former Soviet Union and the states of Eastern Europe. The Cubans are also no longer fighting in Angola where there is now peace among the former warring parties. With the almost total demise of communism, there is not much revolution in Latin America to support, even if Cuba could afford it.
>
> Yet the United States has not relented and has even added an additional demand – that the Castro regime must permit multi-party politics in Cuba if the US economic embargo is to be lifted.
>
> This changing of criteria for the lifting of its economic embargo by the United States has been interpreted by some as an indication that the US is not prepared to accept a Cuba controlled by Castro.

Rumors of purges and arrests, and of possible coup attempts keep this part of the Cold War warm, and the possibility of confrontation alive.

Cuba's Foreign Minister, Ricardo Alarcon de Quesada, charged in August at the summit of the Non-aligned Movement in Jakarta, Indonesia, that private armies are training in the United States to infiltrate his country. He added that he suspects that they're being backed by the Bush administration. According to a CANA-Reuter report published in the SUN on Saturday of September 5th,

Alarcon said, "Washington has stepped up its campaign against Cuba in the hope that its economic plight would spark an uprising against President Fidel Castro."

But it's not only the economic embargo that the United States is using to try to change the political situation in Cuba. Broadcasting has been one of the weapons used in this war. The United States Information Agency launched TV Marti – a program of pre-dawn telecasting beamed at Cuba from Miami. The *Daily Nation* reported on August 4th that a committee which advised the US government on its international broadcasting recommended "that TV Marti be shut down and Radio Free Europe phased out" the main reason being that "what was logical during the Cold War doesn't make sense now." The other reason is that the U.S. would save 18 million dollars by shutting down TV Marti. The committee chairman is quoted as saying that it "is simply not cost effective" since it consists of only two hours of programming which is jammed consistently, so that few people in Cuba actually see it.

In the prologue to his book *America and the Cold War,* published in 1969, Richard J. Walton wrote:

> There is no one likely to read this book who has not been affected by the Cold War in one way or another, and even if it were somehow to end tomorrow – which is highly improbable – its effect would be felt for decades. An American need only look at the racial conflict, the disintegrating cities, the disrupted society, to see legacies of the Cold War – legacies that were not even imagined in its early days. In both nations thought, energy, and money, even moral purpose, have been diverted from imperative domestic concerns to the prosecution of this conflict.

It is not only the "imperative domestic concerns" of the superpowers that have been neglected because of the diversion of funds to build up arsenals for the Cold War conflict. The domestic concerns of countries which were or are dependent on the industrialised nations for economic assistance have also been neglected.

Many of the countries of the anglophone Caribbean in the post-Independence era are undergoing serious economic difficulty. Some of them have entered structural adjustment programs with international lending agencies like the International Monetary Fund and the World Bank, and some like Grenada have devised their own programs without the help of these agencies. Social scientists point to direct and indirect results of these programs – growing unemployment, the decline of the public sector, and the general reduction in the standard of living of the population. In societies where many households are headed by women, the ones who bear the brunt of this social dislocation are women and their dependent children. These days children are learning about the IMF around the same time that they're learning their ABCs. "Privatisation" is a key concept in this changing economic environment. Cash-strapped governments are forced to sell off national assets, sometimes on unfavourable terms. Some of these assets were acquired during the heady days of Independence.

At a time when some people are questioning the validity of that independence, the US ambassador to Barbados and the Eastern Caribbean challenged the independent line that some countries of the region have been taking with regard to their foreign policy. During a speech to a private club in Barbados the ambassador chided Caribbean countries for their voting record at the UN The editorial of *The Sunday SUN* put it this way:

> The ambassador is reported as giving Barbados notice that if it wants to have clout and support in Washington, it had better begin to demonstrate its friendship by such tangible actions as voting with the United States in the United Nations.

The *Daily Nation* reacted with an editorial entitled "Big brother is watching" on July 7th. It read in part:

> There is no doubt that successive governments of Barbados are unlikely to discount the weight and importance of the fact that the United States is a superpower, indeed, the sole superpower in the world, and that Barbados lives within the area of its underbelly. There are too many day-to-day reminders of that dependence.

Living in the "underbelly" of the United States also means living in the footprint of US domestic satellites, which can be accessed by people in the Caribbean who own satellite dishes – individual homeowners and operators of businesses like bars and hotels. So that in addition to the regular American programs offered on local stations, Caribbean viewers are inundated with the satellite fare direct from the source.

This "cultural domination" is a fact of life. The challenge to journalists in the region is to see how we can use this technology to show our own people images of themselves and help to preserve cultures and traditions which may be under threat.

The Caribbean Broadcasting Union is one organization which is making a valiant attempt to counter this influence by pooling the resources of its member stations. The CBU coordinates a daily satellite TV news exchange where television stations in Barbados, Curacao, Jamaica, Suriname and Trinidad and Tobago share their top news items on the CARIBVISION news exchange. The CBU also produces a weekly magazine program called CARIBSCOPE, which includes features on all aspects of life in the region contributed by various member stations, as well as a monthly cultural entertainment program – *Caribbean Night* – which is distributed via satellite.

In addition to these regular programs, the CBI coordinates and provides extended satellite coverage of major events like the annual summit of Caribbean leaders, and the regional cultural festival – *Carifesta* – which was just held at the end of August.

Unfortunately, because the television stations participating in the news exchange are state-owned, there is now a trend to offer only "positive" stories for fear of affecting the tourism trade on which most of the economies depend.

But the media environment in the Caribbean has changed dramatically in the last few years, with licenses being granted to private television stations in Trinidad and Tobago and Jamaica. This has meant competition in a market previously monopolized by the state, and this could result in an improvement in the quality of news reporting, or it could lead to a deterioration in standards if profit is the only motivation.

Concerns not only about how we see ourselves but also about how others view us have always been part of the debate about the imbalance in the flow of information internationally. The only developments in the Caribbean which appear to merit international attention have been stories like the US invasion of Grenada, the attempted coup in Trinidad and Tobago, and the devastation of Jamaica by Hurricane Gilbert.

In an effort to help correct this imbalance, the One World group of broadcasters organized the first international television newscast produced and presented by journalists from the developing world for mainly European audiences. I had the honor to join journalists from Bangladesh, Egypt and Zimbabwe for this experiment called "South by South," in the studios of R.T.B.F. in Brussels in May this year. Although there were some minor problems with the production of the program, the organizers were pleased with the outcome and have labelled it a success, based on public reaction.

But that was only a beginning. There are other stories about the Caribbean that need to be told; stories about how our economies are affected by the recession in North America, about what impact the North American Free Trade Agreement will have for manufacturers in the region, and what a single European market will mean for Caribbean producers of agricultural products which are sold in Europe.

And the countries of the industrialized world shouldn't be the only concern of developing countries like those in the Caribbean. Developing countries in different regions of the world need to exchange news and programs among themselves. It is efforts like these and those of responsible agencies like Gemini that will make reporting after the Cold War a more balanced and less biased undertaking.

The Media and the Third World

Mohamad Hamaludin, Managing Editor, *Miami Times*

The exploitation of natural resources, an ever-present determinant in international relations, will be the primary driving force in a world without the immediate threat of a nuclear holocaust.

The existence of two nuclear superpowers provided a bargaining chip, however small, for the under-developed nations. The collapse of the Soviet Union now leaves such countries at the mercy of the victor, the United States (and the rest of the West), whose national underpinning is predatory capitalism in which most moral persuasions are subordinated to the profit motive.

Even in the best of times, predatory exploitation of the natural resources of smaller countries has been harsh. The huge drain on the world's resources that was witnessed in the East-West confrontation means that it will become worse. The speed with which the Western nations, led by the United States, moved to crush Iraq was an early indication that threats to territorial preserves will not be tolerated.

This is what will eventually become the "New World Order" that President George Bush of the United States spoke of shortly after the Iraqi army was pounded into surrender by overwhelming ferocity. It will be compounded by the fact that while the Western nations aggressively promote democracy, the world has never been run through democratic institutions.

The world governing mechanisms are the United Nations Security Council and the global economic arrangements of the Bretton Woods Treaty which established such institutions as the International Monetary Fund and the International Bank for Reconstruction and Development. Not only are these the exclusive preserve of the developed nations, to use as they see fit, but also they have a sorry history of bullying the rest of the world into fitting into a Western mold of "democracy" and economic planning.

There is little on the horizon to give comfort to those who believe that the New World Order should include a revamping of these global governmental regimes to make them more democratic. Instead, the world will be reshaped into a global economy in which there will continue to be unchecked centres of power, mainly North America and Europe, and the "barbarians" in the rest of the world. In the purest sense, it will be an elevation of the old-style colonial model, this time with the plantation owners in the developed countries ruling the colonized and keeping the "barbarians" at the gate.

A few under-developed countries will fare better than the others in this scheme of things, depending on the extent of their technological development and their history of assertiveness over their natural resources. The Asian nations, including India, will be among them. It will, however, be open season on others.

The English-speaking Caribbean will have little role in any of this because it does not have natural resources. Its connection with the new global economy will most likely be as a magnified playground for those from the power centres. Any pretensions the sub-region has had to strategic significance disappeared with the end of the Cold War.

Ironically, the English-speaking Caribbean has had the most enduring tradition of democracy in all the Third World and even that story was never told. The contrast between this British-influenced sub-region and others where other developed nations have held sway has been remarkable, but untold. The extent to which the Caribbean can influence the formation of the New World Order will depend almost entirely on its willingness to turn toward what, in the 1950s was known as the "continental destiny." Without forging links with Latin America, it will continue to be at the mercy of the power-centres for trade and aid concessions.

That connection has to take place quickly because the North American Free Trade Agreement (NAFTA), which is to be put in place to group Canada, the United States and Mexico, is the forerunner of a wider pact that will link North America with the rest of the Americas. The Caribbean will be in a position to benefit to the extent that it had the foresight to turn away from the power centres to neighbors next-door.

The future of the Caribbean is the major story for the rest of the century. While the media has been focusing on the outcomes of studies such as the one done by the West Indies Commission under Alister McIntyre and Sonny Ramphal, there has not been much examination of the "continental destiny" theory. And it is a fascinating one, for it also raises the issue of a cultural affinity that cuts across the problems of language.

Judging by those who have traditionally held the reins of power in Latin America, it is difficult to appreciate that there is a very large population of people of African descent, just as there is in the Caribbean. Brazil, for instance, has the largest such population in the world, after Nigeria.

The power-centres have installed dictators and other tyrants in Latin America who have looked toward the United States and Europe as the future. Even in the most recent meeting among countries in Latin America and Spain and Portugal, no leader was black.

At a wider level, one way for the Third World to counter the accelerated ravishing of its resources is through reviving the "South-South" economic plan of action that was timorously attempted and then abandoned in the mid-to-late 70s, following the OPEC oil embargo and the ascendancy of the Non-aligned Movement.

Linking the economics of the smaller nations in as many areas as possible – air and sea transportation, bartering, where necessary, convertible currencies, technology exchange and so on – was all spelled out in the "new economic order." The plan failed because of the machinations of the West, which saw it as a creature of the Soviet Union, and because the Arab nations did not provide the capital to finance it, choosing instead to invest in real estate in London and New York and Paris.

An economic arrangement among the Non-aligned nations is still possible but it would be much more difficult now because of the inter-relationships that have developed among the more developed nations and the western economies. And, indeed, it is very doubtful that the political will exists.

Is any of this being told by the media? The answer is it is not. One reason, of course, could be that the media do not see it quite this way. But the more probable reason is the nature of the journalism that would tell the story – the western media.

Western reporters do not actively produce thoughtful stories about the Third World, with the possible exception of the British. Top-rated American journalists can earn over $1 million (US) a year and spend a whole week exploring the spelling propensities of the Vice President of the United States, while it is left to British reporters to tell the world about the Iran-Contra deal and the horrors of the famine first in Ethiopia and now in Somalia.

There are two basic principles on which American media operate. One is to entertain, which is the main pillar because, as seen with television, they command the largest share of the public and so bring in the most money. The other principle is the relationship of the story to national policy.

It is only when an issue is elevated to national scope that it draws media attention, as happened when black americans and others decided to propel apartheid and racist South Africa to the front of national consciousness. The result was that a president as popular as Ronald Reagan found his South African policy rejected by Congress. A similar exercise is now being attempted for Haiti, where the Bush administration has a questionable policy of forcing refugees back home without allowing them a chance to make a case for political asylum.

The past decade has also witnessed the more overt identification of American media as corporations concerned with profits and this has had a considerable influence on how and when they report stories and what stories they cover. This trend can be expected to strengthen, not diminish, because of the emphasis on the bottom line, and stories about the Third World will continue to have lessening priority. Regardless of how fine the stories reported by journalists from the Third World and even from the West, they will continue to have little meaning unless there are outlets for them.

Media outlets in the West must therefore be identified and persuaded to provide additional, not necessarily alternative, stories. For example, the *Miami Times*, which is a 70-year-old black newspaper, has allowed its pages to be used to report just such stories, while not neglecting its primary, local focus.

The *Miami Times* was among the few (if there were any others) American newspapers that carried the two-part series on the appalling conditions in which black Brazilians live, at a time when the rest of the media was paying exclusive attention to the Earth Summit and its significance to the environment. The *Miami Times* thought that taking care of people is an inextricable part of the environmental agenda.

There are "ethnic" newspapers as well as television and radio stations that can provide just such an outlet for stories that would not otherwise be available to American readers. For instance, when Nelson Mandela visited the United States in the middle of 1990, people in Miami knew very well who he was and what he stood for – so much so that when Miami government officials refused to accord Mr. Mandela an official welcome because of opposition to his friendship with Yasser Arafat and Fidel Castro, black Miamians called a boycott of the area's crucial tourism industry on July 7, 1990. It is still going on; it thrust the South African leader and his cause to the forefront of a local agenda.

Unless the capital is available to start up a news agency or to greatly expand one or two now existing in the Third World, there is little alternative to the main sources of international news, such as AP, Reuters and AFP. But even they can be influenced into giving a new dimension to their reporting once the informational need is created. But even if there are other news agencies supplying news, ultimately it is the demand for such information that determines whether an editor sends the copy to a page.

An exchange of news among Third World countries and agencies is always a possibility but unless there is a specific reason for such news sharing, it becomes academic, a waste of resources and, ultimately counterproductive.

For instance, unless there is an intention for the Caribbean to link up with Latin America or for the wider Non-aligned nations to jump-start the "new economic order," it matters little whether there is a sharing of news. While it can be argued that such an exchange can help lay the groundwork for a public opinion base, there is no indication that as clear a relationship exists between Third World media and their impact on public opinion and government decisions as between the American media and their effect on public opinion.

One hope is that, with more developing countries turning away from authoritarianism and embracing even some early, tentative steps toward democracy, the media will become less restricted and so can offer reports that can lay the basis for an informed public opinion.

That will, however, depend largely on the *bona fides* of those who own the media and whether they are switching from one master – the dictatorship – to another, the Western power-centres.

For, in the final analysis, the media are the most vital institution in support of a regime, whether it be democratic or tyrannical. It takes an inordinate amount of courage for many Third World journalists and publishers to resist, often at penalty of death, the tyranny exercised over their nations. It is just as courageous for them to resist the temptation to align themselves with the power centres and help in shaping the new master-plantation style of world government that looms ahead.

Derek Ingram
Gemini News Service

William Saidi
Sunday Times, Zimbabwe

(From left) Satinder Kumar, Director, University of Regina School of Journalism and Communications, Derek Ingram, Gemini News Service. The School and Gemini were the sponsors of the conference.

(From left) Zhu Yinghuang, *China Daily,* Bethel Njoku, Gemini, Gerald Knight, *Guardian,* U.K.

(From left) Carma Livingstone, Melanie Braaten, Clarisse Klassen, University of Regina Journalism Students, Anjum Niaz, *Dawn,* Pakistan

(From left) Ngozi Anayaegbunam (Nigeria), Nujma Yaqzan (University of Regina Journalism student), Brenda Kossowan (Gemini Fellow), Padmaja Padman, Malaysia, Sharon Marshall, Barbados

"The Western Perspective," from left Bill Cunningham, former Max Bell professor, Bernard Proulx, Radio Quebec, Norman Webster, *Montreal Gazette,* Daniel Nelson PANOS Institute, Barry Wilson, *Western Producer,* Patrick Nagel, Southam News, Scott Honeyman, *Vancouver Sun*

(From left) Joseph Ealadona, Papua New Guinea and Ernest Moloi, Botswana

(From left) Mohamed Hamaludin, *Miami Times*, Charles Quist-Adade, Ghana, Joe Thloloe, *Sowetan*

(From left) Knowlton Nash, Max Bell Professor, University of Regina School of Journalism and Communications, Satinder Kumar, Director, School of Journalism and Kuldip Nayar, India

Delegates line up at the microphone to "attack" panelists

Saskatchewan farmer Don Horseman explains the intricacies of grain to a group of delegates

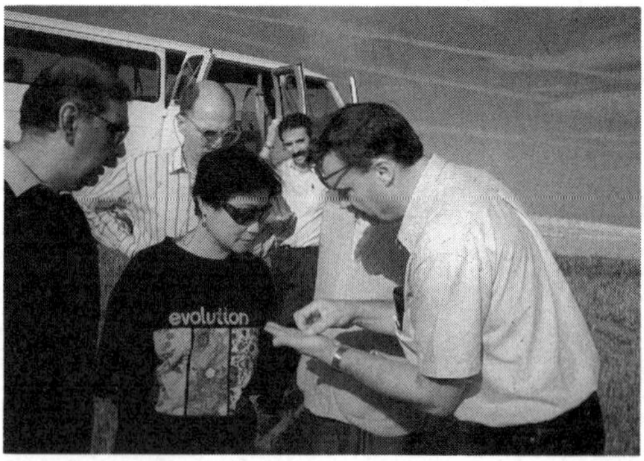

Larry Todd of the School of Journalism and also a part-time farmer gives yet another explanation of Saskatchewan grain to Abby Tan of the Phillipines, Jai Parasram of CBC Newsworld, Danny Nelson, PANOS Institute (U.K.) while Luis Tricot (Chile) looks on

(From left) Gerry Sperling, School of Journalism and Department of Political Science, University of Regina, Maggie Siggins, author and former Max Bell Professor and Bethel Njoku, Gemini News Service

(From left) Sharon Marshall, Caribbean Broadcasting Union, Barbados, and Rex Nettleford, University of the West Indies

Luis Tricot, Freelancer, Santiago, Chile

Noele Hall, Regina singer songwriter

Ngozi Anyaebunam, Nigeria, on Don Horseman's Saskatchewan grain farm outside Fort Qu'Appelle

Clyde Sanger, Director of Communications, North-South Institute, Ottawa

Rex Nettleford, University of the West Indies

Roger Dumilie, Director, International Non-Government Organization Division, Canadian International Development Agency

Padmaja Padman, *New Straits Times*, Malaysia, and Gillian Forrester, former Gemini Fellow

5

Asia and the Pacific
Economic Power and Media Innovation

Anjum Niaz
Senior Editor, *Dawn*, Pakistan

> Life moves on, whether we act as cowards or heroes. Everything we shut our eyes to, everything we run away from, everything we deny, denigrate or despise, serves to defeat us in the end. What seems nasty, painful, evil, can become a source of beauty, joy and strength, if faced with an open mind. Every moment is a golden one for he who has the vision to recognize it as such.

So said the American writer, Henry Miller, way back in 1957. Today, it applies more than ever before, to us, the people in the media. But the question is: do we have the vision to recognize life in its entirety? Can we transcend the geopolitical barriers of time and space, cultures and religions, races and languages to make sense of the world around us? Can we with open minds bring beauty, joy and strength to our own people in our own region?

In Pakistan, as a working journalist for the last ten years, I am often assailed with questions: "What's happening?" "What's going to happen?" "Is martial law going to return?" "Will India attack?" "Will we get Kashmir?" "What will happen in the next budget after a flood havoc which just occurred in Pakistan recently?" Those who query are a well-informed, well-educated lot, but obviously puzzled.

While world affairs don't pose comprehension problems for them thanks to the extensive media global coverage, it's the current events in our country – in our region, that leave them hopelessly confused. Good journalism doesn't only consist of locating news and reporting it accurately. It involves seeing the meaning behind it and reporting it in a way that unravels a story and reveals its significance.

Yes, indeed, stories in Pakistan today are pregnant with revelations which certainly deserve a deeper look and a better display then they receive. What we get instead are statements of people in authority exhorting, sermonizing, admonishing, promising a better tomorrow. Day after day we are fed the same fare, while the realities on the ground get starker and starker.

Third World people (especially in South Asia) are held hostage to a history which has a habit of recycling itself – throwing up dictatorships, militancy, inefficiency, corruption, and natural calamities with a sickening repetition that sentences the South Asians to lives of imprisonment, of rigorous labour, disease, ignorance and grinding poverty.

While a privileged few live off the fruits of labour, the media often miss major journalistic opportunities by failing to investigate, follow-up and report the moral, social, and political repercussions contained in the shibboleths mouthed endlessly by these chattering classes and their actions which keep Pakistan poor, underdeveloped, over-populated and illiterate.

For all the criticism that the press receives, it is worth remembering that where our honorable members of Parliament fail to debate issues of vital national importance, it's the press that does so; where issues of graft and corruption fail to be raised in Parliament it is the press that does so; and where the key task of national agenda-setting escapes the busy lives of the elected representatives, it's the press that steps in to do so, articulating and debating issues sometimes at great risk. The press still seems to have some notion of the public interest according to the first woman editor of a daily in Asia, Ms. Meleeha Hodhi, who edits *The News* from Islamabad.

At the risk of stating the obvious, the independent press would seriously need to investigate, examine, assess, expose, analyze, debate, and most importantly, follow up on stories that are vital to the well-being, progress and security of our nation. It has to challenge the status quo and press for social change.

What's the real story behind our nuclear capability? Do we or don't we have a bomb? Why must the West call it an "Islamic bomb"? Do bombs have religion? Our nuclear wizard, who wouldn't talk to Pakistani pressmen, happily spillled the beans to an Indian journalist (present here among us today) some years ago. But the nuclear issue is still hushed up.

Whether we have gone nuclear or not, one thing is for certain – development in Pakistan is on hold. While we boast of an impressive growth rate, we have failed to translate this into human progress. According to the UNDP's (United Nations Development Program) Human Development Report of 1991, out of 160 developing countries, Pakistan ranks 120th! The Human Development Index says:

- There are 54.6 million Pakistanis without access to health care
- There are 67.5 million Pakistanis without access to safe drinking water
- 97.6 million Pakistanis without access to sanitation
- There are 12 million children who are malnourished
- 56 million illiterate adults
- 25.7 million children out of school
- 36.8 million Pakistanis living below the poverty line

Haven't the media enough ammunition to fire away at the policy-makers and decision-makers for a change in the status quo? Someone has to be held accountable for the fact that "in Pakistan, the illegitimate private gain from one's public position is unofficially estimated at 4 percent of the Gross National Product."

Inequality between rich and poor, men and women, different regions and different ethnic groups is one of the most striking features of South Asia.

Mr. V.P. Singh, former Indian Prime Minister and presently Leader of the Opposition, said while he was in Pakistan recently, "Where does our small arms race lead to except to the burdening of the people who need more food, more schools, hospitals, roads and canals? Does it make any sense to turn these schools, hospitals and roads into tanks, warplanes and dynamite? With the cost of a tank we can build perhaps a hundred primary schools, with the cost of a fighter plane we could build three thousand of them."

It was heartening to hear him say this, but the big question is what stopped Mr. Singh from translating the above rhetoric into action when he was in government?

Development journalism needs firmer roots in South Asia to arm the media for tackling the above stories. Presently development reporting is not a serious business with the editors or the reporters, and it is often relegated to the lowest rung of the newspapers. Data, finances and expertise are perhaps some of the reasons that have kept development journalism from flowering. While editors sit in their ivory towers and reporters grapple with crime and politics, stories of ordinary lives are lost somewhere in between.

Let's take the women in Pakistan. The majority are unlettered, ignorant, house-bound, male-dominated, under-privileged and over-burdened. There are only two women in parliament today, few women in key positions in the government and public sectors. And yet, contradictions abound. Pakistan was the first Muslim country to have a woman prime minister. We have a woman ambassador in Washington. Sadly, stories on women are being missed. The media, instead of reflecting change, must provoke it.

Women must be in charge of their fertility and must be free to decide their family size. In Pakistan today, there is a 60 percent awareness of modern family planning methods, yet only 15 percent of married couples of reproductive age practise family planning. Why? While there are several cultural, social, political and religions reasons, the main one is the population control program itself.

It has never taken off! In spite of pious proclamations from people who have manned it for the last thirty years, it is shell-shocked. We don't need demographic dynamos in the media to expose the shortcomings of this program. We need sincere interested and motivated men and women out in the field looking closely at the service delivery systems.

Pakistan grows at a rate of 3.3 percent every year. Strong religious and male biases keep the Program from picking up. The media must be alert to such regressive forces which keep women bereft of legal, social and human rights. It is also the duty of editors to ensure systematic and continous coverage.

At the recent Earth Summit in Rio de Janeiro, Pakistan, as chair of the Group of 77 (which consists of 129 developing countries), made all the right kind of noises concerning environment and development. Pakistan's Prime Minister was the first head of government from a developing country to make a firm commitment on population control.

The media missed this story in Pakistan.

Speaking about the UN Conference on Environment and Development (UNCED) in Rio, the media here must mobilize and question the government by saying, "You went to Rio, you made commitments to environment and development – what have you done about it? What measures are you taking? What are you doing for us?"

The government can't turn back and say, "We don't have the financial resources, or the GEF (Global Environmental Fund) is making life difficult for us so we can't implement Agenda 21 (the 800 page plan for the 21st century regarding the relationship between evnironment and economy) – as pointed out by Jamsheed Marker, Pakistan's ambassador to the UN, the man who played a key role at UNCED in negotiations between developed and developing countries. He is angry at the North for ordering the South to restructure its economic and social institutions.

> If we re-structure our economies are you willing to re-structure your debt burdens? It's monstrous that today there are reverse flows of $160 billion annually from the developing countries to the developed countries.
>
> Haven't you made enough money from us? Isn't it time that you were a little fairer to us? If that happened we wouldn't need extra aid. We wouldn't need your aid at all. But until you re-strucutre your trading patterns, remove your trade barriers on textiles, improve access to markets, ensure fairer pricing, facilitate the flow of new capital and sophsiticated technology to us, we will need funds from you to meet our needs.

This statement by Ambassador Marker, the spokesman for the G-77 at the United Nations, says it all. Right down from the affluent North and the western press, matters concerning the Third World are not viewed in their right prespective. While power politics after the Cold War are at play in the North making the public figures ignore the plight of the poor South, the western media seems to have also washed its hands of us.

Some sentiments reverberated at the 10th Non-aligned Movement Summit held in Jakarta in September, 1992 where it was felt that the threat to the sovereignty of Third World countries was larger now because the US was interested in a total over-lordship in order to keep Japan and the West European countries from harbouring any economic ambitions.

What would be Pakistan's place in the New World Order? With the end of the Cold War, America's raison d'être for a pampered Pakaistan, as a front line state, has ceased to exist. Now we are under increasing pressure from the Americans regarding our nuclear program, Kashmir, military expenditures and drugs.

The media in the West does not appear to be neutral either. It betrays a certain air of superiority or ignorance. "The Western media is racist with a bias against the black or the brown man who is often portrayed as a fool or a crook. You'll notice the spokesperson on TV is always blonde, blue-eyed and white," comments Dr. Akbar S. Ahmed, a prominent Pakistani social scientist and visiting professor at Cambridge University.

Many think the western media see Islam as a threatening force, a force of disorder and anarchy. 80 percent of the people polled in England and America say Islam is the next enemy after Communism. Akbar Ahmed says. "Every time I appear on a chat show in England I am asked, 'You're a Muslim. Are you a fundamentalist?'" The BBC TV series on Asian Families seems to pick up on the negative side of Islam by portraying Muslims as decadent, orthodox, fanatics, terrorists and bigots who are always praying. CNN finds nothing worthwhile from our part of the world to report unless a major catastrophe hits us like the recent country-wide floods.

Marshall McLuhan's famous dictum about TV being the "message" seems a little dated. Today, the media as a whole is the "Master." There is no two-way traffic. The Third World looks West, but the West looks to itself.

Allow me to end with Henry Miller once again:

> Life is constantly providing us with new funds, new resources, even when we are reduced to immobility. In life's ledger, there is no such thing as frozen assets.

Padmaja Padman,

New Straits Times, Malaysia

> I think it is in our hands to do something for ourselves. We are no less than them as journalists. We don't have to wait for them forever to show us the way to go out and decide what it is we need to know about ourselves. We can tell them. And there are many ways that we can do it.

I just want to illustrate some of the things I have seen in the last nine months and then to go on to some ways that people in Asia, the Pacific region and the rest of the developing world can actually take control of their own destinies without depending too much on the western media.

In February this year (1992), seventy wives or women representatives of heads of state or government met in Geneva for a summit. They were going to discuss what women could do for other women to sort of give them basic economic activities to better their lot in life and to upgrade the quality of their lives. The idea was that if you could do this for the women at the basic level, then you could do that with their families or the immediate communities.

What really happened at this was many of those who came from the western media wandered around the hall asking the delegates the most obvious questions: "Why are you meeting in Geneva? It's so expensive." "Why don't you give the money that you'd have spent on this conference to the women?" And the answer was, "Well, we need the international exposure. We could do it on a small scale, but you wouldn't come to our country, so we had to come to yours." And similarly, they also asked if the First Ladies really thought they had the power to effect the changes. They said, "You're all dependent on your husbands. How sure are you that you going to actually do something about this?" And then they went on to say to us how much the rural women were actually earning, and they said, "Please translate that to pounds sterling, or US dollars for us." And, of course, they went into immediate shock. "What! Three hundred dollars US a year! That's not much!" But they didn't understand what kind of backgrounds these women were coming from.

The journalists from the developing world (there were quite a number of us there as well) had other concerns. We were saying, "How sure are we that these activities that you are talking about are actually going to be translated into action fairly quickly?" and "Can these programs be sustained in the long-run?" and "Why didn't we think of economic empowerment for rural areas before this?"

From this, you can see that there is as wide a gap as ever in the way we all look at an issue. This is not going to change and indeed, it should not because the complexity of world affairs deserves more respect than a homogenous view.

What I'd really like to see is that there is fair and accurate reporting where the truth is given prominence. Let your readers make up their minds as to what should be done or shouldn't be done. I think that's always been the basics of journalism and we shouldn't actually go beyond that.

Economic reporting used to provide a very solid base for this because it was very objective. You couldn't go beyond the facts a lot. You could just analyze the situation for what it was. But in the so-called New World Order, I think this has changed. Now economics has become the big thing in the power play. What I think we're really dealing with here is a lot of willful ignorance because we are not going out of our way to find out how we should be dealing with these situations. And we're actually denying the truth – all of us. We are all being manipulated in one way or another by our governments, our business communities. We all have parochial views. We all have our own self-interests at heart. And somewhere along the way, I think we have forgotten that we just owe it to our public to tell them the truth.

What's really happened is that the economic developments in the Asia Pacific area have largely been ignored in the last couple of years. In this sense, I think the western media is not quite prepared for what's actually come up there at the moment. You have a very young, very vibrant grouping of economies. They're doing very well, and suddenly, everyone is waking up to this fact. You don't know how to deal with it. You're all coming around and saying, "Tell me, how do you do this?"

Well, there is a story there. But why isn't this story being told in the West, especially in a time when the industrial economies are in recession and you have major problems with unemployment? Everyone is trying to work towards economic groupings and we all actually face the same problems in the end, but it's being told from a different perspective.

You have the usual success stories of the East Asian economies: Japan, Korea, Taiwan, Hong Kong, Singapore, Malaysia, too. And these stories are not being told. They're just there for the Asia Pacific countries to talk about – I think not even for a large part of the developing world to talk about.

You find the Asia Pacific countries are actually going for very proactive economic policies. They're promoting investment on a large scale. For the first time, they themselves are beginning to invest in other young economies such as in Vietnam. We want to know now, why is it that these stories are not important enough to the West? Is it because of the political manipulations at the western end? Are the governments so insecure that they cannot tell the story without their own shortcomings being exposed by comparison? Or is it really something that had been said yesterday to me by someone – that ordinary western readers are not exactly interested in what's going on in another part of the world, unless it's something to do with a catastrophe, disease, pestilence which is like war, rioting, looting, whatever. Why are these success stories not of any importance to ordinary people who might actually benefit from them?

Last week, a Malaysian delegation came out to London. Two hundred and eighty representatives of British companies attended a one-day seminar. They were very well informed and I'm pretty sure that they didn't get that information from the British newspapers, because nothing has been said in the British newspapers in the last nine months about anything that was going on in Malaysia. But these people had connections because some of them had traditionally built up economic ties, they had companies based in Malaysia, and they knew what they were talking about and they were interested. Because they weren't getting anywhere in their own economies, they wanted to go out and invest someplace else. They were looking at a whole lot of possibilities.

So you have an interest, even if it is a business interest. So far, business issues have been handled basically by financial publications. Why isn't this important enough to get into the general news section, where the ordinary person who is not likely to read a financial paper can get as much attention?

I know that the western press has got its own problems. We all have those problems. We have space constraints, we have priorities for news, and we have managements that don't change. And so everyone is kept in perpetual ignorance. Do we continue doing that? I think that's what we have to look at in the aftermath of the Cold War. To what extent do we hold back information from our public, and to what extent do we address the fact that they need to know? We can't carry everything; we can't cover everything, but we can try to give them as much as we can.

Western governments have talked about environmental degradation in the developing world and have been insisting that economic development should be done on a sustainable basis.

There was greater reality expressed on this issue when developing countries met in Kuala Lampur earlier this year (1992) at an environmental conference, than all the hype floated at the Rio Earth Summit in June. News coverage of the Kuala Lampur conference in the British press was almost nil – whatever there was, appeared seriously jaundiced and our side of the story was never really told.

Ditto with the Asean Ministeral Meeting in Singapore and the Non-aligned Movement summit in Jakarta. These were not just political meetings, because the leaders had already recognized that the way forward would be to strengthen domestic and regional economic ties to avoid over-dependence on foreign trade and aid. But for the sum total of copy generated by those British newspapers that did send out reporters, they might as well have saved their money and left the job to agencies like Gemini which have an independent insight into the news.

The Asia-Pacific economies have never been in a better position to break the old economic order and to stop current powers from talking down to them. We hold many of the advantages in terms of human resources, natural resources and a willingness to adjust quickly to changing needs and to learn new technology.

A lot of the West doesn't actually know what's going on in the East, and as a result, they're caught unprepared every time when someone comes up and says, "OK, now we've taken a position. We're going to press for the reconstruction of the Security Council of the United Nations." And everyone's wondering, "Who are these people?" These people are something like two-thirds of the world. They're not going to sit there and wait anymore and say, "Carry on running the world as you've been running it." We want our share now. So I think it is important for the western public to be informed about this.

I've said something about trying to get out of the system. I think the Asia Pacific countries have it in them to actually break away from the old order and become a very relevant part of the new order. They're going to stop a lot of people from talking down to them. They have the human resources, they have the natural resources, and they have the willingness to adjust very quickly to changing needs, which is something I think the West has forgotten over the years.

More importantly, we have to talk about us as journalists from the Asia Pacific, from the rest of the developing world. What can we do? Have we, ourselves, kept up with the changes? I don't think we have as much as we should have. I'm going to throw a lot of unconventional ideas around. You can agree, you can disagree, you can talk about it . . . whatever.

I say we should stop moaning about the West. There's no point; they're not going to change – not for a long, long while. I think it is in our hands to do something for ourselves. We are no less than them as journalists. We don't have to wait for them forever to show us the way to go out and decide what it is we need to know about ourselves. We can tell them. And there are many ways that we can do it.

We all speak at least one international language. We are in a very unique position to meet people. And we can go out and tell our stories on a one-to-one basis, we can have talks, we can do networking with associations, the Union of Journalists and we can always make the information available to the western journalists. I really don't believe that any one of them is so mean that they cannot open their minds to the information that is available. They can't really get to the information, so they give up and go back and perpetuate what they already know. So we can do that as individuals.

The developing world is not short of people with technical expertise and experience in economic development, while some of our countries have a little spare cash now and then to provide aid. None of us has an obsession to link aid and trade with human rights practises, good governance and democracy.

As much as developing economies could start helping one another, we as journalists could try and create our own image and establish credibility within the world press.

The other thing we can do, I think, is set up some kind of economic news service as opposed to the general news service. And here we can link up to different parts of the developing world. We can collate the information and we can make this available to people who need to make use of it. We can give our own analyses of economic situations, and this information, if available, is going to mean that publishers or newspaper organizations or forecasting organizations can actually pick up on the information and use it fairly quickly without expending their own resources on having to go out and get it.

For our own part at home, I think we have a very important role: to make sure that our bureaucrats are kept on their toes. We have to have data banks, we have to have information, we have to have statistics, and we have to be able to analyze and criticize our own policies before this is done for us by people who can't understand or people who won't understand.

Think about it.

Joseph Ealodona

Broadcasting Commission, Papua New Guinea

> Maybe nothing is newsworthy except the tourist agencies telling many western people of beautiful girls and white beaches and coconut trees.

I'm from Papua New Guinea, a little nation in the South Pacific. I don't know if many of you know about the South Pacific. It's down south. It's made up of beautiful girls and coconut trees, small islands, white beaches. Well, the tourism agencies say that.

Papua New Guinea has 800 languages. It's generally quite hard to put out news that many of them will understand. We're going to talk about economic power and media innovation. I'll just briefly explain how we disseminate news to our people down there. I write English news and it's translated into local languages and then it goes out. If you study language, it changes slightly, so maybe many of them don't get what we really write.

I'm quite a new journalist and I feel I'm privileged to stand out here in front of many of you experienced journalists.

We're talking about the Cold War. To many of us in the Pacific Islands, we ask, "What is the Cold War?" We don't know much about the Cold War except that we're bombarded by news from the western media that comes through BBC and ABC telling us of the Cold War. Because only recently, we realized that they are dumping nuclear waste in the Pacific. As a young Pacific Island journalist, I think journalism is developing and we are looking toward helping our governments criticize those western nations that are dumping nuclear waste in the Pacific. I'm not a political activist.

The shift of economic power is to bigger western countries that run our economy and tell us what to do. We don't know what to report except to criticize the western governments for dumping nuclear waste in the Pacific.

Only recently we've come to realize what the Cold War is. It has ended in Europe, maybe it has ended, but it has not ended in the Pacific; it's beginning because of the dumping of nuclear waste. Only recently France stopped its testing in the Pacific for one year on the grounds that America must stop before they stop completely. Japan is now trying to transport some nuclear leftovers from Europe through the Pacific, through to Japan. That's what we know about the Cold War. That's what we are reporting about. Telling small island Pacific people the dangers of this nuclear waste – we don't want it to come to us.

That is why I said that the Cold War, although it has ended, though it has had much effect in other countries, really hasn't as much effect on us except for the aftereffects of it. It still remains a frightening prospect for small island nations like us because of what we think the bigger nations will do after the Cold War.

The western media – I don't know why it's happening – it reports to its audience only on newsworthy things and not on many other good things that are happening in the developing world, such as in the South Pacific. According to White, General Secretary of the International Federation of Journalists):

> In most regions of the world, the provision of newspapers, periodicals, radio and television is taken for granted. In doing so, it is also assumed that news is being made available to the people in one form or another. In the South Pacific, these assumptions simply make no sense. Scattered across millions of square kilometres, the world's largest ocean, are thousands of small island nations on which live barely one and a half million people, and only the existence of Papua New Guinea, on the Pacific's western rim, gives the region a society with both a large land mass and a proportionally large population. In the island mini-states and colonial territories that dot the South Pacific, the lack of a developed territory-wide infrastructure, the legacy of colony leasing, an absence in many instances of a viable and national market, have greatly hindered the growth of an independent media.

In the South Pacific, many small nations rely solely on broadcast media and radio networks. Those radio networks depend heavily on BBC and ABC. And that's why I say we are bombarded with western news almost daily.

The media in the Pacific is still young, climbing out of its colonial hangover that many developed nations have put on us. Therefore, most journalists are relatively young, still needing more experience in the world of reporting. I'm glad that I'm here, maybe the only small Pacific island journalist to be here, to such a gathering.

You know, in the Pacific, it's the same old problem – like one African said yesterday, western journalism isn't really understanding our way of living. I really don't want to blame them for not understanding us. Maybe, it should be we who should change to make them understand us more.

So it appears that the foreign journalists write stories out of the Pacific and at times do not really give the true story of what's happening. There's only a few foreign journalists who cover the Pacific fairly and accurately. The others – we call them "fly-in and fly-out journalists" – journalists who fly in when there's trouble. When there was a military coup in Fiji, they flew in just to report what at that time was happening and not what created the situation.

They flew into Papua New Guinea to cover the Bougainville break away movement, like what's happening here in Canada. But in my country, the secessionist movement has gone into an armed conflict. I've been in there a couple of times. Some bullets have missed me. It's a good experience to go into such situations.

Many foreign reports do not really see the root cause of problems that come out from developing nations, and I refer to the Pacific.

Some years ago, my country's foreign minister, Sir Michael T. Somare, proposed to bring in a code of conduct for journalists. His reasons were clear. It's in this magazine. I will quote it. He said,

> For some time now, leaders, officials, and citizens of foreign island countries have voiced concern about the role and activities of media organizations and the personnel operating in the Pacific. But too often, media reports of events in the Pacific Island countries are extremely biased and even damaging at times to Pacific Island governments and people. [We continue, as nations in the Pacific, properly to] uphold the principles of freedom of expression and the freedom of media.

The government believes, then, that the media organizations and their personnel must be encouraged by the government of Pacific Island nations to conduct their activities in the region responsibly. To adhere to the principles of freedom of expression and freedom of the press while at the same time demonstrating sensitivity and respect for the views and inspirations of the Island people or the indigenous people of the South Pacific. I see nothing wrong with that. I'm only afraid as a journalist that it may become a form of news censoring for us. This proposed code of ethics has yet to be discussed by politicians in the Pacific.

I have not really delved into our sub-theme of Economic Power and Media Innovation. It is obvious that the United States, Japan, and Germany are controlling the world economy and if I go deep into that, I might have a headache after this.

Many things have gone unheard in the South Pacific side of the world. Maybe nothing is newsworthy except the tourist agencies telling many western people of beautiful girls and white beaches and coconut trees. I deliberately said "unheard" because I believe the BBC, ABC, and some other media agencies that operate from the Pacific run something about the South Pacific, but maybe it's of no interest to the bigger western world.

For example, only recently my country was asked to recognize the PLO. Very sensitive. They haven't decided on anything yet. This hasn't even gone through cabinet. We know the PLO only as terrorist people. But maybe they are a form of freedom fighters who want to form a country. But we don't know about that. The United States is telling us that they're fighters, they're rebels, they're terrorists. But that's something that's not being reported much in our world. Maybe we will recognize PLO and maybe in the end, some years later it might explode into something big – the PLO gets hold of the Pacific.

So journalism in the Pacific is rapidly developing.

As a young journalist, I believe in what a fellow journalist friend of mine said, "Freedom of the media is not absolute; it entails responsibility in that journalists should respect views and aspirations of indigenous peoples." It means not only reporting the protests, the warfare and the demonstrations, but also reporting the development and the better shaping of a country that is wanting to develop. It is here that I see a New World Order.

If the Cold War is really over, reporting developing nations from a fair and accurate perspective should become a must.

We've seen that what this seminar hopes to come up with is a network of news distribution. We have one in the Pacific called Pacific News Network (PAC News) for both print and radio media broadcasts for all island nations. I believe this meeting talked about setting up a network that should be modelled after Gemini News to distribute fair and accurate news coming up from the developing world.

Open Forum

Kuldip Nayar (India):

In our part of the world, newspapers have not been able to adapt to the new technology or have not been able to buy new technology because it's very expensive. Machines are very expensive and they are out of date after six months. Big papers are in a position in India where they have been able to buy these machines. But normally speaking in my country, since there are a myriad of languages, it is not possible for the newspapers to have this technology.

In many parts of the world, technology is so costly. I remember the comment that Saddam did a lot of damage to the Third World countries and to the Middle East. But there is a very interesting observation. Oil is cheap, but technology is costly, meaning that we in those parts of the world where we have the raw materials, that still remain cheap, but technology is going up and up in cost.

Ernest Moloi (Botswana Guardian):

Madam Niaz, you say you are assailed with questions from members of the public. It is a clear indication that people do read your newspapers and that you are keeping up with events in your country. So I want to know, do you give them an in-depth story so that you are not all the time being asked questions like, "What is happening?" "What is going to happen?"

Anjum Niaz:

Unfortunately, in Pakistan, in-depth reporting is not that much a practice, especially in the daily papers where you have to be meeting a deadline. And, also the problem of lack of reporters to send into certain areas. There are – I'm sorry to say – very few in-depth stories that come out from the daily pages.

But we do, on the other hand, have monthly magazines, and they are doing a terrific job in carrying investigative in-depth stories.

Ngozi Anyaegbunam:

Mrs. Niaz, you said the Third World looks to the West but the West looks to itself. Mrs. Padman said we should stop moaning about the West and think about what to do to help ourselves. I think we are all saying the same thing. I would like you to elaborate on that. Joseph said that they are dumping toxic waste on us. Somehow in desperate ways we are all saying the same thing.

I've read in a lot of foreign magazines where they talk about "compassion fatigue." They are tired of us now, especially because you cannot continue to help somebody who is not helping himself. We have poor leadership, corrupt leadership. If the little you are given you have not properly managed, of course whoever is giving it to you will resent giving you more.

I was discussing "compassion fatigue" with a group of journalists last night. I was the only black. They are all white. They are very young – I'm older than all of them. Somehow we were able to relate to one another and were just talking very openly. You could never have had a more open conversation – they were so candid about their views and I was somehow able to get some feelings from them. There is something that we have not realized – those of us in the Third World – which is that the "compassion fatigue" is getting to an extent where they are thinking of a way to not just fob us off, but to get us back to the old imperialistic situation. If you can't manage your lives, they'll take over your lives for you, and maybe we'll go back to the days of imperialism.

Anjum Niaz:

I think we need to take a look at our own courtyard. In Pakistan, and I'm sure all the other Third World countries – the governments have functions for the foreign media. For instance, the Prime Minister or the President will be very happy to speak to a BBC correspondent, will be happy to speak to someone from the *New York Times*. In fact, the press spokespersons of these people are always chasing them and always entertaining them. They make them feel as if they are really some terrific – God's gift to us in Pakistan. As opposed to the local media, the local reporters, the local press who are kept at bay. I don't know why in this regard there is already discrimination. The foreign media gets the top seats and the most prominent places and the local media have no access to interviews or things like that.

I'll give you an example. In Pakistan we have had some very young girls in their twenties come out representing very prestigious papers in the UK and in America who came out and were wined and dined and they were flattered by our ministers, by our army, by our people. And then what do they do? They go back and they write books. And those books are an insult – they just laugh. They laugh about how they were treated or about how the Pakistani males were all the time busy chasing them. I think it is quite disgusting, but this is what it is. This has been the trend. So, first of all, I think that we should question our own government's attitude towards it.

The newspapers are quite happy to quote figures from BBC, Voice of America, at a local rally. They are not willing to rely on local reporters reports that there were about 10 000 people. BBC says that there were 10 000 people. Now why are we, ourselves, giving them so much importance, so much elevation? Really, I think we have to look at it in that way.

The third thing is about subscribing to news agencies. My newspaper is happy to spend lots of foreign exchange subscribing to *Washington Post, Los Angeles Times,* and we are carrying huge stories – for them, for these stories, we find space. We print them very happily. But, if a local person was wanting to do those kind of stories, he would not be encouraged and would not really be paid the kind of money that we pay to the agencies.

Kuldip Nayar:

Have you ever protested against this in your own paper?

Anjum Niaz:

No.

Kuldip Nayar:

So that explains it.

Anjum Niaz:

No. How can I protest when the press barons and the editors themselves think that this is what is going to sell the paper? We are for some reason on a bandwagon here where the editors and the publishers and the press barons feel we must get these prestigious services. Take for example, the local correspondent in India and Pakistan for the *New York Times.* She has been the most important person in Pakistan besides the President. People followed her all around and made sure that they caught hold of her and maybe she might have spent some time and maybe she would have reported back a little news item on Pakistan or whatever. So I think that we really need to train our own people. We are not being fair. We are, in that way, not allowing the flowering of local talent. That, I think, is criminal to me.

Kuldip Nayar:

One explanation I have is that I think we have been too near our slavery and have not been able to get out of that complex yet. Why would a correspondent from Africa come and not be given the same treatment as a person from London or Europe would? So it's within us – something like that.

Since you say that you are never protesting – I think we all have to protest against this.

Padmaja Padman:

My question was how can we stop moaning and do something for ourselves. The western media is not portraying us in the developing world the way we want to be seen – they're not giving us any dignity, they're not telling the truth about us, and they are generally not interested in coming out to get to know us. All I'm saying here is why do we wait for them to understand? It's very hard for them because they come from a completely different environment. They don't have sufficient exposure to what's going on. As anybody who's been a foreign correspondent knows, it takes years for you to really understand what the situation is really like in any one particular country. Just when you understand, they pull you out and send you home and send somebody back to start all over again.

So this is where we in our own countries are in the position to project ourselves and, as journalists, to project ourselves without the hype of patriotism and without the propaganda of our governments. We all know that happens, so we have to cut through to the truth and we have to be able to tell the truth about ourselves. When we do this, then perhaps we can gain international respect and credibility, and maybe we can finally make somebody else understand what we're all about. So this is why I say it has to start from us.

Murray Burt:

I want to address two points made by Kuldip Nayar regarding technology and since the topic is innovation, the innovation that technology offers.

In India's case, Mr. Nayar, the greatest impediment was Indian policy on allowing the import of much media technology, a policy that changed in its last budget with some hope.

The other point I would like to make to you is that I think it would be disastrous for the Third World to invite the Western world to send its cast-offs of media technology. It's happened in Africa and it's absolutely unnecessary. Technology is far from getting more expensive – it's getting much cheaper and I would desperately caution that you don't ask for the West's cast-offs. You'll be the loser.

Duart Farquarson:

I think it's important as you are in western Canada that we stop generalizing about "the West" and I don't mean western Canada; I mean the West. You're casting this phobia and you're talking about the *New York Times* and the *Washington Post* and so on. As someone who's been a foreign correspondent in the field, I've had to deal with that. That's the phenomenon, that's the real world that we live in. We all have to deal with it. We have a Prime Minister who often gives interviews to the *New York Times* when he won't give them to Canadians. Now does this make us a developing country as was suggested yesterday? I don't think so, but there's a point of reality here.

I was very impressed by Mrs. Niaz's initial paper because she revealed so well all the problems of her country and criticized her own media for not doing the job that she'd like to see them do for it. You were truly talking about comforting the afflicted and afflicting the comfortable to use the old cliché. That impressed me because yesterday we heard so much about how the western media comes in and it only sees the bad things, it doesn't see the good things. Everything you mentioned was bad. There was no good news there. That is the news – that's what you're dealing with, and that's what correspondents often have to deal with too.

The quote that was mentioned before – that the Third World looks to the West but the West looks to itself. I think that in parts of the world that I know, that's not true. I think in the Middle East, in many of the Arab Muslim countries, quite the opposite is the case. In the case of Iran, the whole Iranian revolution was primarily about getting rid of the Shah for many good reasons. The Islamic Fundamentalist Revolution came after that and was part of the machinery that did it, but it is very much a rejection of western values and a looking to the strengths, as they're seen in Iran, of the traditional Iranian culture. It's looking inward very much. I think the West is becoming more and more conscious of that.

Again, I would like to say, don't generalize about western reporters going in. A lot of us here who have been around various places find ourselves running differently from Americans. That's why we need more Canadians in the field plugging for Canadian foreign correspondents.

Unidentified Questioner:

A question to Joseph. Towards the end of his presentation he mentioned very briefly about the PAC News which is one of the innovations in the Pacific and he didn't go into too much detail. I was wondering if he could share some more information on how it actually operates.

Joseph Ealodona:

Pacific News Service is made up of many island radio stations and print media. What happens is that we have this faxing system. They write stories for their own stations or media. The same story is faxed to my station from say, Fiji, and we use the story with the local perspective. We don't really change it. The local understanding of it is there, but we just maybe change a few words and put "in Fiji" and all that. It's funded by Germany. It's quite helpful to many Pacific Island nations who want to learn and know more about each other. It's basically a news writing, news sending service.

Wafula Oguttu:

My question goes to Padmaja. While I fully embrace your concept, as for the Third World relying on ourselves, I have a problem. The western journalist presides over the world's news network. Supposing we go back home, back to the drawing board and we attempt to do things on our own. How do we penetrate this network – the world's news network? How do we go in there? Do we stand a chance of getting through? How do we go in there on our own? It's good, we can do a story in Uganda, but then how does this story in Uganda go right around the world?

Padmaja Padman:

It's also all our problem. I just basically feel that if the story is worth telling and if the story is well told, then even if it appears in our own newspapers, it doesn't have to go very far beyond that because we have international wire agencies operating in our own areas. You have AFP, anybody else who is around. They could pick up the stories and those stories could actually be fleshed out.

The other thing is that many newspaper organizations actually have arrangements for lifting rights from one another's newspapers. Although that doesn't come very much from the developing world, it's more so from the developed world at the moment, I think if we can continue to impress people that we can do our stories well, I think those arrangements can come in.

I don't suggest it's going to be easy. I don't suggest it's going to be done in a really short time. If we can tell those stories, I don't think there is any newspaper from the developing world which would not prefer to pick up a story and use it rather than send a correspondent, go through all the expense of basing him somewhere and trying to get him to understand things, to make his contacts, to get the story done when it can be done so easily locally.

Kuldip Nayar:

If I may add, in India, some regional papers are exchanging their news stories among themselves. Is it possible that we could have the same arrangement among the Third World countries – exchanging? Because, after all, all of us use English copy as the basic material. So language will not be a barrier that way. It's only the transmission part. That experiment has succeeded in India. Five, six newspapers, they're regional language newspapers, so they are exchanging information among themselves. They give credit to the paper which has given the story. And it has worked well there.

Jill Forrester:

I just wondered if Joseph could describe more of your relationship with the people that speak the other languages – your stories get translated into their languages – is there much demand for stories from those people?

Joseph Ealodona:

We have some 800 different languages and if I write my news in English, it has to be translated back into the local language.

Most of what is going down through people is not world news. It's just development news. Many of them are agriculture news of what the government can do to help them and all that. We are using it to inform our people that this is happening. They're very simple (maybe four paragraphs only) in their local language. It's nothing much on world news and all that.

Jill Forrester:

What about the people in the villages or more remote areas, are their stories getting told?

Joseph Eleadona:

I'll refer to Papua New Guinea; we're like Canada, we have provinces and premiers. We have about 19 – 20 provinces, and we have reporters based in each province. We don't really travel out to the provinces because we have a local reporter there who knows much of what's happening in the province.

Once in a while the villagers come out and express their concern that they don't know what the government is doing to them. They use the media. They find it really hard to get through to the top people to talk to them. So they use us, the media, to express their frustration and that's how they use their provincial reporters. They can speak in their language to him, but he writes it in English to us, and then we put it out.

Clyde Sanger:

Just to cap what you said. I was really impressed when I went into the legislature in Port Moresby and saw that there was simultaneous translation, not just in English and French as there could be in Canada, but you have, I think, six languages that you've translated parliament into simultaneously. So you have your problems in this way.

Just picking up on two points, Mrs. Niaz. You worry about visiting journalists. I think someone answered you to quite an extent in saying that Mulroney talks to the *New York Times* but doesn't talk to Canadians.

I'm the Canada correspondent for *The Economist.* Mr. Robert Bourassa settles down to dinners with the foreign editor of *The Economist* who comes out here maybe once a year. I don't get that sort of access. You have to live with this. But it happens all over the world and you can complain about it or you can work the system.

My last point is about the gatekeepers on papers. We've talked a lot about foreign correspondents coming into a place without the background and some have been longer in places like Patrick Nagle and so on than others and get to know the area as well as any outsider can. But you have then to deal with the people inside the paper, the gatekeepers, the world editors. Thank goodness what is happening in Canada now is that people who have had experience in various parts of the world have moved into senior positions. They have that wider view. I think there's a maturing process that's going on and things are getting better.

Wafula Oguttu:

I think we are using some wrong words here. Words like bashing and moaning with respect to western journalists. I think they're not appropriate words. We are not moaning about western journalists. We are not bashing them. We simply want them to understand us, our predicament. The BBC, Joseph was talking about BBC, or *The New York Times* or *The Washington Post,* these papers are powerful papers, so if they understand our problem, then they will reflect our issues from that perspective.

Because we can't break off immediately, we can't. We're not abdicating our responsibility so that the western journalists should do everything for us, no. But we can't at the same time just blow a whistle and say we are taking new stock there, and we are taking over.

One question which I would like to put to the western journalists who are here is, if we formed our own local syndicates for news, would you be willing to buy our information? Madam Niaz is talking about an Islamic bomb. Why is it that you choose these words to have an "Islamic" bomb or these people are "pro-this"? When we are writing about the West, why don't we say "capitalist" bomb? Why do you use these labels? Are you conscious of them? Because they are dehumanizing us. They make us have nothing of our own.

Sat Kumar:

My question is for both Mr. Nayar and Mrs. Niaz. When I left India in 1968, it was my firm belief that up to that point, because English was the language of the intelligentsia and the ruling class, it was largely irrelevant to the people of India and that the English press was largely irrelevant to the ordinary people of India. It meant nothing to them; most of them did not read it. Not only that, the creative work in India, the literature, the poetry, and everything is in other languages – it's not in English. Should I have any reason to believe that it's any more relevant now than it was then?

Kuldip Nayar:

Well, I wouldn't say that things have changed very much in the sense only that English is now a compulsory language in our schools. This has been for the last three decades. Those people who are really in parliament, are in the bureaucracy, are part of political leadership, they are very much influenced by English.

I wouldn't say that other people are not relevant. They are. And I think there is an effort now. For example, Hindi is becoming very important in our country. But still those who are really at the helm of affairs know English very well, are familiar with English. And then English is the *lingua franca* around the world.

Mohamad Hamaludin:

When we talk about bashing the western journalists, and of course I know of that because I used to do it at one time in Guyana when I was more of a nationalistic Guyanese than I am now. We always hear that most of the ills of the Third World rest on the shoulders of the foreign correspondents. But since I've come I've gotten more mature, more grey, and my questions now would be, "Who cares? Why should a Third World country care that much about what a western or eastern or northern journalist goes back and writes for his constituency?"

You care because you have things that you don't want people to hear or to read about because it might affect the flow of aid. If you put your house in order and you do your own business, it's like what you do in your own home or family. What do you care what they say about you? If you are thin-skinned, you probably will be. But very often, more than not, what you try to do is to be sure that you have a good image.

When the ministers and the government start to wine and dine the correspondents from the *New York Times* and *Washington Post* and ABC, they are actually trying to give a good impression and the false hope (if you know how western journalists operate) that they will go back and write a nice puff piece and then you're going to get an additional $100 million from Washington. It doesn't really work that way.

So the best bet is in fact to conduct your business in the way you see fit. Get rid of some of the dictators, don't try to buy the wheel from the West because it leaves you with a $450 billion debt as in Latin America. Try to re-invent the wheel – there's nothing wrong with that. The West tells you, "Don't" because they've got the wheel. But you should try to reinvent it and perhaps in that way when a western journalist comes they'll say, "Hey, Castro has discovered the horse and cart again." I don't know, I might be wrong, but I just want to make that point.

Kuldip Nayar:

I think you have a point. Not only that. We journalists, if we appear in the *New York Times* or *Times of London* or *Guardian*, we save that clipping for our grandchildren.

Gerald Knight (*Guardian*):

One thing I haven't heard mentioned at all so far are the readers. Hopefully, most of you are writing with the reader in mind. There are journalists, unfortunately, who write with nobody in mind. But most people are trying to address an audience. That's what we have to consider.

The audience for foreign news is very small. There are five broad sheet news papers in Britain which have very high readership figures for newspapers as you know. They sell 2.5 million copies per day. Maybe each is read by two people. The UK population is approaching 60 million. Every day there are 5 million people reading a serious newspaper in the UK and each of those newspapers has a foreign section.

But if you think about the number of countries affiliated to the United Nations, if each country was to be mentioned in turn, there'd be probably two mentions per year. The space just doesn't exist for all the demands which I've heard. I say demands in a nice way. But the space doesn't exist to do it, because every time there's a big story, it forces the smaller stories off the page.

The people who worked over here will tell you how frustrating it is. They're filing all the time. They're filing something which is important. But when it gets to the other end, something else has happened elsewhere in the world and it pushes it off. That's why stories are not covered.

The other thing you've got to remember is that foreign news doesn't sell newspapers. It has an interest to some people, but the vast majority of people, and I'm sure this applies right across the world, are not terribly interested in foreign news. That's why so little of it gets into the newspapers.

These are some of the things that you need to consider. It's the practicalities of journalism; it's the practicalities of what's available in the media which affects the things that get reported; why some things are not reported. Comments I picked up: If there was a good story in Uganda, would it be used if it could be got? Now the answer is, if it was a good story and it was the best story of the type of its day, yes it would be used. But just think of how many other stories it's likely to be competing with. I think these are the things you've got to take into account.

Other dangerous things are uses of phrases like "the western media." What is the "western" media. What is the "west"? Is Japan in the west? Is Singapore in the west? Is Malaysia in the west? Is Taiwan in the west? Economically, they are. How do they rate? Japan has hardly been mentioned. The coming industrial power of the world. The fixation has been on the United States.

"Global village" and other words which don't really mean anything. "Global village" sounds good if you live in a village, you know everybody and they have the same sort of lifestyle as you do. You know them intimately. We may live in a global village, but we don't know each other intimately; we don't have the same sort of lifestyles. In some ways, it makes it harder for things to be reported because the more you learn about people, the more complex it becomes. So, saying it's a "global village" and therefore we can instantly talk about each other is just not true. We need to forget these broad concepts.

Finally on technology, I must stress that technology is getting cheaper and simpler. I must back up the previous speaker. It was, in India for example, the policy of the government to keep the technology out, which they've now reversed. In Pakistan, it was different. Governments often affect these things and they do it for what they consider good reasons, but the result is that India has now got a little bit left behind in the technology race. It'll probably change now because it can be brought in. But you certainly don't want the old technology; you want the best technology. And the best technology is generally the cheapest technology.

The other thing you've got to remember is how this technology works. As you know, a television reporter with a small dish can report anywhere in the world, so news becomes instant. We haven't heard much about television. We've tended to concentrate on press, but most of the images we get of the rest of the world, wherever we are, come through television. Television is a whole different set of challenges because you can say, in fact, that the camera always lies. Selective images. People go for what they call the sexy image. That's the impression you get. So we're bombarded with these images. I'd like to hear some of the panel or panels later address what they think about television coverage because that's far more important in the coverage of the developing world.

Kuldip Nayar:

That's the problem. The West makes news in our parts of the world and we do not make news in your part of the world. So that is the basic situation. So when you are saying that you'll carry the news, if it is news. That is our whole concept.

Our whole basic discussion is, what is news? Is this what you think is the news? Or isn't what is happening in our part of the world, what we are striving to meet our own demands and challenges, meeting secession movements, terrorism, all these things which are the product of what you in the west have done? So you cannot shrug your shoulders now and say, "You don't make news." We do make news that should get in if you were to really understand us, appreciate us.

Anjum Niaz:

Just to talk about the television. Very recently there was an air crash, a Pakistan International airliner crashed, and the news that kept flashing from Skybase (I think it's called Skybase) was "Thirty British Dead" and nothing else. I think it was so insensitive. I mean, after all, there were other people in that plane and there were other people who died. No mention of the crew. I, being a Pakistani, I was in Frankfurt, and I was just dying to get some information about the air crash, but it was just this family of missionaries and after every fifteen minutes, we were being flashed that this missionary who had three children and a wife who was having a fourth and they perished in the crash. So I thought that that was really so callous, not to mention the other people and what happened.

Second, the BBC news series that is telecast to us in Pakistan every Saturday, the Asian part, it's always, again, brides of the Koran. I don't know. We in Pakistan haven't seen anything like this. But these people have picked up and said they are married to the Holy Koran. It was news to all of us. I wanted to make sure who those women are here because they really didn't look as if they were married to the Koran; they looked very happy. So these are the things that have to be investigated and explored. Or the Asian prostitutes in London, about these Indian, Pakistani girls, and how they solicit. There are other good stories, positive stories, which need to be picked up.

Gerald Knight:

The point I was trying to make is that newspapers, wherever they are, are written with an audience in mind and, unfortunately, that determines what will be written. And in our British newspapers, it's a sad fact that in a crash in Pakistan, people will be interested in – were there any Britons aboard?

Three days ago, two helicopters collided over the Niagara Falls. In one of them were four German tourists. Now it was reported, "Two Helicopters Crash." In Germany it would have been, "Four German Tourists Killed in Helicopter Crash." That's just the way the world is. You have to confront this. It's what actually happened.

6

China
Must Press Freedom Inevitably Follow Dynamic Economic Growth?

Gerald B. Sperling,
Professor of Journalism and Political Science, University of Regina

The region that we are going to be discussing in this panel does not only include China; it also includes other very important parts of East Asia such as Singapore, Burma, and the Philippines.

I have had some personal experience with the Soviet Union in its heyday, when it still had not reached its peak as a superpower and the rot that was eating at it from within was not evident – I'm speaking of the years of Nikita Khrushchev and the transition to Leonid Brezhnev. What characterized the former Soviet Union in its last years, in contrast to the People's Republic of China, was the effort to reform its political structure profoundly before economic reform had been effected. China, on the other hand, has been engaged in a complex process that has seen gradual economic reform accomplished somewhat in advance of political changes, "yi bu, yi bu," or step by step as the great Chinese Premier, Zhou Enlai put it.

The results have been remarkable. Communism, in name at least, persists in China. The Communist Party is still in charge and economic growth and a rapid increase in the standard of living of the vast majority of the Chinese populace, that is the peasants, is palpable. Political reform is problematic to say the least. Whenever political reform has advanced too far; whenever press freedom or demands for democratic reforms have advanced too far in the view of China's aging leadership, economic reform has been temporarily halted. The iron fist of the state has been used to crush those who have been interrupting and introducing instability and creating disunity in their view.

I am not for the moment, let me state this clearly, justifying the actions of the Chinese state in Tiananmen in 1989. However, if one looks at what happened in Eastern Europe since 1989, one can see that perhaps these old Chinese men had some foresight. The triumph of capitalism in the old Soviet Union has not resulted in prosperity; it has not resulted in an unstoppable engine of economic growth. It has unleashed insidious political forces that had been contained by the old communist state: forces such as fascism, anti-semitism, national hatred, and peculiar longings to create the old Czarist monarchy. Has the political system changed all that much?

We recently had a delegation at the University of Regina from Ukraine. They commented that in almost every state in the new Commonwealth of Independent States, the new leadership were members of the old **nomenclatura**, that is, they were former communist leaders who now called themselves democrats. And in most cases, this "new leadership" is characterized by the same lack of any ideological commitment that they had demonstrated when they were communist leaders. Absolute chaos could be just around the corner.

But they do have freedom of the press which we read a lot about. I won't go into this topic except to note that representation from the old Soviet Union should probably be here at this conference. From being a society that could feed and clothe itself, from being a place which was industrialized, it has now degenerated into a place where 90% of the population lives below its poverty line. I think that such poverty is a principal characteristic of underdevelopment.

So, the capitalist triumphalism of George Bush and Brian Mulroney is something of a shell, because while the world did have some knowledge of the transition of capitalism to socialism, any understanding of going in the other direction, is woefully lacking.

Hopefully our two speakers on the China subject, all of whom have experienced life in societies which have undergone deep economic change, will be able to illuminate the affect that this has had on the prospects for an open and a free press.

It's my pleasure now to introduce my old friend, Zhu Yinghuang. Zhu has had a long and productive career as a journalist. He has a masters degree in journalism from Stanford University. He is now Deputy Editor of *China Daily,* a fascinating and at times, scrappy English language newspaper that has borne witness to economic reform in China with accuracy and sympathy and has, at times, been on the cutting edge of China's gradual move toward a politically more open society.

Zhu Yinghuang
Deputy Editor *China Daily,* Beijing

Chinese in general are rather suspicious of this concept of press freedom. I think that they have some reasons. One reason is that this concept of press freedom was originated, created, and has often been abused too much by the West to the extent that it is used to prove that this is the best part of a Western social system. And also to the extent that it is often used as a weapon or as a stick to strike at some Third World countries.

I first of all would like to remind you of two facts. One is that my English might be broken, so pardon me if I can't explain myself very clearly and I don't understand your questions. Second is the fact that China has 1.1 billion people, because I made a terrible mistake in the written paper I have submitted for this conference and where I wrote 1.2 billion. Because of this mistake, if China now has 100 million people more, that would be terrible. That means we would be repeating Chairman Mao's mistake in the 1950s. And I guess Professor Gerry (Sperling) will grade me down from "A" to "B" or even "C."

In fact, China has now 1.14 billion people, and the government is trying to keep the population under 1.2 billion by the year 2 000. In the name of 1.1 billion people, I probably deserve 10 hours talking about China, but for the sake of democracy, I shall shrink it to 10 minutes. Let me make three points as briefly as possible.

I believe the end of the Cold War has not changed what is called the old international information communication order. We have seen dramatic changes over the past several years including the collapse of communism in Eastern Europe and the former Soviet Union, the victory of the allied forces headed by the United States in the Gulf War, the spring turmoil in 1989 in Beijing, and the continuously widening gap between the North and the South.

All of this has confronted journalists in the world, especially in the Third World countries with more difficult and new challenges. So I believe that there is a long, long way to go before we can talk about, before we can see a re- birth of a new world information order.

After the Cold War, people have been talking a lot about the New World Order. What should this New World Order be like? People have different opinions and are pushing in different directions. Therefore, I believe it is very important for people to exchange views on this subject, especially among journalists whose mission is to inform the people about what is really going on around this troubled world. In this, I would really thank our hosts, the School of Journalism of the University of Regina for this initiative and its other fruitful international exchange programs. I would also like to thank the Gemini News Service which has for the past 25 years been dedicated to the improving Third World reporting.

I understand this session is not only for China, but also for Singapore, Burma and the Philippines – again, I would like to thank the hosts that we have one section for this area. Not only because China is a developing country, which as some other Third World countries, has been victimized by this old world information order, but also because China is undergoing rapid changes which, themselves, are affecting a lot of changes including the journalistic practices in my country.

Must the Press Freedom Inevitably follow Dynamic Economic Growth? My answer is a "yes" and a "no." I say "yes" because economic growth in China, especially when it was brought about by reforming the old economic system and opening wider to the outside world, will inevitably bring changes in other non-economic fields including our political system, government administration, people's social and cultural lives, their way of thinking, and also the roles and functions played by the mass media.

There is no doubt China's economy has been developing at an unprecedented pace. The latest of figures, especially since the early spring this year (1992) when our senior leader, Deng Xiaoping, called on the whole nation to accelerate the reform and opening. The latest figures shows that China's G.N.P. surged by 12 percent during the first half of this year. Our industrial growth hit 18% in August which is very impressive. In fact, the average China G.N.P. growth was around 9 ppercent over the past 13 years, that is, ever since China adopted it's policy of reform and opening. By the way, statistics released by our government used to be not that reliable, but these figures have been confirmed by the World Bank and I.M.F.

Also, it is true that economic growth has brought changes in many other fields. People's ideas, ways of life, and on top of that, political reform, will definitely follow in the direction of building up a more sound democratic and legal system, although not necessarily after the model of the West.

There has also been much change in the mass media. Anyone familiar with the Chinese media a decade ago, if you go to Beijing now, you'll find they are very different. But I believe that like political reform, press reform will be a slow and gradual process to the extent that it will not jeopardize economic reform and opening, and certainly will not be as drastic as what some people in the West have wished.

I say "no" to the question because of this definition: press freedom. The definition is never clear and often controversial. Chinese, in general, are rather suspicious of this concept of press freedom. I think they have some reasons. One reason is that this concept of press freedom was originated, created, and has often been abused too much by the West to the extent that it is used to prove that this is the best part of a Western social system. And also to the extent that it is often used as a weapon or as a stick to strike at some Third World countries. The other reason is that we believe there is no such an absolute thing as freedom in the world. All press, all media, either in the West or East are constrained and to a certain degree controlled either by the government or by money or by a certain interest group. A third reason, is have we ever asked what this freedom and democracy is for? We cannot just simply say that we want freedom for freedom's sake. We've got to have a goal – an aim. I believe the freedom of democracy must serve to help people live a better life.

I'm not saying we already have enough freedom and democracy in China, which is not the case. I want to make it clear. But, we are improving and we don't want to turn the boat over.

Finally, the question is who should give the verdict as to which country has the freedom and which country doesn't have the freedom. As with the social system, it is basically a problem with the people there in that country. People should have the right to choose what kind of social system they want. If they don't like it, they will change it. Of course, it doesn't mean that between us we can't exchange views, ideas on an equal basis. Nor does it mean that we should not learn from the West. China is learning a lot from the West including press management. Whatever is good for China, we should learn.

To cut it short, the answer to that question is, I believe the economic growth and other changes in China will definitely bring more press freedom in the Chinese media, but not necessarily after the model so strongly advocated by the West.

Gerald Sperling:

Cultural imperialism has triumphed because of the ability of Zhu, like a good protestant, to be so punctual with his delivery. He has not used one second more than the time allotted.

Our next speaker is Scott Simmie, who is a graduate of our School of Journalism and Communications. Scott is a Gemini fellow. He has also worked in China. He was at CCTV (China Central Television) and he is co-author of a book on the Tiananmen incident which the *New York Review of Books,* considered the best on the subject. Without further ado, I introduce Scott Simmie.

Scott Simmie
(CBC-TV News Toronto)

> After Tiananmen there was incredible anger from many Chinese at the government. And the answer is to allow economic reforms to push along, allow people to improve their lives, improve their standards of living in other while still keeping a lid on the press. They have allowed greater artistic tolerance but Chinese know and respect that there is a line that they're not to cross.

I suppose before I start, I should give you an idea about what I did in China. I don't come to you as any sort of sinologist or expert on the country. I went to work for China Central Television in a position that's called "foreign expert" where you're hired basically as a form of linguistic carpenter and you help to edit scripts, train reporters, and that sort of thing.

When I first went in the fall of 1986, they were about to launch an English language nightly news program. I went because I had some experience in television and helped them launch that, that year. I stayed there for two years and then returned to China to report in spring of 1989 during the student movement.

So, on to today's topic: Will Economic Reform Inevitably Lead to Press Freedom? For me, in China in particular, it's an assumption that's often made and to many it's a fairly reasonable assumption because to a certain extent it does make common sense. Most of us in this room have grown up with a fair variety of choices in our lives. Not just speaking of political choice but the choice of where you're going to live, where you're going to work, what type of education you'd like to take, access to university, those sorts of things.

Traditionally, many of those choices have not been so easy in China. There's tremendous competition for universities, there are relatively limited job opportunities; I'm not speaking of China right now, but at the point when I was there. There are tremendous pay inequities. The story that most of us chatted about in China at that time: a cab driver might make more money than a brain surgeon. So those choices have traditionally not been so easy. For example, even the number of children that you'll have. Many of the basic and fundamental choices that we can make in many countries in the world. So when Deng Xiaoping introduced at first limited and then faster economic reforms beginning in 1979, a lot of people found suddenly that they could make more decisions in their own lives, whether it was a peasant who was suddenly able to sell excess produce or a person who wanted to change jobs.

For example, there's now a job market in Beijing. It's much easier for them to actually go and allow market forces to determine if they have the skills if the opportunities are available. And so suddenly they can make those kinds of decisions which they haven't traditionally been able to make. So according to the theory, the greater freedom in the economic sphere will lead to greater pressures for the ability to make decisions in other aspects of their lives and in political aspects.

That was a connection that many made during the democracy movement in spring of 1989. I certainly remember there were huge, huge demonstrations outside of all of the state run media, whether it was Xinhuashe (the New China News Agency), or China Central Television. There were literally tens of thousands of people denouncing the state-run press agencies as telling lies. And in fact, during that spring, there was a brief period when there was total press freedom.

Many of the reporters that I knew in China found it the most liberating period in their lives – that's what they told me. Because they did have the freedom to go and cover a story as they saw it; and that's quite a change from the way things operated at the point in time when I was there. I guess that lasted about three weeks until the declaration of martial law after which about the only thing you could report in China was that martial law had been declared. And, of course, on June 4 when the army did move in to clear the students, we saw again that power does stem from a barrel of a gun, at least on that particular night in China. And there was one person who I know who worked for Radio Beijing who that morning went on the shortwave service and tried to write a balanced account of what happened, although it was fairly loaded – and understandably so – and he called on people who are "friends of China around the world" to condemn what had happened and to try to reach out to help the people who had suffered. Hours later, the police were at his house, he was detained and I believe imprisoned for a period of time. For this man, journalism was his life. He is not back at Radio Beijing. Although he remains on the payroll, he is not working there right now.

For many journalists, I suppose, that served as both a warning and an inspiration. It was funny (well, not that funny actually) because I returned to Toronto about a week after the killings, and at that point the Chinese government had said that no-one had died in Tiananmen Square, which may technically be true. I was called by some colleagues at CBC and asked if I would come in and describe what I had seen that night, and indeed I had seen people shot on the perimeter of Tiananmen Square. So I went on television and basically described what I had seen to refute what the Chinese government's version of the events was, which is the way things work sometimes in the Western media.

The moment I got off the air, there was a telephone call for me in the newsroom. I picked up the phone and it was a person identifying themselves as the second secretary of the Chinese consulate in Toronto. In fact, I was threatened. I was told that the Chinese had been watching me ever since I had returned to Canada, that I used to be regarded as a friend of China, but now they know that I'm not, and that they would continue to watch me very carefully. I suppose my initial reaction was to say, "Let me put you on hold," and record the call and try to do a story with it. But because I also had some very close friends of mine from China, including some people I had sponsored to live in Canada, for some reason I decided it was best to just forget about it.

At any rate, to back up a bit and get more on topic. When I first began work at CCTV, I was quite stunned by the censorship, whether it was self-censorship or imposed from above. On a typical day, the lineup of our show would be taken to the party secretary in the building about two hours before we planned on taping. If we had planned to run an item on students demonstrating in Seoul, he would take that off the lineup. Labour unrest in France would be taken off and deemed "too sensitive." My colleagues seemed to accept all this. I didn't challenge them on it. It wasn't my role to do that. That's not why I was there.

But then after I'd been in China for a while, I noticed certain subtle acts of defiance. I remember we had a newsfeed from the Visnews Agency and there were visuals of some European trekkers who had been caught in a terrible storm in Tibet, and on the Visnews feed, they were saying, "My goodness, it was terrible. We nearly died, but the Tibetans were wonderful. They helped us, they fed us, they clothed us, they sheltered us, and without them we likely would not have survived. In fact we tried to get some help from Chinese authorities and they didn't seem very interested in our plight." So we were pondering whether we should run this because it was a somewhat interesting story.

Well, the work unit leader, given the sensitivity of Beijing's relations with Tibet, decided that the best thing to do would be to take this video tape and trim it half-way through so that we had the Europeans saying what wonderful people Tibetans are and wasn't it great that they helped us, and no mention of the fact that they had not received help from the Chinese side. One of the people that I worked with who was anchoring that day flatly refused and said, "I will not read that on the air." I was quite surprised by this. And, in the end, nothing went on the air. There was no story of the trekkers of Tibet or of the storm. Over time, after I had stayed there for a while, I realized that this defiance was not new.

During the 1950s in the Hundred Flowers Campaign, where people were encouraged to speak out, many people were jailed or tortured or lost a lot, perhaps everything except their dignity. We saw similar purges at other points in Chinese history, and it dawned on me while I was preparing this that these were people who had not enjoyed the economic reforms during the 1980s. These were people who had lived in a very different China when the only economic reforms were generally disastrous policies by Mao.

So that "desire," whether it is a desire for basic freedom of personal expression, those desires appear to have been there, although muted, without economic reform. So I don't think we can specifically point to economic reform as the driving force.

For governments intent on stability, though, those voices represent a threat. For the Chinese government, in fact for many Chinese people, they remember the unrest whether it's the Cultural Revolution or during other periods, and that instability is a threat and it's something that most people don't want to go through again.

Not actually just individual voices but for the Chinese government right now, it faces threats of technology. All along, places like Shenzhen, which borders with Hong Kong, you'll see people tune in routinely to radio and television from Hong Kong. Shortwave – many people have shortwaves in China. Fax machines played quite a role during the student movement and afterwards with people faxing information. So it's increasingly difficult for China to isolate itself. And with its desire for economic reform, in fact China doesn't want a completely hermetically sealed environment, it's impossible. It's a difficult balancing act.

In fact, with so many students it's becoming increasingly difficult because so many students have gone abroad since 1979. Fewer than 1/3 have come back. So the government is now offering incentive programs, sometimes the promise of a car, an apartment, freedom to choose a place to live, and a pledge of no retribution. So it's clearly trying to get these people back for economic reasons, and yet these people are people who have lived in other countries where perhaps they do, perhaps they don't, but often do, enjoy the increased political freedom.

For a government also that is concerned with unity, as I mentioned, the idea of complete freedom of the press is almost impossible if you look at regional areas. In Tibet, for example, the government feels that Tibet has always been an inalienable part of China and many Tibetans feel that China has no business there. So, can you imagine a free press in Tibet run by Tibetans? It's not likely. Nor is it likely in a place like Urumchi (capital city of Xinjiang province in China's far west). In a nation with 55 minority nationalities, many of whom who have their own interests, their own distinct identities, it opens up a whole and very unpleasant can of worms for the government.

So, at least for now, I think we will see a speeding of economic reforms. The government found it was sitting on somewhat of a tinder box, I think. After Tiananmen there was incredible anger from many Chinese at the government. And the answer is to allow economic reforms to push along, allow people to improve their lives, improve their standards of living in other areas, while still keeping a lid on the press. They have allowed greater artistic tolerance but Chinese know and respect that there is a line that they're not to cross. There was a TV writer I saw who was interviewed just the other day. He said, "I live inside a cage; when the cage gets smaller, I get smaller; when the cage gets larger, I get larger."

So for the moment, I suppose it appears that the cage is still there from a Western point of view, and economic freedoms and those choices are very valuable to many, many Chinese who have lived with not a great standard of living.

A very close friend of mine was just back in Beijing for six weeks this summer (1992) and said that things have improved dramatically – that China is far better than it was prior to Tiananmen. The standard of living, the things people are able to buy, the money they're able to make. In fact, they've coined new phrases; "make money quick people." The concern now among many Chinese is not political but economic. They want to get ahead and get on with their lives and leave the political fight for another day.

In closing, this is a country where time is not measured the same way as we measure time here. The Chinese are a very patient lot.

I do sympathize with the government. It does face a lot of difficulties, a very wide country, and a lot of different people with different interests. But for the moment, as far as the press is concerned, we may see some gradual loosening of it. But I think in China power stems not just from the barrel of the gun, but from the glow of the TV set.

Gerald Sperling:

I would like to introduce Abby Tan, a Singaporian who lives in Manila, who freelances both for the *Times of London* and for Gemini. She has also done some work for the *L.A. Times.* She's been the previous Philippine correspondent for the *Straits Times* and for the *Washington Post.*

I would just say by way of an opening, that the Philippines certainly has experienced a political revolution and an explosion of press freedom over the past few years. Manila newspapers appear to breed with one another and multiply. Singapore has always had a peculiar relationship to the media, especially in recent years. It's battles with the *Far Eastern Economic Review* and the *Wall Street Journal* are legend. Burma is an enigma which perhaps Abby Tan can unravel since she apparently visits there fairly often.

Abby Tan

The chairman has allowed me to cross the South China Sea to talk about a country I know a little bit better, the Philippines. Having lived in the Philippines for more than 10 years, when I say "we" I mean the Philippines.

Now the topic is intriguing from Manila's perspective. Must press freedom inevitably follow dynamic economic growth? In the Philippines we begin in the opposite direction. We have press freedom first. Dynamic economic growth is nowhere to be seen yet. So we are quite different. The Philippines is really the odd man out in the Asia Pacific region. Other economies have grown, the dragon economies have prospered: South Korea, Taiwan, Hong Kong, Malaysia, Thailand, etc. In fact, the whole of the Association of Southeast Asian Nations of which the Philippines is a member.

The Philippines certainly has often been referred to as a "sick" man of Asia. To understand why, perhaps I have to recap very briefly its recent history. In the Philippines, democracy was restored in 1986 following 20 years of dictatorship of Ferdinand Marcos. But the fledgling democracy under Corazon Aquino underwent a period of great turmoil and instability. We went through eight military rebellions and coup attempts in six years. That wiped out all economic growth. When Mrs. Aquino took power in 1986, the economy then had sunk under Ferdinand Marcos. By 1986 when she became President, the economy was minus 0. After she took over, the economy grew very slowly, 1%, 2%, and they reached up to 5% in her third year of rule. When she left in the middle of this year, she was back to square one. The economy was minus 0 growth.

The press in the Philippines, I think it must be the most free in Asia. There is absolutely no government control at all, either censorship or any form of government interference over the newspapers or television or radio. Censorship is exercised only by the owners or the advertisers. Most of the owners of Philippine media are either politicians or big business men who have massive interests to protect and they only interfere with the content when their private interests are involved – not the public interests. In the Philippines, you will find that there is no policing body to control or guide media like the press council that you know in other countries. There's no such thing. We do have a movie and television censorship board, but it is unable to exercise any power or any control over television or radio.

So what you see on TV is sometimes appalling violence. You will see men blazing away with their M-16 guns, killing their wives or girlfriends, beating up their wives and families, and they get away with those things. It is absolutely appalling. And no-one stands and says, "Why is this going on?" And I think Filipinos are not raising their voices at this moment except a few people I meet in private who do ask the same questions.

I think this is perhaps a reaction to the censorship that we went through under the Marcos regime. The democracy that we had under Mrs. Aquino is an opposite reaction to everything that we went through under the dictatorship.

In the face of the lack of economic growth, the topic perhaps should be reversed. Must dynamic economic growth follow press freedom?

After years of Corazon Aquino's shaky rule, many Filipinos have looked with great envy at the dragon economies of Asia and say, "Maybe there's too much democracy in the Philippines." And towards the end, there was really some general yearning for the return of strongman rule. It was reflected even in the media that perhaps the Philippines should have an Lee Kuan Yew or somebody similar that can establish some control. But I don't know if there will be dynamic economic growth in the Philippines after the change of leadership. We had an election in May, and a new President, Fidel Ramos took over in June. What seems clear is that there might be economic growth – not necessarily dynamic in the Philippines, but that takes a little longer in the country.

What is reporting like in the Philippines in the post Cold War situation? By the time Fidel Ramos took over after a long protracted election (I think we must have the longest election in the whole world, three months of campaigning and six weeks of counting before he was proclaimed) . . . by the time he took power on June 30, the Philippines had disappeared from the Western media. The reasons are quite obvious: there had been a continuous flow of events. First of all, the end of the Cold War coincided with the Philippines giving up the military bases of the Americans. By that, the Philippines lost its strategic value to the Western powers. Then the recession came and that cut back a lot of Western media, especially the American television networks. They had offices in Manila. By that time, a lot of them had closed their bureaus and moved elsewhere to other parts of Asia and Europe and the Middle East. Also there were other big events: Sarajevo, Somalia, etc., and in spite of the constant volcanic problem and natural calamities in the Philippines, that couldn't compete any more with bigger events in our world.

With the lack of emphasis on the Philippines, I must say that the Philippines had its fair share of bad press in the past 26 years, since Marcos and Corazon Aquino. Now that the Cold War has ended and there is not too much focus on the Philippines, it might be good for the country I think. Because with so much bad press in the past, the Philippines was unable to attract a lot of foreign investment. It suffered terribly from that, because of its instability and bad press. Now with Ramos in power, we do have a sudden period of stability. The President has not made any major blunders yet. So we do have a very peaceful, stable period right now, which can also be interpreted as extremely boring from the media perspective.

But then, in the final analysis, I think it's not press freedom that really blocks the Philippines' economic growth. I think it has to do with the political leadership because there was none for six years, unfortunately. But one good thing that has come out from the end of the Cold War is that you will find that with the bases gone, the American influence in the Philippines has receded a great deal. I remember during the whole five to six months of our election campaign, there was not a single mention of the U.S., the U.S. Embassy or the U.S. diplomats present.

In previous elections that we went through, every election time is an emotional time for the media where they blame the Americans for everything – for every problem that they had and every problem they couldn't fix. The Americans were always a whipping boy, they were always to blame for every problem in the Philippines. In the last election, you will find that there was no such mention at all of the Americans. So I could breathe a sigh of relief and say that at last the Philippines have nobody to blame for their problems except for themselves. Now they could trust their own destiny and fix their own problems.

If the chairman would allow me to briefly touch on my hometown, Singapore for just two minutes . . .

In Singapore, we also had a change of Prime Minister. A younger man took over, Mr. Goh Chok Tong, from our old strongman, Mr. Lee Kuan Yew who was in power for 32 years or so. The new Prime Minister decided he wanted a kinder, gentler society which means taking away the rough edges of the authoritarian rule. So he had begun to relax. He allowed more soft porn movies, more magazines to come in. The press was allowed to be a little bit more critical which everybody thought was a wonderful change. And then suddenly, a couple of weeks ago, the internal security department, which is the police that take charge of political offenders, raided the *Business Times,* which is the sister publication of the *Straits,* the only newspaper monopoly in Singapore. The offending article? The *Business Times* had published six weeks before the raid, a story about Singapore's second quarter G.N.P. growth statistics which was a few percentage points below target of the government. The newspaper got raided. The government wanted to find out who was the source of the leak.

You've got to understand that in the Singapore context, government information is considered secret. The government, in raiding the office of the *Business Times*, invoked the Official Secrets Act, meaning to say, any information of the government is considered secret until released by the government. So this information on the second quarter G.N.P., was considered a state secret. In other countries you would think that this is ridiculous. Who cares about G.N.P. growth, especially the second quarter? But in Singapore, it matters. Of course, the press got rather flustered by this incident. The point here is that the press at this moment doesn't know how far it can go. How far is the government going to allow them to go? They thought that things were changing. This raid proved that it has not, and also proved that the government itself is not quite sure how far they're going to allow the press, how much freedom they're going to give the press. By the law of progression, therefore, you would think that yes, press freedom should follow dynamic economic growth, but the Singapore experience shows that no, they're not quite sure – it won't necessarily follow.

On that note, Mr. Chairman, I rest my case.

Gerald Sperling:

The floor is now open to questions.

Open Forum

Allan Thompson:

I'm with the *Toronto Star* newspaper. I have to admit that I've never been anywhere near China. I'm a victim of the media as you claim you are. Most of what I know about China would come from the media. I was interested by your paper.* In your content analysis, you found that something in the order of 3 out of 4 of your stories that you examined were negative in tone. My recollections from 1979 and the beginning of the economic reforms and the decade after that was quite different. I'm sure if you did your content analysis sometime in the 1970s, I remember it seemed as if every television correspondent in China was doing stories on rock music coming to China and people dancing and people learning about abstract art and economic reforms. Your content analysis, I think, would have been almost completely the reverse, if not 70%, 80% or 90% of the stories being quite positive, cheerful. And I would submit that that press or media honeymoon with China certainly seemed to end in 1989, but I would also challenge your suggestion that there were no grounds for divorce at that time. I think that if there has been a change in the media coverage of China, something obviously happened between 1979 and now. The tenor of the coverage is

*Zhu Yinghunag's paper follows on page 164

completely different. I'd maybe like to hear from the panel. Scott, as well, I think has some thoughts on that.

Zhu Yinghuang:

I think you have a point. First of all, in my paper I have made it very clear that this is not necessarily the typical 10-day kind of coverage by the news agencies, because I chose five days for August and five days in September – just ten days. It might not be that typical. Another factor is within these ten days, there was somewhat of an unusually great number of China stories by the four agencies because of some events.

The second point is that I agree that there was a period of euphoria in the 1970s, that coverage about China was quite good and quite arousing because at that time, some people in the West really believed that China was the only socialist country going capitalist, which , unfortunately, was not true. But they believed that, and they thought that was good. And the Soviet Union was there.

The second thing is that I believe that the United States and some Western countries or some politicians were actually playing "China cards," as we called them at that time because of geographical and political reasons that China could be used as an ally against another superpower, the Soviet Union. After the collapse of communism in the Soviet Union, there is no Soviet Union existing there, so that does mean a lot of change.

I cannot deny the fact that some people in the West, especially some politicians, believe that now China is the only stronghold of communism. And they are waiting to see the collapse of their communism in the world, then the whole world will be capitalist.

China's point of view is that whether this social system is good or not, it is up to the people to decide. No other country should interfere in the internal affairs of this particular country (China).

Another event was Tiananmen Square. Again, before Tiananmen Square, some people in the West had this illusion that China was changing so fast in the direction they really wished for. As I said, a lot of foreign correspondents who stayed in Beijing did not really have that sense of tradition and history about China. They did not really know what was going on.

Talking about Tiananmen Square, I understand that Scott was in Tiananmen at that time. I understand that he observed, and especially I appreciate his observation of today's China's situation, but this is a very difficult issue. I think history will gradually reveal more clearly all the truth. And certainly this was a tragedy. Nobody could deny that the killing was a bad thing, even the government officials couldn't say that it was a good thing.

Today, for some people, it was something that you could never forget. I will never forget it. But for many, they believe this is something in the past. Chinese like to look forward instead of just looking back.

Why should we argue all the time over whether we should use the gun or not? Because the government also had a point, especially since the world situation has changed so much in the last three years that the people begin to see it in a new, different light in which a lot of people believe that the students went too far and a lot of students on the square didn't know what they wanted. They didn't know what democracy or freedom was; they just believed that freedom means, "I can do what I want." That's not freedom. A lot of Chinese, especially people my age or older than I, did have different approaches to the whole issue because we have experienced the Cultural Revolution. Just like Scott said, the people in China don't want to go through it again.

You said that before the Tiananmen incident, there was total press freedom. Actually there was another period when there was really total press freedom – that was during the Cultural Revolution. Anybody could just post up a poster on the wall criticizing anybody. If you don't like the professor, you just pull him out and criticize and humiliate him. If you don't like these books, just burn them. You could do whatever you like.

I was a Red Guard during that period. I could travel around the country free. Wherever you went, there was a station receiving you. They provided you with the housing, with the food, because we were making revolution. The country suffered. China lost ten years and the economy was on the brink of total collapse. That's why a lot of people don't really like to see chaos. That's why the government has a point in convincing people that whether you like it or not, stability is the most important thing for China. If you want to have economic growth, you must have stability.

Kuldip Nayar:

On this point, Tiananmen Square, would you tell me how did China Daily cover this incident. And, too, if this incident did not meet your approval because reading between the lines, I think you were uncomfortable about that, did you protest it?

Zhu Yinghuang:

For the first part, as one of the editors of the paper when students were on the square, our guideline was very clear because I was in charge of the reporters covering the event. I told my young reporters, "Go to the Tiananmen square, mix up with these students and leaders and find out what is really happening and come back and write what is really happening." But I warned them to not take sides because a lot of people were cautious. China already has had too many "mass movements." Wherever there is a mass movement, there are "black hands" behind it – political elements with all kinds of motives.

Actually, the Tiananmen incident and the students movement was also a reflection of the power struggle in the top authorities. And not to mention the involvement of some foreign elements also, including the CIA. So we wanted our reporters to go to the Square and to come back and write what is happening. I think *China Daily* covered it very objectively and low-key. We didn't play it up, we didn't play it down, while some other Chinese newspapers seemed to me to be going a little bit too far because they were overly sympathetic with the students and did a lot of stories encouraging students. This was before the killing.

Right after the killing, I'm sorry to say that we didn't have any way to protest, although a lot of people in my newsroom could not understand why it should happen. That was true, because nobody could believe that the Chinese army would shoot guns.

It is very tragic that some people were marching in the street and the army began to shoot. A young man, when he was hit by a bullet, he just shouted to his fellows, "Hey, guys, this is real!" because nobody could believe that the army would shoot. But the government had a point because nothing like this had ever happened since 1949 when new China was founded – nothing at all, and nobody had ever seen tanks rolling into Beijing. And also, the army, the police, they explained that they really didn't have rubber bullets or what is called a water cannon that could stop these people. Besides, there were so many people, students and sympathetic citizens that there was no way for the army to get into the square.

Answering the second question, I think the Chinese press covering the Tiananmen Square itself was quite a failure in the sense that for one thing, they were also carried away a lot by what students were striving for – freedom and democracy. But in fact, a lot of people really didn't know what they wanted. When the students first started, the target was the then Premier, Li Peng, then it was shifted away. Mainly, it was about corruption in the government, about the economic situation in China because the economy was growing sso fast. Then there was very high inflation and also the widening gap between the rich and the poor – all those kinds of social problems. I think even the students did not think they would like to overthrow Cmmunist Party rule or overthrow the government. But the government was cornered to a point that they believed that there was no other way to stop it. I think even Henry Kissinger once said he couldn't believe any government in the world could tolerate a group of people gathering in the centre of the city for nearly one month. And the government was patient, and their patience was limited.

So, in answering your question, I think the press, we protested in the way that we believed what we could do. Naturally, on the day of that massacre, no newspaper could be printed because the whole city was paralyzed. No traffic was seen in the streets, and the people . . . a lot of newspapers just closed down and stopped publication.

Unidentified questioner:

Miss Tan, I was very heartened by your own contribution with respect to the way you addressed the topic of the panel. There are people who still (many media practitioners) who still assume that there is an organic correlation between the free press and economic growth. We are told daily by columnists in my part of the world that the Asian tigers ought to be the model. I mean Singapore, Taiwan, South Korea, etc. Now these are places, if I may say so, I have visited one or two of them, and quite frankly, I'm not so sure that that's my idea of the kind of society that I would want to live in because I find that they are pretty closed societies. But, I'm interested to hear you say that in Singapore, which is usually presented as the model of Third World development, what happened to the press there. I'm equally interested to hear you say that the inverse virtually presents itself in the Philippines. I mean, it's freedom even "anarchy" as far as the press is concerned. Yet you went on to give us an idea about the profile of ownership, that many of the politicians own the press or big interest people, does that make the press any freer than if the government itself as such did?

Abby Tan:

It's only free vis à vis the government. They are free to criticize the government and the government does not control the press. But it is not free in relation to the ownership and to the advertisers.

Rex Nettleford:

Well, I'm glad you say that, because one has to think of power centres in societies because the press pretends that it is free if it is able to criticize the government but cannot criticize the business sector. So I'm glad for that.

Gerald Sperling:

This, of course, is not something that would really apply in places like Canada. Mr. Webster?

Norman Webster (Editor, *Montreal Gazette*):

I was a correspondent in China for two years from 1969 to 1971, so I'm an old, old China hand. The turning of guns in Tiananmen Square was not the first time it happened since 1949. There's the small case of Tibet which I don't think should ever be forgotten.

Now I want to go on, however, to say that I'm not here to dump on Mr. Yinghuang. I think we should have listened very carefully to the way he phrased answers to questions. He's in an extraordinarily difficult position – the sort of position that editors of Canadian papers are not. The sorts of pressures he has to deal with every day would perhaps crush some of us, and I think we have to be sympathetic to the sorts of things he has to deal with on a daily basis. I wanted, however, to pick a bone with the analysis which we've got here because I think it somewhat misrepresents things. For example, we're talking about so-called human rights issues and this particular so-called human rights issue which deformed the coverage of the Western agencies. The other panelist, Mr. Simmie, noted that thousands of Chinese students are studying abroad and only 1/3 have come back. This is an enormous brain drain which is really hurting China.

They're trying to get students to come back and indeed have promised that there will be no retribution. One of them did come back and was arrested for trying to establish in Peking a branch of the Democracy for China Fund – the sort of thing that most of us would consider innocuous. Authorities could not stomach that. They arrested him and it is not surprising that this got enormous coverage in the Western media because it went directly counter to what the authorities were saying and it spoke greatly to the whole fall-out for Tiananmen. In addition to which, he was accompanied by Ross Terrill, who is perhaps the best known sinologist in the Western world.

So I think that to indicate that perhaps by using this incident, that the Western agencies are somehow trying to blacken the name of China (if you'll pardon the expression) is misleading.

I wanted to make one more point. Again in the paper, you speak about a spirit of euphoria among politicians and press magnates who wish to see the collapse of communism in China. I submit that it's not Western politicians and press magnates or even Western editors who are trying to see the collapse of communism in China, it's the people of China who are trying to see if not the collapse of communism, the collapse of dictatorship by a gerontocracy.

I think it's important that we note the Western agencies who've taken a lot of stuff today (and some of it deserved) are not necessarily out there whacking governments because they don't like the people of the country. Indeed, the things that they are writing are very often in defence of the rights of the people of the country. And I say right here the rights of the people of China.

Unidentified questioner:

You like the people of China, but how do you know the people of China don't like the government?

Norman Webster:

Well, I would submit that there's a good way to do that – it's known as democracy however you define it. Free elections and free press if you want a couple of simple answers.

Gerald Sperling:

I hope that you don't have Ross Terrill organizing those elections. I wonder if he was surprised that that student got arrested. If he was, then it shows what kind of great sinologist he is.

Charles Quist Adade:

I was the Gemini news correspondent in St. Petersburg of the former Soviet Union. Could you tell us how Africa is covered by your paper, because my ten-year stay in the former Soviet Union demonstrated to me that the so-called socialist internationalism and sympathy for people struggling against Western capitalist exploitation by the so-called communist media proved totally wrong. I want to find out if your paper also goes according to the socialist ideology.

Zhu Yinghuang:

We are criticizing the old news order. Unfortunately, a paper like *China Daily* cannot get out of it. Because we are getting all the news from agencies. We are quite aware of the fact that even *China Daily* has not covered news from the Third World countries enough, although we have a column just for Third World, its called Third World Column, maybe twice a week. And this column is brief. And these briefs tell of development and economic progress of some Third World countries. If there is any difference, this is the difference: all the other world news stories are mainly dominated by AP, FP, UPI and Reuters. And we, right now cannot get out of it. We also use some Xinhua(New China News Agency) stories, but Xinhua is not powerful enough to compete with these four news agencies. We want to see more improvement.

Maggie Siggins:

I'm a freelance writer here in Regina. I'm trying to get my mind around these kinds of definitions of free press. It seems to me somewhat like being a little bit pregnant, actually. When I worked in China, I taught graduate student journalists who knew how to speak English and they were at the graduate school level. I went there with all the preconceived ideas of a Western journalist and I have no idea how else I was supposed to teach what journalism was all about. It wasn't only me. I could see this happening all over the place. Foreign experts had been hired to come into China to teach journalism in English and all the ideas that went along with that. It was no surprise to me at all that Tiananmen happened, not the shooting of the students, but the protest movement, mainly because of the educated ones who had been taught these ideas now for ten years. I sense a great confusion not only in China but also in some of the other Asian countries that I visited, and Miss Tan mentioned that in the case of Singapore, exactly what freedom of the press means to them. I'm wondering really if there is any other definition except that you allow the journalist to tell the story the way he wants to, whether his master is the owner of a press or his master is the government. I'm really trying to understand at this point what China wants in the way of freedom of the press. Maybe all of you could answer that.

Zhu Yinghuang:

Freedom of the press. This concept, this phrase was created by the West. This was introduced from the West to China. China is a country with 2,000 years of feudalist rule. There was no such thing in the past, but the people definitely believe – I think Miss Tan has a very interesting point in inverting the order of the question – because freedom of the press and economic growth are interrelated. If you have freedom of the press, not necessarily in the Western concept but in our concept, that means we should allow more free flow of information. People should be allowed to express themselves, but not to the extent that you sabotage stability. You are a human being not because you have eyes, you have a nose, you have feet, and you have a brain. You are a human being because you are a human being living in the community. So Western philosophy is more of an, as I understand it, individualism, while we're more of a collectivism. You are a human being because you have to think of others, you have to think of your neighbours. So, in that case, we want to have more freedom of the press which means more free flow of information and that people are participating in state affairs. The Chinese have their own way of doing such things. This is also the fact.

The function of media changed a lot, because in the past *People's Daily* was regarded by many people as a central party document. There are people in the world who read newspapers from front page to back page because they were reading it as a document because that was the voice from the party from the top authorities. They were telling you what to do and what not to do. That was the past. The function was mainly educational.

But now the function has changed. People's concepts have changed a lot. Newspaper people had realized that the newspaper should be informative, should be critical and should be entertaining. If you go to China today, you go to the bookstores and newspaper stores, you just collect all these newspapers and you will find kinds of stories, all kinds of investigative stories and the photos are bigger. Layout has changed a lot with big headlines. Also the number of publications have increased. In 1976, that was the end of the Cultural Revolution, China had only 237 newspapers. Now China has 1,600 newspapers plus several thousand magazines and journals. And the radio stations has jumped by 8 times, TV stations jumped by 7 times. These are the facts.

Also I want to emphasize one point. I believe Chinese people, not only intellectuals and students, are much better informed about world affairs than some people in the United States. Not only are Chinese newspapers carrying much, much more international news, but also we have a paper called *Reference News.* It is considered internal circulation, but anybody can have access to that newspaper. Originally, it was four pages, but now it has expanded to eight pages without much editing. It's just a translation of all the news from all over the world. And people read them every day. So they know what's going on around the world, including scandals in the British Royal families, anything.

Scott Simmie:

I guess I'd just like to address Maggie's question, this definition of freedom of the press. Certainly from having worked with Chinese journalists for a couple of years, I think the definition is not so much as the freedom to criticize and challenge the government and such as the freedom from self-censorship which is so big there. I mean these are journalists who would like to go out and do a challenging story.

I remember one colleague of mine who had done a lot of research on a building, a joint venture hotel which had been built in Beijing, and the Chinese government is very proud of its joint ventures because it shows how the economy is reforming and how foreign countries are willing to invest. Well, this was a very large building that had been constructed, but it was actually off-kilter, it was slightly off centre, and so the elevators wouldn't go up and down and the building had remained empty at that stage. So, it was a very interesting story. This was a multimillion dollar structure sitting right in the middle of Beijing and it was unoccupied. So she wanted to work on this story. She did the research. She did the groundwork, and the pre-interviews. She came in very excited one day and said, "Scott I'm going to do a story on this." I said that it was great.

The work unit leader said, "You're going to a story on what? It's very sensitive. I don't know if we should do a story on that." For her, it was a crushing blow because this was a real spark of a journalistic enterprise. For her, that was her freedom of the press – to be able to pursue a story without someone looking over her shoulder.

Unidentified questioner:

I want to invite Abby Tan to say something about Burma. It's very rare that we do have a journalist who's visited there very much, and yet there is a Canadian interest in that the Canadian friends of Burma are looking for democracy there and also PetroCanada, the government oil corporation who has invested quite a lot of money.

Abby Tan:

There's no real press in Burma as you would think normally. The only press activities are radio and TV stations owned by the government, and a newspaper owned by the government. I noticed there was only one newspaper there called the *People's Working Daily*, and you cannot say that that is a newspaper in the true sense of the word. It functions more like a bulletin board of the government. You pick up the paper and you read a story that says, "The Chairman of the State Law and Order Restoration Council held a meeting with Minister so and so. General so and so turned up. His aide turned up. His secretary, Lieutenant so and so turned up . . . " and you read on and on and on. About ten inches. And all you saw are names of people who were present in the meeting. And you say, well, where's the story, what is the meeting about? You don't get the answer. The English was there – the English was perfect. The content was zero. That is the press in Burma.

So the newspapers and television can only carry statements from the government, and they just repeat what the government says. There's no attempt to say what the story is. Even when they brought diplomats and journalists to the border to investigate the problem of the Muslim refugees going to Bangladesh, all I could read was a list of names of diplomats who went there and not what they discovered or what they said or what they saw. None of that happened.

But where the foreign press is concerned, you know that Burma has kept out the foreign press until lately. I went there twice this year in March-April and July-August, and there had been quite a change since then regarding the foreign press. When I was there in March-April, hardly any journalists could get in, and almost none could have access to the government officials. Between that time of my two visits, there had been some changes. The government decided to release political prisoners and allow the dissident Mrs. Aung San Suu Kyi's husband and family to visit her. They could now see her. The reason was because they had to organize a constitutional convention to write a constitution by December, they had to start work on that, so they needed the cooperation of all the political dissidents, and they couldn't get their cooperation as long as the leaders were in prison. That was one reason.

On my second visit I had realized that they were issuing visas to Western journalists to visit Burma but access to offices is a separate thing but they were allowed in, which was a big change. But the reason I found out was because Burma, the government, decided that they had to open up because they wanted foreign investments. They could not get foreign investments last year. Their target was 16% and they only got 6%. They realized that they had compete with Vietnam and Cambodia. Before investments were rushing to Vietnam and Cambodia and just giving Burma a miss because their image was so negative.

They had to, in my stories, pick up the rough edges of the military. And they're trying to put on a smiling face. In fact, when I interviewed the officials, I noticed a change. They had put on a smiling mask. But behind the mask, of course, you still see the very tough Burmese. But the change was for a reason. They're now allowing more journalists to enter.

Anjum Niaz:

My question is for Mr. Zhu. I want to ask of another kind of freedom – the freedom to determine one's family size.

China, in the past, has been very strict about one- child families. There have been cases, of course, of abortion. And China blamed the Western media again that it was the propaganda of the Western media with the result that America cut off certain aid to the UN because of the Chinese family planning program. I want to ask you, what is the status now, and what role did the press play during this period?

Zhu Yinghuang:

I think the press in general is totally for this government policy of family planning. I think this will not be a question for the majority of Chinese, although some rural people, when they have money, want to have a second child. Also, in minority areas including Tibet, all the areas where minority people live, we don't have that policy. They can give birth to as many children as they want. But for Mandarin people the policy is being carried out rather strictly because this is a fact; whatever your economy develops, you have such a big population, you have to feed them and house them and clothe them. This is the biggest headache.

People ask me what is the biggest question with China. I would say population. Even so, China's population is increasing by 16 million a year. You have to remember this basic fact. China has 22-25 percent of the world population but only 7 percent of the cultivated land. So nobody can support that big a population.

The government bans any forced abortion.

Anjum Niaz:

But the Western media brought out news stories about women who wanted to have their second child and they were being forced to go and abort.

Zhu Yinghuang:

There were rural areas, because there's a strange thing in China that we have such a population, if we want to achieve something, very often the government will give quotas. In this village this year, you can only have 5 children born. So some rural officials are going against the government regulation. They may use some illegal means to force abortion. But this is totally banned by the government. But that issue was, again, played up too much by the Western media.

Rick Boychuk:

Having witnessed the functioning of what I consider a dangerously free press in Manila, what struck me more than anything else was, in a country where there's great poverty, you also see how easy it is to corrupt journalists in the sense that they're badly paid and therefore easily bought. I wonder if you could give us some sense of whether the same applies in China – are journalists in fact badly paid and do you worry about the corruption of your writers for your newspaper?

Zhu Yinghuang:

You seem to know the inside story of the newsrooms now. *China Daily* is confronted with the big headache, that is, all our young reporters know English. They can find better jobs in the foreign venture hotels or foreign company offices in Beijing which means they work at 10 to 20 times more than what they get at *China Daily.* Some of them are doing a second job and we cannot stop it because the government regulation now is that you are allowed to do a second job. So the bad thing is that some people get sloppy and lazy while doing their first job during office hours and get really busy and hard working after office hours. The only way is that if the *China Daily* could get rich, we would have a big attraction for really competent reporters.

Written Submissions

China Through the Eyes of "Big Four"

Zhu Yinghuang Deputy Editor-in-Chief, *China Daily,* Beijing

Ten years ago, UNESCO published the MacBride Report, "Many Voices – One World," which was hailed as a milestone in the endeavors of the Third World countries "towards a new, more just and more efficient world information and communication order." Today, can say the situation has improved as the MacBride Committee members once wished? Have the changes in the past decade brought the world nearer to the establishment of that new order?

The past ten years have witnessed dramatic changes in the world situation: the "collapse of communism" in Eastern Europe and the former Soviet Union, the end of the Cold War era when two superpowers vied for world leadership, the "victory" for the allied forces headed by the United States in the Gulf war, and the ongoing Yugoslavian civil war. All those have led the people to believe that the world is at a historical turning point and needs a "new international political and economic order." But what should this new world order be like? People have different views and are pushing in different directions.

It is the same with the prolonged debate on establishing a new world information and communication order, as it is only an adjunct to the modern international political and economic establishment, in which hegemonism and power politics still prevail.

Thus harsh realities remain where the old order of "imbalance" and ""distortion" exist: the means of discriminating information are largely dominated and monopolized by a few developed western countries; over 80 percent of international news is circulated by the "Big Four" news agencies while disproportionately little news from Third World countries finds its way into world circulation; the press portrayal of the Third World, often accused of being one-way, biased and distorted, is generally out of tune with the values, interests, aspirations and actual circumstances of these countries. In spite of a certain degree of consensus reached between Est and West on the necessity of restructuring the international information flow and the progress, however tardy, in this direction, the status of the world information and communication order has so far remained practically unchanged. Rather, the deficiency of the old system have become all the more glaring and intolerable with the ending of the Cold War, the continuously widening gap between the wealthy North and poor South, and with the innovation of new media technologies backed up by economic power.

Life many other Third World countries, China has, on the one hand, been victimized by this unjust and inequitable world information order, and on the other hand, been making strenuous attempts to diminish the disadvantages imposed by the old order and to portray a more truthful image of itself in the world community.

Right after I received the letter of invitation to participate in this conference, I set about collecting all the China stories filed by the "Big Four" news agencies (Reuter, AP, UPI and AFP*) between August 27 and September 5, 1992. The idea was to have a ten day survey on those agencies reporting on China and to do a content analysis. Although the period chosen was too short to support a substantial argument, and the sorts of stories selected by those agencies depends largely on the specific happenings during those ten days, the survey results can, nevertheless, serve as a clue to what those foreign agencies were most interested in and what they tended to miss while reporting China in that time.

The following may help illustrate the survey results:

Total number of stories:	286
Period of time:	August 27-September 5, 1992
Agencies:	Reuter, Associated Press, United Press International, Agence France Presse.
Subject matter:	
	1. Foreign Relations: 96 stories (33.6% of total)
	2. Domestic Politics: 72 stories (25.1%)
	3. Business and Trade: 66 stories(23.1%)
	4. Human Interest: 52 stories (18.2%)

Positive vs Negative (good or neutral vs bad news):

Under category 2 (Domestic Policy):	21 positive; 51 negative (negative 70.8%)
Under category 4 (Human Interest):	10 positive; 42 negative (negative 80.8%)

Here are some of my reflections, if not conclusions, on the survey results:

First, a total of 286 stories filed by the four news agencies within ten days is by no means a small number, although this might not be a typical ten day volume. Of the total, 171 stories have the dateline of China's capital, which shows those agencies' correspondents stationed in Beijing were busy. Also interesting is the fact that one third of the stories are on China's foreign relations. Of those 96, 33 were directly related to the United States.

To my mind, this finding shows that for one thing, China, as the world's most populous and fast-developing country, is playing an increasingly important role in world affairs, which can not be ignored by anyone, and for another, China has been steadily making progress in improving its relations with other countries. China remains one of the focal points for international news coverage. During the period of examiination major diplomatic issues included: the opening of the Chinese embassy in Seoul, ex-Japanese Prime Minister Tanaka's visit to Beijing, China's concern over the Iraq "no-fly zone," and announcements of upcoming visits to China by the Iranian President, the President of the Republic of Korea, the Russian President and the new Hong Kong Governor.

However, two events stand out: one is China's strong protest against the US selling F-16 fighters to Taiwan, and the other is China expelling one American sinologist and two French journalists involved in the case of a Chinese dissident engaged in illegal activities. Both events have significantly affected Sino-US relations, which accounts for the great number of US-related China stories in the period.

Second, never in the history of China coverage by foreign agencies has there been so much attention to China's business and trade ties with foreign countries. Nearly a quarter of the China stories were on this subject, which is certainly rather encouraging. In recent years, particularly since the beginning of this year (1992) when senior leader Deng Xiaoping called on the nation to accelerate reform and openness to the outside world, the whole nation has concentrated on economic development. With more areas and businesses opened to foreign investors, the environment and infrastructure greatly improved and more flexible and favorable policies adopted, China is undoubtedly becoming one of the most attractive markets and business partners for foreigners.

Business reporting by the agencies was, generally speaking, quite fair and objective during this period, which saw such coverage as "Sino-Russian border trade," "China to buy eight British aircraft," "Singapore Maritime to purchase China-made, high-powered tugs," "China offering interest-free loans to Bangladesh," and "nine more foreign banks allowed to open branches in China."

On thing is noticeable: while the Chinese press has been carrying lots of success stories of foreign-funded enterprises in various areas, and when the State statistics show over 70% of foreign-funded enterprises in China are making profits, foreign agency correspondents in Beijing seldom pick up such stories. However, the survey found one story by UPI that deliberately and in detail, played up a "bitter public feud between Chinese and foreign managers in a luxury hotel," which the story claimed "offers an unusual window to reveal the danger of investing in China."

Third, categories 2 and 4 can perhaps best reveal the mentality and approach of these agencies in reporting stories inside China.

At a time when China is accelerating its pace of reform and opening, and when even Chinese newspapers find themselves lacking space to cover so many new measures, policies and accomplishments, a lot of which related to foreign investment and cooperation, it is interesting, though not surprising, to observe the focus of attention of foreign agencies in covering events in China.

A quick glance at the front pages of Beijing's *People's Daily* during the ten days reveals such headlines as: "China successfully retrieves a scientific experiment satellite," "China builds more harbors and airports to improve investment environment," "China seeks better co-operation with aerospace industries of foreign countries," "the Standing Committee of the National People's Congress examines the draft law on limited liability corporations," "China speeds up transition toward a market economy," "prices of over 600 production materials set free to fluctuate according to market needs." "China opens its wild west to neighboring countries" . . . , etc. All those failed to find their way into foreign agencies' stories.

According to the survey, 51 of 72 domestic political stories filed by those agencies are on the negative side. Of those, 42 are on so-called "human rights" issues. When Chinese police detained a returned Chinese dissident who is charged with engaging in illegal activities, a total of 28 stories on that issue alone were filed by these agencies.

For most Chinese, it is hard to understand why foreign agencies like to make such a fuss over the issue. While holding that human rights and fundamental freedom for all mankind should be universally respected, China believes, "What comes first for developing countries are the rights to independence, to subsistence and to development." For China, the utmost thing on the agenda is not only to feed, clothe and house its 1.2 billion people, but also rapidly to raise their living standards. The world today is diverse. Each country has the right to choose independently its social, political and economic system and development model in accordance with its own conditions and the best interests of the country and the world.

The emphasis of agency reports on "the lack of human rights" and political democracy has always been the tack of Western agencies. This reflects the value systems and biases of Western civilization, which on the one hand stress the "good of pluralism," yet on the other hand show a desire to make the whole world into their own image – thereby negating the concept of pluralism. There have been times when a more tolerant approach prevailed in the interest of "finding common aground against a common enemy," but in the wake of June 1989 and the subsequent collapse of the former Soviet Union and Eastern Europe – the end of the Cold War era – there was a spirit of euphoria among politicians and press magnates who wished to see the "collapse of communism in China."

Good, objective journalism – the kind of journalism that will build up its own credibility – must be based on an objective approach, reporting not only what publishers wish would happen, but what is the actual situation and what is likely to happen. Only in this way will reporting and newspapers stand on undefeatable ground.

The "human rights" coverage is a typical example of how China news disseminated by the western agencies reflect the interests, preferences and news values of the western media.

Another example is seen in category 4, where of 52 stories, 42 are negative, further divided into eight crime stories, 26 disaster stories and 18 assorted others. While Chinese newspapers also reported these events (in fact, many of these were picked up from *China Daily* or other Chinese-language newspapers), they never make up a large proportion of news coverage.

Human interest is the stuff of good stories. Misfortune and human suffering are often the easiest to report. But isn't it strange than when China had been struck by serious floods last year (but fortunately not much loss of life) people overseas hardly knew about those floods. Also stories that highlight the goodness and selflessness of people are also poignant and moving tales, yet western agencies seldom report on them. People may ask: if "human interest" stories just mean disasters, crimes, drug wars, pollution, "a father killing his infant daughter," or "a man arrested for stripping a neighbour's wife naked" (both AFP stories), where is the hope for mankind?

True, the issue is more complex than sheer rhetoric can describe: It can be a problem of the definition of news, a problem of news being made "sensational" to be marketable as a commodity, or a problem of prejudice and ignorance on the part of the reporters in covering a country they do not really know much about. But for China, a country desperate to improve its economy and develop friendly relations and economic ties with other countries on the basis of equality and mutual benefit and understanding, what image have those foreign agencies portrayed in the world community if they just pile up all those overwhelmingly gloomy stories in the world media?

Damages are already there. For example, while some people in the West hailed the reporting on China's "Tiananmen demonstration" in 1989 as a "triumph" for coverage of international crisis, some more serious-minded and far-sighted academics and journalists at Harvard's Kennedy School of Government have found in a recent study that that coverage bred some serious and lasting misconceptions about China, and "that distortions caused by the media prism had an unnaturally disruptive impact on public opinion and policy making in both countries." Reviewing the "Study of US Press Coverage of the Beijing Spring of 1989" completed by the Joan Shorenstein Barone Centre on the Press, Politics and Public Policy (June, 1992), a *Boston Globe* writer, Michael Kenny said, "As long as American political leaders and American public opinion continue to see China through the prism of Tiananmen, the chance for rebuilding a constructive relationship with a China that is neither dominated by students and intellectuals nor a mirror of American political systems, is diminished," (August 2, 1992).

We journalists, in a profession with a respected status and a noble mission, shuld really bear this question in mind: shouldn't we be more responsible in reporting news of our neighbors, who only want peace and development, in a more accurate and truthful manner so that our audience will not be misled again because of the prisms we create?

Bells In Hell

Little girl grows up and wants a voice like a bell.
She does one or two things wrong
And everybody says she headed straight for hell.
And she says mamma, mamma, mamma, mamma are there bells in Hell.

Chorus

And I say help me, help me, help me
To make sense of it all.

Young man dies far away from where he was born
On one side there is love
On the other there is scorn
He says mamma, mamma, mamma, mamma was I born in scorn.

Chorus

That old man over there used to be some mother's child.
Now he just survives
Like something in the wild
He says mamma, mamma, mamma, mamma was I wild as a child.

Chorus

I am an old woman whose voice peals like a bell
I've know one or two days
Oh Lord they came straight from Hell
And I say mamma, mamma, mamma, mamma I've rung those bells in Hell

Chorus

Song by Regina Singer-Songwriter, Noele Hall

7

Whose World Order?

Journalism, History and the White Male Perspective

Maggie Siggins, Saskatchewan Writer and Journalist

It's often been said that journalism is a moment ago's history. I believe there's a much stronger link between the historian and work-a-day journalist than is usually acknowledged. On the one hand, the journalist's cultural template, ideas about his or her own society and that of the world, is set early on by the work of historians, in school textbooks and movies and novels in the great intellectual debates of our time. On the other hand, I believe historians are much more indebted to journalists than they would like to admit. An exposé by a hard-nosed reporter of a Prime Minister's fraud is often much more significant in the scheme of things than private letters or secret documents of that same politician.

Although they often squabble, the historian and the journalist are really siblings of the same family. In my most recent project, I find myself in that strange netherworld of the journalist having to deal almost entirely with historical fact. What I'm doing is a biography of the great Canadian revolutionary, Louis Riel, who was hanged in 1885 right here in Regina for treason against the dominion government. From my current position deep in the 19th century, I must say it's very different. I spend most of my day talking to the dog. It is a very strange experience for a journalist that's used to doing things like interviews, to suddenly be stuck with huge piles of documents for years on end.

Such as that may be, from my current position deep in the 19th century, I am developing an allergy. I can actually find myself wanting to scratch on most days. I'm developing an allergy to the arrogance (and I emphasize the word arrogance) of the usually white, almost always male, European-oriented academic historian. Let me give you an example of why I have become so itchy.

It involves a historian-ethnographer by the name of Marcel Giraud. Giraud is renowned in the Western world for a massive two-volume tome called *Les Métis Canadiens, The Métis in the Canadian West.* Marcel Giraud was born in Southwestern France in 1900 and to my knowledge, he is still alive today. As a young scholar at the University of Paris, he developed a passion for the history of the new world, particularly the French speakers there, and over the next 25 years he accumulated material for his book. During the 1930s, with the help of

Rockefeller Foundation funds, he made two visits to Canada, travelling across the country to study various Métis communities.

During World War II, lucky for him, he was stranded in London where he had access to the Hudson Bay Company's records. Since he was one of those people, and I'm beginning to think that I am not, who thinks paradise is being locked up in a gloomy archive, surrounded by dusty records, the war years for him were very profitable.

At this point I would like to digress. For those of you who aren't Canadian, allow me to treat you to a totally biased capsule history of our country, in particular this part of it, which before Confederation was known as Rupert's Land or the North West Territories. For two centuries, this vast frozen north land (you're lucky it's not so frozen today) was considered of little use except as a place to extract the furs of beaver to make elegant top hats for the European elite. First the French, setting out from the St. Lawrence river basin, explored the West. Then the British perched themselves on the shore of Hudson Bay. The Scots out of Montreal carried on what became essentially Canada's major economic activity. It was a simple enough business that sometimes yielded enormous profits. European goods such as guns, whiskey, and lace trim for dresses were traded to the Indians in exchange for the skins of beaver, otter, fox and other poor little animals. While the English sat like lumps on the rim of the Hudson Bay waiting for native trappers to bring their wares to them, the entrepreneurs out of Montreal were much more aggressive. They transported European-made goods from Lower Canada into the heart of the fur country. The picture (and I think everybody has this picture of the strapping voyageur paddling his nimble but heavily laden canoe, bellowing out boisterous songs) has been forever and indelibly imprinted on the Canadian psyche. To make this business work smoothly, the more independent of the adventurers, primarily French Canadians, although there were some Scots, began spending more and more time in the heart of darkest Canada.

One of our most distinguished journalist historians, Peter C. Newman, who has written three marvellous volumes on the fur trade, describes these strange winterers as they became known. He says, "To the few outsiders who visited the domain – and there were very few – the traders seemed a species apart – men who had voluntarily stepped outside the bounds of civilized society."

Now, in order to survive in the northern wilderness, these madmen quickly formed liaisons with Indian women. The "country wives," as they were labelled, pounded the corn for their husbands' breakfasts, dressed the furs they collected, cut out from moose skin their moccasins, repaired their canoes. Soon their mixed blood children became a prominent feature of the fur trade and with them developed a very unique culture indeed.

What is particular about Canada's Metis is that for as long as the fur trade flourished, well into the 19th century, they were a highly successful people, so much so that they considered themselves an independent nation with their own language called Michif (half Cree and half French), history and culture.

Okay, there's your history of Canada. You'll notice I left out all the whites altogether except for the voyageur. Now back to our friend the French historian who moved from London back to Paris.

Marcel Giraud's huge 1400 page opus was published in 1948. Although it was right after the war and there was a severe shortage of paper, the academic community thought this work of such significance, such magnificence, that publication should not be delayed. Accolades poured in from all over the world. Even Canadian historians, whom you think might be a bit jealous, heaped praise on it. The eminent military historian, George Stanley, said "It was a magnificent contribution both to Canadian history and Canadian sociology." And as for Giraud, he found himself being awarded a most prestigious academic position, which normally would have taken many, many years to corner.

Giraud's volumes are found in the bibliography of every kind of writing on the Métis from that of the most modern radical kind of historian to work published by the Metis associations themselves.

So it is with a certain amount of interest and anticipation that I tackled *Les Métis Canadiens* this summer. What I found – let me just say that I was unpleasantly shocked by what I read. It seems to me that what Giraud had done was to have taken the 1 million or so facts that he had dug up and mold them into a rigid hierarchy (I want to stress that word) according to his cultural perceptions. At the top of the ladder was French civilization, with Britain not far behind. The Canadians are quite a way down, and they're followed by the Métis, at least that side of them that is French. At the bottom of the heap is the so-called primitive Indian.

I want to quote just one passage from his first volume to give you the flavor of his work. Note his judgmental and condescending attitude towards the subject matter, and please excuse the rotund language.

> The lack of frankness which Europeans attributed to the Métis found expression in the perpetual oscillations of his conduct. And the impression he gave of betraying one after another, the causes for which he declared his support. But here we must see not so much a deliberate or spontaneous process of deception as a reflection of his emotional temperament of his unsettled upbringing in contact with two cultures only superficially assimilated. Hence comes that weakness of will which was manifest not only in the hesitations of his behaviour and the lack of conviction with which he defended his own interests, but also his propensity for drinking. The freedom of his manners, in a phrase, by the complete absence of any clearly defined morality.

Now he described the Métis, and this is a description of about 1820 just as they were conquering the West and their culture was really flourishing. Now I have no time here, or patience, to argue with Giraud. It's enough to say that my research reveals that he was entirely out to lunch on most of his broad generalizations. Interestingly, Giraud considered himself and was considered by others as sympathetic towards the Métis people. He displayed no such warm – heartedness towards natives. His description of so-called "barbarian proclivities" is in my estimation outright hate literature. I don't see how you could call it anything else. And if you put the word Dane or Jew or anything pretty well in the western hemisphere in place for Indian, you would very quickly see that this indeed was hate literature.

Now if these were the grumpings of a single unimaginative academic, there wouldn't be much to worry about. But Giraud's ideas have prevailed through the years. In 1986 at a time when it was very difficult to get things published in this country, the University of Alberta published an English version *Métis of the Canadian West,* translated by one of Canada's most eminent men of letters, George Woodcock. Now I don't think this book should be suppressed or taken out of the libraries, but I always felt if they had just kept it in French, it wouldn't have been quite so accessible.

Moreover, Giraud's attitude and philosophy, and here I'm finally coming to my point, have seeped into the popular and journalistic commentary. For years, almost nothing was written in our newspapers or magazines or broadcast on our electronic media about the Métis. Never mind that they have one of the most interesting cultures this country has ever produced. Now that native issues are fashionable among the cultural elite, we hear more but seldom without the condescension meant for a people defeated and subjugated.

I believe most journalists in this country have no idea of the true history of these people. And right now in Canada, there are as many as three million who consider themselves as Métis. The journalists know nothing of this group's successes, nothing of their profound contribution to the country, and this of course is directly reflected in the work of these journalists.

It's difficult for anyone, including journalists and historians to carry the baggage of their own culture to any situation. This seems to me to be human nature. Of course you're going to take your own experiences and your own education to any of the work that you're going to do. But what bothers me, and really bothers me to the point where I start to get scratchy just thinking about it, is the judgmental quality. The sentencing of any people considered "other" to a position of inferiority, the inability to look at a culture within it's own milieux. As a feminist, I see this as the paternalism dominating the Christian, Islamic and Confucian cultures, the chauvinism which has resulted in the terror of the World Bank, the devastation of our environment, and the horror of nuclear war.

We as journalists must be on guard against what must be a really deeply inbred human trait – the judging of others, while blindly accepting the values of our own culture.

I keep thinking of Marcel Giraud writing about the unique savagery and barbarity of North American Indian tribal warfare just at the time that the gates of Auschwitz were being opened and the civilized European was beginning to realize the full consequence of the holocaust.

(Maggie Siggins has worked in Canadian newspapers and television in her journalistic career. She has written seven major books. She is the 1992 recipient of the Governor General's Literary Award for Non-fiction for the book, *Revenge of the Land* which is also about to be made into a movie. Her well-known book, *Love and Hate,* about a prominent Saskatchewan politician who murdered his wife, was made into a television movie and has been shown in Canada, Britain and the United States and around the world where it drew record viewers. In her work, Maggie Siggins has created a powerful blend of history, journalism and drama. She was also the visiting Max Bell professor at the School of Journalism and Communications at the University of Regina in 1983-84).

Whose World Order?

Knowlton Nash, Journalist and Max Bell professor,
School of Journalism and Communications, University of Regina

My own sense, frankly, is that behind that phrase, [the New World Order] there really is nothing, or at least, not very much. In spite of a good deal of apprehension, I think there really is no great conspiracy or scheme or plan or even much thought given, in Washington, about details of any new world order. There is just no real substantive policy for a new world order that's discernible coming out of Washington and the U.S. government today.

Nor for that matter is there anything discernible in the relationship to a new world order being structured in London or Bonn or Paris or Tokyo or Moscow. All of those countries and all or their leaders are utterly pre-occupied these days with their economic relationships with each other and with their own domestic economic and social and political issues.

I thought that possibly this past week when George Bush was to address the United Nations, he might begin to at least draw the outline of his New World Order. But that didn't happen. In fact, I was struck by the front page headline in the *New York Times* (Norman Webster's favourite newspaper and mine too, I have to say) reporting the speech which said: "Bush, In Address to UN, Urges More Vigor In Keeping The Peace." Then, in the subhead, the *Times* said, "But He Does Not Offer Money or Staff, Nor to Pay U.S. Debts."

The latter point refers to the fact that the United States has refused to pay its debts to the United Nations and now owes the U.N. about $733 million – the biggest U.N. debtor of all.

What Mr. Bush did say was that he, in principle, supported expanding the United Nations' role in peace-keeping. He said that he had ordered the U.S. military to start more training for possible peace-keeping actions. His comments, though, fell far short of the recommendations of the U.N. Secretary General and were greeted by what the *New York Times* called "polite applause."

What struck me is that nowhere in his speech to the world body did he use the phrase "New World Order." There was no reference there whatsoever. And that was a bit unusual because Mr. Bush is often given to using colourful, rhetorical flourishes in his speeches. The reason there was no mention of it, I suspect, may have been the return to the White House of James Baker who, as Secretary of State, was always a bit uneasy with sweeping Presidential generalizations about foreign policy. And besides, Mr. Baker is now running Mr. Bush's presidential election campaign, he may well calculate that a "New World Order" is not an especially vote-grabbing slogan right now.

In fact, the United States is simply obsessed with domestic navel-gazing in its election campaign. Foreign policy, let alone a New World Order, is nowhere to be seen in the Bush-Clinton and now, Perot campaign.

And if you believe the opinion polls, the public matches the apparent leadership indifference to the substance of any New World Order. In one poll in the U.S., a mere 1% of the people said foreign policy should be the main concern of the president. No wonder Bush and Clinton and Perot are not talking very much about foreign policy in their campaigns. As a result of all of this, the U.S. media, the Western media, seems to have lost interest in the Third World.

What's happening in the United States is that the Americans are really unsure of what their role should be in this new, non-cold war world. All the old cold war sloganeering about the "evil Empire," "massive retaliation," "going to the brink," and being "eyeball to eyeball" . . . all of that has been tossed into the ashcan of history. The cold war pawns and surrogates in the Caribbean or Africa or Asia or the Middle East no longer have any foster parents in Washington or Moscow. It's a whole new world out there. Suddenly, there are not two superpowers growling at each other across the Iron Curtain, but only one superpower. So the Americans are now struggling to learn how to live without an enemy. The United States is really trying to redefine just exactly what its compelling national interests are. Until that's done, we won't know what shape there will be to any "New World Order."

Kuldip Nayar told us that the order that usually emerges is the order of the victors, but in this case, the cold war victors really don't know what they want.

The phrase, "New World Order" is not an entirely new one for American Presidents. In fact, the last president to use a variation of that phrase was President Warren Harding who talked of "The New Order in the World" back in 1921, and he called for international law and understanding. Unhappily, despite Harding's words, Harding's actions had the opposite effect. His policies led to a return to isolationism of the United States with a vigorous anti-foreigner tone reflected in everything from immigration policies to higher tariffs.

About a quarter of a century later, another American president got involved in a New World Order, although he didn't call it that. He was President Harry Truman. He tended to act rather than talk, especially with his programs like the Marshall Plan and his Point Four foreign aid scheme to aid Third World countries.

There has been a good deal of criticism of the United States at our conference – a good bit of it justified, but to my mind, both the Marshall Plan and the Point Four probably represented the most generous, the most selfless acts of any nation in history. There undoubtedly were some self-serving elements in both programs, but Truman's commitment and the support that he was able to generate from the congress and from the American taxpayers to foot the bill, were simply unique and mightily impressive. All the more so because Truman faced a public that, not totally unlike today, was generally anxious for at least some disengagement from the world. But Truman was committed to an internationalist philosophy.

I was living and working in Washington with an international organization for the last year or so of Truman's presidency and it was an exhilarating time for anyone involved in world aid and trade. Probably we were naive, but there was a very real feeling that, with international cooperation, you could do almost anything at all – heal the sick and feed the hungry, end wars and stop illiteracy, lessen poverty, give hope. There was a wonderful sense of the possible, an infectious, irrepressible and, I suppose, innocent spirit of optimism that we could change the world, that the red, black and pale horses of the apocalypse could be made to disappear. As I think of it, maybe that was a form of Western arrogance, although I'm not sure how you can be naive and arrogant at the same time, but certainly we were, I guess, naive because those horses of war and famine and death are still galloping around the world these days.

The brinkmanship confrontations of the Cold War may be over – just as World War II was over in Truman's day, but now the question mark comes over which way the United States will go as we approach the 21st century. Will it be the way of President Harding in the 1920's of self- centered isolationism, or the Truman way of enlightened internationalism?

As I noted earlier, concern about defining new U.S. world interests – articulating a New World Order – is way down the American priority list.In fact, it's way down on the priority list for most other industrialized countries as well – perhaps not quite out of sight, but essentially an issue to be dealt with rhetorical ad hoc'ery and immediate economic benefits that can be gained.

Most of us in the so-called Western world are, I think, increasingly self-centred these days. Look at Europe with its pre-occupying, almost exclusionary, concerns with its economic troubles ... Maastricht, a European currency and the future, or the non-future of a united Europe. There is room for consideration these days of little else for Major or Mitterand or Kohl. Or, indeed, look at domestic pre-occupations of Yeltsin in Moscow or Miyazawa in Tokyo. And certainly here in Canada we are looking inward, possessed with our constitutional debate on the future of the nation and alarmed about our flagging economy.

Through the mist of these pre-occupying domestic concerns, it is possible to discern – or to make an educated guess – at the beginnings of what might evolve as a "New World Order."

As I said earlier, one thing President Bush talked about at the United Nations last week was strengthening the U.N.'s peace-keeping role in the world. That's a change – a sign – that the United States has no intention of, by itself, being the policeman of the world. No matter who is elected President in November – George Bush or Bill Clinton – I think the U.S. is going to seek international colouration through the U.N. for most, if not all, peace-keeping efforts. Someone mentioned yesterday the danger of the U.N. being hijacked by the West, and I suppose that is a possibility. Part of this new approach likely will see the Americans pulling back somewhat from stationing its NATO troops in Europe – just as Canada is scaling back its NATO European commitments.

Clearly, though, the shape of any New World Order is going to be more economic than military. American public opinion, and public opinion in most of the industrialized countries, has shifted from defining national security in military terms to defining it in economic terms. We've moved from ideology to pragmatism. Maybe we've moved from the Hot War to the Cold War to the Profit War.

From now on, I suspect that the U.S., when promoting democracy collides with economic interests, will give priority to economic interests. The American magazine *Business Week* recently noted that increasingly in developing nations of the world, prosperity is given priority over democracy. The magazine suggests that the U.S. is increasingly looking favourably on this in places like China, for example, where Washington now seems to feel democratic progress will have to be pushed by economic improvement. There is a sense among many U.S. policy makers that if you push prosperity, you will get democracy, but if you push democracy first, it may take longer to get prosperity.

Also, the distribution of foreign aid in general is going to change in the United States. Hitherto, aid was often ideologically based on Cold War considerations but from now on, decisions on aid will be much more pragmatically based. And as some have noted here in our meetings, that removes the leverage that some Third World countries had in the Cold war, playing one side off against the other to get more aid.

And it's pragmatism that is the underlying motivation for the efforts to reduce trade barriers, whether through the international mechanism of GATT or, if that fails, through the development of trading blocks in North and South

America, in Europe and perhaps in Asia. The question mark hovering over all of this, however, is whether the industrialized nations will, in the process, open their markets to substantially more Third World trade.

The question is, in any New World Order, will aid and trade with the Third World be blunted or reduced, or diverted, by a Western policy of trying to invigorate the economies of Eastern Europe. George Bush, the other day, announced a $1 billion fund of grants and credits to help U.S. business invest in Eastern Europe, but he said the money will be coming from existing foreign aid programs. That means clearly that somebody else is going to get less. And that somebody else could be the Third World countries.

Whether it's trade, foreign aid, or peace-keeping efforts, they'll all be affected by whatever "New World Order" emerges over the next few years. For the last 45 years, they've all been seen through the geopolitical prism of the Cold War, which, in a way, made it easier for the policy-makers. They could just do the opposite from the other guy . . . if the bad guys do this, we'll do that. It was punch and counter-punch.

And in many ways, it also made easier the job of being a journalist. The media, or at least some of the Western media, often essentially just kept a score card on which side – Washington or Moscow – was ahead.

But for the policy makers now and for journalists, that game is over. Our job in this business of journalism is suddenly a lot more complex – a lot more difficult because reporting on any New World Order, whatever it's shape, will demand more skill and more knowledge from the media. We, and especially we in the Western media, need to be much more knowledgeable – much more sensitive – to nuances and subtleties in our international coverage. And that's a challenge, especially right now in these recessionary days because much of the Western media coverage of the world is increasingly that of a fireman's role – rushing out from London or New York or Toronto to cover a breaking story with only at best, a superficial background and knowledge of the political, social and economic reality of the area being covered. Increasingly, we fall back on journalistic fire brigades rather than full-time bureaus located around the world.

While my organization, the CBC, has certainly the best broadcast coverage of international affairs of any Canadian organization and better than most of the print media as well, nevertheless, there are vast parts of the world where CBC doesn't have a full-time bureau – in Latin America, in much of Africa, Southeast Asia. We do, of course, send in people from time to time to take the pulse of an unstaffed region, but we, as well as other Western news organizations, simply don't do enough. That, of course, is why the Gemini News Service can be so valuable in helping both to fill the gap and provide a different perspective. But Western news organizations should do much more – have more people stationed around the world, soaking up the reality of Southeast Asia or Central Africa, so their reportage can be more valuable for the public.

The convulsive changes of the last couple of years has transformed the world's political landscape. The question is will it be an American or Western New World Order, or an "Order" that belongs to everybody. In all this, there is a critical part for journalists to play in explaining *whose* New World Order and what it's all about. It is only through the media – through what we do – that the world will know what is going on. And what we do is to provide the raw data for the public debate. The quality of that public debate depends on the quality of our reporting and on the quantity too. We do need to do very much more. And to paraphrase what we heard musically earlier tonight, journalistically speaking, it's better to have too much too soon, than too little too late.

Thank you very much.

(Knowlton Nash is a distinguished Canadian journalist who began his career with the *Toronto Globe and Mail* in 1947. He began freelancing in the 1950s for the Canadian Broadcasting Corporation from Washington and became the CBC Washington correspondent in 1961. Reporting for radio and television, he covered many of the momentous historic events of the time – the Bay of Pigs, the Cuban Missile Crisis, revolution, civil war and politics in South and Latin America, and the Vietnam War. Knowlton Nash has also served in various management positions within CBC Radio and Television during his career. More recently, in his career, as anchor of CBC Television's "The National," Knowlton Nash became one of the most well known and respected journalists in Canada. He has also written numerous books about his experiences as a journalist, his newest book is called , *Visions of Canada* and he is now working on a history of the Canadian Broadcasting Corporation. Knowlton Nash is also a recipient of the Order of Canada. He is the (1992-93) visiting Max Bell professor at the School of Journalism at the University of Regina).

Creolization and Creative Chaos

Rex Nettleford, Communications Scholar and Pro Vice-Chancellor, University of West Indies, Jamaica.

Ladies and gentlemen, I don't quite know what to say about how I feel following Knowlton Nash in his own territory. But first of all, I would like to say how very happy I am to be in Regina. When I told some of my colleagues I was going to Regina, one or two of them said, "Where is that?" And I said "In Saskatchewan." They said, "Oh." There you are.

I have been attending a very stimulating and challenging exercise over the past two days. Human beings have to keep talking. I think it is a good thing it was held in Regina. I kept saying to both Clyde Sanger, my old friend, and Derek Ingram what a wonderful city this is (I said "town" but then was corrected). The people haven't lost their innocence. They're obscenely guileless and just beautiful to be with. I shall report this as well. Now, let me warn you, you might just be flooded with immigrants you don't exactly want.

It's difficult, of course, when Derek wrote to me many months ago to tell me of the plans for this meeting in Regina and what the topic was, I reacted in the way that one of my colleagues and Ms. Marshall from Barbados reacted in her presentation yesterday. As far as we in the Caribbean are concerned, the Cold War is nowhere yet finished.

But I said that in one sense it is finished. What I've been saying since 1989, that now that Europe has it's own Third World in Eastern Europe, now places like the Caribbean and Africa are in for a warm time, because if we thought we were exploited way back in the 16th century, we are now going to face something worse. We are going to be treated with total indifference – and that is worse than being exploited. Some of that has been coming through in the discussions over the past two days.

I, and others like myself, have been grappling, with something which is far more fundamental than what either Mr. Bush or his likely successor (which could be himself) is cooking up in the Oval Office. I, and others like myself, have been concerned with the year 1992. It's a very important year for all of us on this side of the Atlantic. I shall have to leave my African brothers and sisters out of this for a while. You happen to be one of the "Old World" peoples who came here and usurped this part of the world. But those of us who have come and have had our being on this side of the Atlantic have some serious thoughts to weigh and ponder down the decade into the 21st century. The economic determinism to which Knowlton Nash referred is obviously part of it, but even behind and beyond that is something which is much deeper. If there are any native Americans in here, you are included too. All of us who have made this (either by force or voluntarily) hemisphere our habitat over the past 500 years have some very serious decisions to make about ourselves, including the citizens of the United States who have managed to "hi-jack" the word "American." The United States is only one part of the Americas. All of us who live and have our being in this hemisphere are Americans. We are the creatures of 500 years of a particular process with colliding cultures which have ended up with a new sense and sensibility. It is in this sense that we are a new world – not in Mr. Reagan's or Mr. Bush's sense. There's a new sense and sensibility which has, in turn, affected the people across the Atlantic.

The way history has been written since 1492, we are led to believe that it has been a one-way exercise, that we have been civilized by the importations from across the Atlantic. Of course, we have chosen to ignore the Pacific totally. The notion that the West *is* the North Atlantic and that, in fact, people in North America have chosen to identify with the other side of the Atlantic and, in so doing, ignore the dynamism of their own existence over the past 500 years, is part of our problem. We are *all* Creoles. Native bred and native born. Those of us who regard ourselves as Englishmen overseas or Scotsmen overseas or Ukrainians overseas or Africans overseas, or Spaniards and Portuguese overseas have to think again. That is why any attempt to, in a unilateral way, decide that Euro-America is some mainstream on this side of the Atlantic and everything else is secondary and are tributaries to feed into that mainstream, will create trouble for all of us for a long time to come.

People like myself and certainly those of us from the Caribbean who are deemed to be "ethnic" – that dreadful word which has crept into trans-Atlantic vocabulary – you're either white or ethnic – I've never been able to understand that – people like ourselves have come around to the view that we are not interested in entering anybody's main stream. The New World Order for us is one in which people like ourselves are going to help determine that main stream. It's a fundamental difference and it is critical that we all understand it.

I often say to white Americans . . . I often say to them, "The day you are able genuinely to feel that you are as Negrified as I am Europeanized, then we are in business. You are a Creole; you have entered the New World Order."

How do we say and mean that I am part African, part Asian, part native American, part European, and totally American. That's what we in the Caribbean are learning to say. We are learning to say we are part Indian (meaning East Indian), part African, part European, part native American (where they still live), but totally Caribbean. We are learning to say goodbye to our motherland, to sing, "goodbye motherland" without losing our ancestral connections, but having a sense of place and purpose, rooted in 500 years of a peculiar kind of history which has done a great deal to enrich human development.

There are those of us, of course, who may be of African ancestry and because of the special and the specific occurrences of history through trans-Atlantic slavery, have a particular kind of connection that has to remain for the time being because it is not yet solved. The triumphalist posturing of Western civilization is unfortunately rooted in notions of super-ordinate positions, pre-ordained by people of Caucasian stock as against all others and particularly people of African ancestry. Until that is resolved, the Americas are going to have very serious problems.

The native Americans can at least invoke an ancestral metaphysics and that is very important. You will notice that people like ourselves have not myths of origin. We merely have myths of relations. But in fact, we have to have myths of relations because that is what has made all of us in this room who are not native Africans or native Europeans or native Asians. Everybody who has made this continent, including the Caribbean, home, is a Creole. There is absolutely no difference between a Canadian of whatever racial origin and myself on that score of ancestry. We can, in fact, make reconnections, as we do when we are prepared to declare our positions, particularly if we are in a power situation.

Now with this goes the whole range of cultural indices, whether it is religion, whether it is language – and I've got to tell Canada about the importance of language whether it is kinship patterns, the way you bring up your children; whether it is artistic manifestations; whether we have to go still to Paris or to London to get recognition before we get it here – all of these things. There is no New World Order if those old categories remain. And those take precedence as a kind of logical priority to all the G.N.P.'s and G.D.P.'s that we can think about. Until we have a sense of place and purpose rooted in our own traditions and in our history of the past 500 years at least on the soil of the Americas, we will continue to regard Africans as inferior. We will continue to suspect the Asians as cunning, and we will still have the native Americans in reservations, even if we devise something called "equal opportunity."

None of the things that we have devised in this part of the world to fake cultural equity among peoples of different stock, different racial and cultural backgrounds has worked. We are into multiculturalism which is a kind of near-liberal mechanism. You watch it. It will not make sense in the long run, because the emphasis will be more on the "multi" rather than on the "cultural." It's an excellent device for those of us who are in a power position to maintain our power position. Of course.

The Americans had a thing which they called the "melting pot." They are neatly abandoning that now, because indeed all the different peoples were in that pot, but they were all surrounded by prophylactic shields, so they touched and were side by side, but never really did live together or mix. Brazil continues with the thing about the mixed blood ideal, making absolutely no sense in practical terms. I would strongly recommend to the Canadians that they get rid of that "multi-cultural" policy. Now interestingly enough, I know the "minorities" love the multi-cultural policy because that's the only way to access funds frequently to buy costumes to dance. All of this is rooted in received epistemology, received anthologies, received cosmologies, all of which have to change.

I have taken Columbus very seriously. Not taking sides at all, that is, in terms of whether he was the harbinger of ecocide, ethnicide, or whether he brought civilization to the likes of us. Not at all. That is a quarrel between the people in the North Atlantic having nothing to do with me. Having read a great deal about him, he has a lot of lessons to teach us. For one thing, the notion that that event in 1492 should create a historical situation where we all have been educated to believe that the world started in 1492; well, the native Americans are reminding us that that is nonsense. And in any case, the Africans circumnavigated Africa centuries before 1492.

Columbus was part of a process, but to his lasting credit, there was a root expansion of thought. He was prepared to break all the received wisdom of the time, all seas were navigable. And for people like ourselves, any New World Order has got to be predicated on the belief, the faith, if not the logic, that all seas are navigable; all peoples are equal; all peoples are worth something; that we, people like ourselves, are far more textured than we allow ourselves to be.

I come from a nice little laboratory – not a great many people, but very much the laboratory of the dynamism of this creolization process. It's turbulent. It's a laboratory of turbulence. It's creative chaos. Nothing as obscenely ordered as Regina. If we have a solution, we find a problem. And, the notion of organized chaos surrounding a core set of values, however ill-defined, but somehow strong enough to hold us together, it's in this sense that maybe people like ourselves, on this side of the world, if we really want to accept ourselves and stop faking our identity, may very well be the citizens of the 21st century, because the kind of world we are entering is going to be a world of creative chaos, a world of turbulence.

Telecommunications, you turn on (however bad CNN might be) and you see a war starting in the Gulf. How do you deconstruct something we in the Caribbean were doing long before Mr. Derrida came on the scene, how do you deconstruct all that host of facts and data which assault you? The implications for education are far-reaching. The universities have no money all over the Western world at a time when we need them more than ever, because as generators of knowledge, of knowledge bases which are appropriate to inform policy and inform the way we make decisions about our daily lives, this is something which should have high priority at this time. The school systems are critical. How we educate our people – its not just the journalists. The journalists are merely reflections of the society. They're no different from their colleagues. They're merely pursuing a particular profession. But if they're transmitting things, unless there is a receiver's set which is ready to receive it, they can be as kind about the "Third World" as they are. If the Third World itself and their own people are not in a position to receive and to understand and comprehend what they read, no go.

There is something which the Americans, meaning the people of the United States, are pushing, called global education. The Canadians are part and parcel of that. I'm not referring to geography, of how many rivers and coal mines are in the world. As a good colonial, I learned all of that. I knew about all the rivers in Europe and all the coal mines. I even knew about the tundra. I knew a great deal about Canada. That was one blessing of colonialism. Unfortunately, we have become so provincial at the very time when we need to get our people to understand the interconnectedness of things. Only babies now understand that. All of us who are parents, a child comes to us to ask a series of questions. The child incubates connections, interconnectedness and we are angry because we can't answer them because we have been "well-educated."

All of this, that's the new world that we are talking about. And we must get those very fundamental things in order – new paradigms appropriate to the new reality. What is coming out of the Oval Office is the old weapons in the old armory fighting new wars. And interestingly enough, it is people like us, a Regina more than a Toronto, a Kingston maybe more than a Port of Spain, more than a Washington or a London where they have great founts of wisdom because there is texture.

I know you have one-way streets. Where I come from, we have too. But we're likely to have people driving both ways, and flying over at the same time, and also underneath. We operate on several levels at the same time. It's the kind of world in which we live. The reconnections with the old world, then, are very important in every tableau. Whether we like it or not, this is what is coming, because the world – your own man here from this country spoke about a global village. It's a Canadian who created that phrase. He had been knocked for it. But he was a Canadian from provincial Canada, not from Washington. Why was he able to see it like that? Probably, in his own personal life, the connections that he had, the density of his interrelationship with people, was far greater than that of his counterpart in New York. We frequently underestimate the tremendous opportunities we have. Many of these cities were bigger than Athens. In Western civilization, that's the fount of wisdom. It's the density, the intensity of interaction and interrelationship which allows for the kind of sense and sensibility which will be able to cope with the complexity of complexity and make sense of the noise. And that's what the 21st century is likely to be.

We're already in it, in any case. It has very little to do with what Mr. Bush is talking about. Mr. Bush presides over a great bitter nation. There's debt stress there as there is in Jamaica. We are debt-rich in Jamaica and Trinidad is oil-poor. Alberta has become oil-poor. We understand these contradictions. As one of our poets said, "The contradictory omens are what characterize the kind of world in which we live." And it requires tremendous imagination. The exercise of the creative imagination and the creative intellect to pull through. You don't have to go to Toronto to have it. It can be had right in Regina. It can be had anywhere where people care to live in human scale development and to take each other seriously. To respect, to go on the basis of cultural equity, on the basis of mutual respect, one for another.

These are the little values that have nothing to do with getting to the moon, nothing to do with the G.D.P.'s and the G.N.P.'s and the what have we. All of which are important, but I'm afraid are a little out of tune and we should have learned over the past 300 years at least, that a lot of those things haven't worked.

The bourgeois dispensation of the 18th century is no more. We need new paradigms, new language. I don't refer to blackmail. The language has to change. There are lots of things which are rooted in prejudices, in cosmologies which do not have any basis in the new reality, in the New World Order which the majority of the world would like to see. I'm afraid much of the New World Order has to do with the re-alignment of the old power to maintain superordinate positions over the traditionally subordinate.

People like myself can't subscribe to that. People like myself want to be able to be part of the dialogue that is going to decide the next half a millennium. Over the last half a millennium, the vast majority of the world were kept out of that dialogue. This is where people in the communications media are so critical. Like teachers, as members of the intelligensia, as themselves opinion leaders, and even generators of knowledge, they have to first of all start with themselves, understand the reality of the world that we live in, because, while Mr. Bush and the superpowers govern, the people will continue to rule. The best laid plans can be sabotaged. Ask us in the Caribbean. Without putting dynamite in a bridge, we can sabotage by neglect.

And these are things which we have to bring people to the centre of the cosmos. I see Mr. Clinton referring to people first. It was the very thing one political party in Jamaica campaigned on. And the very slogan was exactly the same thing. Now I do not want to confuse sequence with consequence. And I'm not saying that Mr. Clinton has taken a leaf out of our book. But it's possible – quite possible. If they learn from Athens, which was smaller than Kingston, why can't they learn from Kingston?

We sell ourselves short and we declare premature closure on the tremendous cultural potential of people like ourselves who have had to make sense of our whole hemisphere. I read the *Globe and Mail*. With due respect to the *New York Times*. I keep saying that the *Globe and Mail* has improved so much, it's a good paper. The English is good. Some of our English "are" bad. We say "the media is," but I read the *Globe and Mail* and in some of its feature articles I'm deeply impressed. I'm sure there are people (your richer cousins to the South) who would feel that those country bumpkins up in Canada can't produce anything. You just think seriously about that. We in the Caribbean don't feel that way. We can see the world as a tapestry, where every thread that runs through is quite distinct, which makes absolutely no sense, except in terms of its relationship one to another. We have to be that sort of people. The people in the metropolises megalopolises are jaded in many instances. And what a city used to do is give humans a reasonabble scale of development. Cities now, in many instances, have gotten far too big to be able to afford that density of interaction and interrelationship between people. In fact, in places like Regina on one level, in places like Canada on another level, in places like the Caribbean, we have to think in concentric circles.

I'm very impressed with what Europe is doing at the moment. Maastricht or no Maastricht. And it is going back to texture. And despite the battle being put on by the Thatcherites and other Brits, they will become European. We, on the other hand, have got to make something of a Commonwealth. What the New World Order is going to be is a series, like a honeycomb thing of different kinds of blocks, interrelating in strange architectural patterns, different to what we had before. Are we ready to be able to be part of that? Not simply just to sit back and report it, but rather to help determine where it goes and what it looks like down the decade into the 21st century.

I speak not with arrogance, but a little bit of confidence that the human being, as long as he or she is allowed the exercise of his or her creative intellect and creative potential, can do anything. And we have to believe that in the way that Columbus did and when he "discovered" us. What we have done in return is to have survived him and we are here being able to live to tell the tale.

It was wonderful to be in Regina. I feel so much at home. Thank you.

(Rex Nettlefored helped set up Gemini News Service 25 years ago. Rex has been a very firm friend of Gemini ever since. He has been a governor of the foundation that owns Gemini for ten years. Rex Nettleford is pro-Chancellor of the University of the West Indies and a very well-known Caribbean scholar, trade union educator, social and cultural historian, and political analyst. He was a founding governor of the International Development Research Centre in Ottawa. Rex Nettleford is a member of the West Indian Commission which has been examining the effects of the Free Trade Agreement (FTA) and the North American Free Trade Agreement (NAFTA) on the Caribbean. He served as a consultant to UNESCO and he's editor of the Caribbean Quarterly and author of many books and finally, a recipient of the Order of Merit).

8

Tomorrow is Another Day

Whose Future Is It Anyway?
Tina Spencer, *Ottawa Citizen*

I work for the *Ottawa Citizen*, it's one of the Western imperialist newspapers that we've all been bashing for a couple of days. We've ended up, somewhat by accident, with a very politically correct panel of people. We've got black, we've got white, we've got women, we've got men, we've got north, we've got south. We've also got two topics to cover, so we'll try our best to get through them and still allow some time for chat afterwards.

I'd like to start by introducing Ernest Moloi. He's a journalist from Botswana from the *Guardian* there. He was a participant in Gemini News Service's Village Reporting Program which, if you know about that, has been quite an ambitious scheme and quite successful. Ernest is going to talk a little bit about women's issues.

Ernest Moloi
Reporter, the *Botswana Guardian*

> But you want to find out why, when reporting on women's issues, for example the current drought, you never find anything, you never hear any story about the women affected by the drought.

We in Botswana are a small press. We have about four private newspapers. There's one daily that is a government owned paper. We have a radio station that's government owned also. Then we have some magazines.

I want to talk a little bit about women's issues. I don't know about "as engines of change," but I believe that women's issues should be given some priority in the press. They should be.

I've heard people here quoting and quoting and quoting other people. I want to just make up a little quotation of mine, "A journalist has a broad and open mind when observing the happenings in his country outside the newsroom. He has grand ideas of how to develop these things into a well balanced article. But all this is shut into oblivion once he goes into the newsroom. He forgets everything." I think there is something about the newsroom which is terrible because you have to comply with other policies and so on.

Women's issues in Botswana are given some coverage. The latest development is the appeals court ruling in favour of Mrs. Unity Dow. Sue Montgomery wrote for Gemini. I haven't seen anything from Gemini regarding the appeals court ruling. This ruling favored Mrs. Unity Dow. You will find that she's taken (and she's my auntie) the government to task over her right as a citizen of Botswana and as an equal before the eyes of the law. She wanted to pass on her citizenship to her children. She's married to an American citizen, but he hasn't declared Botswana citizenship yet. He stayed in the country for the past 12 years, but he's not a citizen of Botswana. Now she wants her children to become Botswanan. As the law stood then, her children were regarded as aliens in her country. They were regarded as Americans really because they have to follow the male citizenship.

So women's issues are given some priority in our press. We believe women are doing a grand job. They are trying to voice their dissent over what traditionally has been accepted as "just." But if you want to find out why, when reporting on women's issues, for example, the current drought, you never find anything, you never hear any story about the women affected by the drought. I believe that journalists can do much better and focus on women on such issues also. Not only about how male farmers are coping with the drought, but also females.

But it is believed that women, in their quest for liberation, should not do that at the expense of their culture. I believe the culture should be a complement to the liberation women are asking for. They shouldn't have to follow the European, the Western model. I believe an African woman is an African women and a European woman is a European woman and an Asian woman is an Asian woman.

Tina Spencer:

Let's switch hats (hemispheres). Let me introduce Teresa Mazatelli, who's the next speaker on the panel. Theresa is one of Derek's protegés from the Gemini IDRC (International Development Research Centre) fellowship program in 1987-1988. She's now a medical reporter in Toronto and she instructed me to say that she's looking to go abroad again. She's going to focus a little bit on women and the North American media which should be of some interest both to North Americans, but also everybody else who wonders what's going on in our newsrooms.

Teresa Mazzitelli
Gemini News Service, *Canadian Family Physician*

The end of the Cold War will not affect the lives of women at Canadian newspapers because there is another Cold War being fought in those very newsrooms. It does not divide along East/West. It divides along male/female.

I am going to follow Ernest's lead and talk about women as well, from a slightly different perspective. I want to talk about women's voices in Canadian newspapers. I want to share with you that I showed [my] paper to two friends of mine, both female, both reporters and one of them said, "I think you should probably not use phrases such as "male dominated model of journalism," "female sensibility," or "feminism." The second one, quite apart from the first, said quite carefully, "Why don't you cut to the chase and just say 'Die, sexist pigs!'" I'm not going to tell you what camp I'm in because that would ruin the ending.

I want to start with a quote; a phrase that a Mexican novelist, Carlos Fuentes uses. That phrase is "literature of the centre." Fuentes uses it to describe the Eurocentric model of writing that he felt obliged to follow early in his career. It was the model set by the West and accepted internationally, so why speak with a distinct, alternative voice when you have a model to imitate?

If we talk about journalism of the centre, we mean journalism of the majority, journalism of the establishment, journalism of the North, and journalism from a male point of view. It's exclusive, and I think it's becoming increasingly less relevant because it no longer reflects its community. It certainly doesn't reflect the Canadian multicultural community.

The end of the Cold War will not affect the lives of women at Canadian newspapers because there is another Cold War being fought in those very newsrooms. It does not divide along East/West. It divides along male/female. Most of the women that I talked to, and I did talk to several in preparing this, said to me that they do not believe that it's necessary to break down the male dominated model of journalism. We need only to add to it, to expand, to draw on female points of view.

What do we need to do this? The first thing we need is women in sufficient numbers in newsrooms. The second thing, we need the confidence to move away from journalism of the centre. Let's be fair. The numbers are improving in this country, they're improving very slowly, but they're not enough. What we need are women at all different levels of the decision-making process in a newsroom. Not just a newsroom that is half female with possibly one or two senior editors who are female, and with any luck a managing editor at the top; that won't work.

I think what you need is a thread of women throughout the process, probably a rope of women would be preferable, but there you are. That, as far as I can see, is the only way to ensure that the story ideas are different, the writing is different, the editing is different, and the placement of that story is different. The women that I spoke to agreed that women will choose the same story as a man, but they will view it differently. They will go to different sources. They will use different examples.

I want to give you some of those examples. Eileen McCabe covered the Gulf War for Southam News. She said to me that the American government briefings did not appeal to her, so she went somewhere else. She went to women rather than to male generals to find out what that war cost. I'm going to quote her because I think it's a great quote. She said, "Nine times out of ten, women will handle the story differently. There are no sub-plots, there is no conspiracy. We're just different." Jan Wong, the *Globe and Mail's* correspondent in Beijing has written eloquently and at length on such social issues as one child families and abortion, matters, I think her predecessors did not focus on. Juliet O'Neill, Southam's Moscow correspondent, wrote about the privatization of business in the former Soviet republic. She used a hairdresser as her example. The tone in that example landed that story on a lot of front pages. All it was was a basic economic story about small business, but it had a very, very different twist.

Departing from journalism of the centre means the freedom not to conform to both a male or predetermined definition of what is news and what is normal. Female sensibility brings an additional perspective to the story. We agree on that. There's a lot of pressure to suppress it, to shave it off, to erase it, to be seen as "tough," as being able to handle a hard political story, a hard economic story. I must confess that I am uncomfortable about using that phrase myself. It sounds patronizing to men, and condescending to women all at the same time. I'm not sure why that is. If somebody could explain it to me, I would appreciate it. But I know, it's my phrase, I'm using it, and that's how I feel about it.

We end up for some reason apologizing for having a female bias. I think it would be more helpful if we recognized that we have accepted a male bias as normal. If we accept that both males and females are working from a position of bias, and we incorporate those two voices, we have a much better chance of achieving a balance.

Feminism in the media. Why? In this country it has resulted in articles on rape, child sexual abuse, wife assault. It has brought those issues to the forefront, to society, for discussion. I think it's fair to say that as a result of that, family violence is now a public issue instead of a private one. I don't know how anyone can see that as a negative development.

I'll go back to female sensibilities. If you erase that, you are not only limiting the scope of the article, but you're cutting your reading audience in half. The *Globe and Mail* recently discovered that even fewer women read it than other newspapers. I'll offer you a theory on why I think that happens; I'm open to any other theories. The *Globe and Mail* is written as the male establishment newspaper. Women, unfortunately, do not see themselves as insiders. So the paper has held in-house focus sessions to discuss this (obviously they see it as a problem, and they're right). Their own staff has decided that one way to tackle this is to quote more women, photograph more women, interview more women. From a marketing point of view, if you want women readers, you have to include them.

Let me leave you with this: If women hold up half the sky, then women could read half the newspapers. That is not happening today in this country. I don't know why. We have the resources, we have the woman-power, we have the freedom. We have a lot of things that I think some of our colleagues from the developing world do not have. We should be much further ahead than we are. We are not reflecting the community. We are not representing half of the constituents.

Tina Spencer:

I'd like to introduce to you now my friend Charles Quist-Adade. He's a journalist from Ghana, who's now a visiting scholar at the University of Windsor here in Canada, but he came here via the Soviet Union where he was based in Leningrad (now St. Petersburg) for nine and one-half years. He wants to talk about the issue of youth. Youth is the next generation of gatekeepers.

Charles Quist-Adade

Former Gemini Correspondent in St. Petersburg, Russia

> It was my coming to understand the real situation on the ground that actually [opened] my eyes.

I'll begin by proposing that there is need for intercultural studies amongst our journalists because the title would begin to respect and afford other cultures the respect they deserve. Every culture is egocentric. We all believe that our mothers are the best mothers in the world. There's nothing wrong with that. It is only when this egocentrism, that this love for our mother, extends to deny the existence of other mothers. Then it becomes very dangerous indeed.

Today as a reporter, tomorrow one becomes the gatekeeper, the news editor, the managing editor. He will have to decide what type of news should appear is which part of the newspaper or magazine. That's why it is very important for us to grasp the need for the respect for other cultures, so that when we become gatekeepers and we get a story from the village in Ghana, we don't say that we don't know we know anything about what is happening in Ghana, so let me either bury it somewhere and bring maybe a story about a Canadian farmer or something. Maybe in the Ghanaian story, a whole village has been cut off from the rest of the world and there is a need to report this. But because we really don't appreciate the need to cover this country, we deprive the world of knowing about what is actually happening in this particular part of the world.

I'll use my personal experiences in the Soviet Union to illustrate my point and that will make me digress a little bit from the youth as engines of change topic.

Before I left Ghana for Russia, I used to reject out of hand in my youthful romanticism anything that I ever read about the Soviet Union in a negative light. I said it was Western, American, orchestrated propaganda against the Soviet Union. Fortunately, I had the opportunity to go to Russia. There I was in St. Petersburg. First of all I was in Donetsk, Ukraine, a very small mining city.

It was after some time that I started to understand the Russian language and interact with the people that I got to know the reality of the Soviet Union. I didn't have the real picture because our (Ghanaian) media, it was a leftist media, especially the government controlled newspapers were always projecting a very romantic of the Soviet Union, and that was what most of us were digesting. It was my coming to understand the real situation on the ground that actually opened my eyes.

This goes to show that there is need for one to be on the ground, to live in the particular environment for quite a time to be able to appreciate, understand and report very objectively. And that speaks to the "fly in and fly out" journalist that somebody talked about.

With the end of the Cold War, there is a saying that, "There are no permanent friends in politics, there are only permanent interests." And this was very well demonstrated after the Cold War ended. It was better demonstrated in the mass media. When Mandela was released from jail after almost three decades, it was news all over the world. It captured the headlines. It was given top billing.

But not in Gorbachev's Soviet Union. Mandela was supported, the ANC was supported and encouraged morally, economically, materially by the former Soviet Union and all of a sudden this man has been released. You would be surprised to know that less than 30 seconds was allotted on the main TV program and that came at the very tail end of the news program and it looked as if it was an oversight. In fact, the sports news of the day was even rated higher. We only saw a flash of Mandela in a black car waving and the anchor just said, "Today, Mandela after 27 years in prison, has been released." That was all.

The following day, probably they carried something, but it was buried on the fifth page, and it was under a commentary. It was just a few paragraphs, a dry biographical sketch of Mandela. And the only thing about his release was the first line, "Yesterday Mandela was released." *Izvestia,* the government newspaper, didn't carry anything on this release. In fact, what it reported was that African nationalists had threatened to kill Mandela if he was released. This is just to show that the former Soviet media didn't have Africans at heart when it was shouting about proletarian internationalism.

In Africa there are a number of people who are still claiming to be on the Left side. We should not always go clamouring after slogans. We should not always close our eyes to realities and must be able to appreciate our land.

In my country we have what we call the ivory tower Marxists. I was one of them. When I was in Ghana, I didn't want to believe that there was anything wrong with Marxism at all. There are a lot of people over there who are behaving this way.

The youth or the future journalists should learn to respect the cultures of others. To be able to write objectively, one needs a longer period of acquaintance with what appears on the ground, what are the new answers of other cultures, for one to be able to write very objectively and inform the world with more balanced and objective information.

Tina Spencer:

Let me introduce you to Elaine Shein. She is a graduate of the journalism program here in Regina and she was one of the Regina Gemini fellowship participants a couple of years back. She now works as an editor/reporter for *Western Producer*, which is the biggest agricultural newspaper in Canada. She also wants to address this question of young reporters, of youth in general and pass on, perhaps, a bit of a hopeful note.

Elaine Shein,

Managing Editor, *Western Producer*

> We're the children of the post Cold War era. The Cold War that affected our parents did more than raise suspicion of what the superpowers could inflict upon each other. That period in history also robbed North America of the opportunity to broaden its perspective of the world.

On my first day in journalism school, my classmates and I were surveyed about our goals and why we had decided to become journalists. At that time, more than half of my class of about 30 students said they were interested in becoming foreign correspondents.

Less than 5 years later, probably less than half of those students remain in journalism. And, in fact, last night, I was talking to one of my classmates who has dropped out of journalism just in the past two weeks. Many of the people in my class are now employed in other careers. None of the former students have become the foreign correspondents that they wanted to at least not yet.

Looking at the statistics does not give the true picture. While the young journalists may not have become the foreign correspondents in a far off bureau, many of them retain a very strong interest in foreign affairs. They are very interested in what is happening around the world, and some of them are now writing local angles to events happening thousands of miles away. Unfortunately, they are not getting the chance to access the information or opportunities needed to put into perspective what is happening.

We're the children of the post Cold War era. The Cold War that affected our parents did more than raise suspicion of what the superpowers could inflict upon each other. That period in history also robbed North America of the opportunity to broaden its perspective of the world.

The young journalists are still suffering the after effects. The United States, and consequently Canada, became insulated. Their views of the world rotated around themselves. Our coverage of news became more self-centred. We concentrated more on what happens to our own country, our province or state, and most importantly it seemed, our own city or village.

The focus of news coverage became the ability to show the average reader how his own personal life will be affected by decisions being made by governments, or the local weather for that day, or in Canada, the latest draft trade in hockey.

By the time my classmates and I entered the journalism program, we were being taught to report on that level. We were not being taught how to analyze what's happening beyond the borders of our city or province, because we were told our readers and listeners are not interested in such matters. This becomes a dangerous approach. The changing world affects everyone, whether it's a drought in Africa, a war in the Middle East, subsidy wars between Europe and the U.S., or aboriginal rights being demanded in Africa, or Australia, or Canada.

The challenge is for the journalists to comprehend the significance of what is happening and then relate the news back to the audiences. The newspapers and other media should be able to prepare people for certain events and explain why it's happening along with how it may affect the readers.

Unfortunately, the young North American journalists didn't have an opportunity to grow up in such an environment. Newspapers, for example, have changed in the last few decades. At the turn of the century, up until perhaps the early 1970s, the events of the world were featured prominently on the front pages. This evolved into what we have today international news featured on page 52 in Section F, or something like that. The North American media works its international news into spurts of priority student riots in China, the Gulf War, Yugoslavia, Somalia have each had their turn in recent time, to be the hot spots for news coverage, but the rest of the world is relatively ignored.

So what does this mean to the young journalists? The journalists are frustrated by the lack of opportunity to cover news from outside their country or often even their beat in a city. Many of us are curious and intrigued by what is happening in the post Cold War era. We realize the incredible opportunities to travel into certain countries and learn about different people, cultures and conflicts. We are energetic, inquisitive and willing to work. But we are faced with a lack of resources, a lack of training, and a lack of commitment from our news organizations.

Few reporters from Canada, young or old, are willing to risk their job stability at this time. I think a good example of that is the IRDC scholarships that a lot of us here have gone on. I found out by talking to someone just last night that only six applications were made this year to go for one year on a scholarship. There were a lot of people interested, but the reason there were only six applications, was because news organizations would not commit themselves to hiring back that reporter one year later.

The journalism scene in Canada is not stable, with more jobs being lost than are being created. Instead of being as mobile as they were in the past, reporters are willing to stay five years or often more with the same news organization. This does not allow new reporters to enter the organization. I mentioned before that a classmate of mine has now dropped out of journalism and you're probably wondering if there are so few jobs why she would consider doing that at this time. She did it because of work conditions, a lack of job security, and disillusionment with what journalism is all about. The employer was no longer interested in the value of news coverage and placed more emphasis on using the resources to get advertising than on covering the news. I know that I keep mentioning that we need resources for covering international journalism, but I guess I'm more concerned about our local coverage of news events and how we're using the resources. It seems that we're closing down bureaus and we might just depend on CNN here, too, for everything, for all our news coverage.

The freelance or full-time reporters are being frustrated by the cuts they are seeing to international coverage. At the Canadian Association of Journalists annual meeting in Edmonton earlier this year, any potential foreign correspondents were strongly discouraged. There were told there are no jobs, and the big newspapers and networks do not consider their bureaus as a high priority. Many have been closed.

Some young reporters have gambled and offered to string stories from other parts of the world. Few are successful in lining up committed editors to their ideas. They are simply told there is no interest in the developing world. Any stories that are used by the news organizations come from large press agencies such as Reuters, Canadian Press, Associated Press, Broadcast News, Christian Science Monitor or the U.S. television networks.

At times, Canadian media organizations have selected journalists and sent them to do stories abroad, but rarely to developing countries. If young reporters are sent, they are often ill-prepared. Again, this is something expressed at the CAJ (Canadian Association of Journalism) conferences I've attended in the past.

The picture isn't entirely bleak for young journalists.

Let's look at my class again. More than a third of them have travelled outside of Canada since we graduated. Some of them have written stories, often freelancing back. All of them expressed different attitudes about the world after they returned. All of them were very interested in doing something with the knowledge and experience they gained usually the first thing was to educate their parents that people in other parts of the world are experiencing the same situations that they are.

As for myself, speaking as a young journalist, I must admit I became more interested in the world after leaving the restrictive perimeters of Canada. I was raised on a farm in Saskatchewan and didn't receive a daily newspaper. I was dependent on radio and television news and documentary programs for my news. While I watched as the world opened up and became more accessible to media, I found my own mind still hadn't opened up. I was very much affected by the insular attitude of Canadian journalism. I was one of those people who were taught that two superpowers were battling for control of the world, and the rest of the world didn't matter. I refused to believe it, but I was not encouraged by the media, the school system or other influences to actively try to learn more about the developing world. Anything I did come across led me to be suspicious that it had an American or Soviet slant on it.

Maybe it's that pessimism that has driven me and now other young journalists to pursue opportunities to find out for ourselves what is happening in the world.

The young people can influence the future of media coverage, but they need to be encouraged. They need to have the opportunity to learn what is good journalism on a global perspective. They need to have the chances to travel or to be exposed to sources who can explain what is happening and why, in other parts of the world. They need to have editors, managing editors, station managers, etc. who allow them opportunities to be exposed to these other forms of information.

The bosses need to be committed to allowing the young journalists to try different work experiences and then invite them to join their news team again. These people could influence the approach of the news organization toward world news. This wouldn't cost a lot of money but it would require a change in attitude. The danger is that if the attitude doesn't change, a new generation of journalists with open minds may continue to desert the profession.

I believe the youth can offer a fresh perspective to covering the world because they have the desire to dismantle the barriers that their parents placed on covering certain parts of the world. Maybe if more young journalists express this desire and somehow show they can make the audiences aware and more interested about what is happening internationally, the journalism of tomorrow can be more than just filling spaces that aren't taken up by ads and commercials.

The media can record more effectively the history of the world and not just the developed world.

Open Discussion

Jill Forrester:

Elaine mentioned how Canadians have this thing about believing the world is right here and nowhere else, and I just wanted to say that Gemini was what opened the world up to me. I started seeing what else is going on.

When I was in London I went to a conference on development economics and I thought, "Oh great! A whole weekend. I'm going to learn about this finally," because people were telling me I was naive. So I went to this room full of British economists and I found myself listening very keenly, but then in about two hours, I was bored stiff. There was one person doing graphs. They were trying to figure out which businesses or sectors of the business community should be privatized first. They were trying to analyze it this way, and I don't know if anybody could follow it. I couldn't.

They had various people analyzing how life changed in all these countries with charts and numbers and graphs, so I listened. Finally, after one of the presentations, this guy at the back got up (I think he was from Ghana) and he said, "Your graph is really nice, but I'm sorry, things don't work that way in our country." So I thought I had found someone who could explain to me where the story was, a person who actually knew what was going on.

This fellow from Ghana explained to me that a few decades ago there weren't the people at the back of the room to stand and say "Excuse me, it doesn't work like that." But more and more, there are more people from those countries who can explain things, who study this for themselves instead of having to rely on the Westerners to come and explain this to them.

I think this applies to what's happening here in Canada with native people. I had the privilege of driving many of the delegates in a van showing them Regina and Saskatchewan, and one of the things they were most interested in was native people. That's what was important. I think we did a poor job of inviting the native peoples. I don't think we invited enough of them.

I just wanted to read this. It's from Chief Dan George who's famous in Canada. He was very accessible to the media, he was on TV a lot, and he was one of the few natives that we white people knew as a face and thought about. I found this while I was researching a paper a couple of years ago. It's from a paper he did called *"My Very Good Dear Friends*:"

> I was born in an age that loved the things of nature and gave them beautiful names like Tes-wall-u-wit instead of dried up names like "Stanley Park." I was born when people loved all nature and spoke to it as though it had a soul. And then the people came. More and more people came, like a crushing rushing wave they came, hurling the years aside. Suddenly I found myself a young man in the midst of the twentieth century. I found myself and my people adrift in this new age, but not a part of it.

He goes on:

> Do you know what it is like to feel that you are of no value to society and those around you? To know that people came to help you but not to work with you, for they knew you had nothing to offer. Do you know what it is like to have your race belittled and to come to learn that you're only a burden to the country? Maybe we didn't have the skills to make a meaningful contribution, but no-one would wait for us to catch up. We were shoved aside because they thought we were dumb and could never learn.
>
> And now you hold out your hand and you beckon to me to come across the street. Come and integrate, you say. But how can I come? I am naked and ashamed. How can I come in dignity. I have no presents; I have no gifts. What is there in my culture you value? My poor treasure you can only scorn. Am I then to come as a beggar and receive all from your omniscient hand? Somehow I must wait. I must delay. I must find myself. I must find my treasure. I must wait until you want something of me, until you need something that is me. Then I can raise my head and say to my wife and family, "Listen, they are calling. They need me. I must go."

I think that we can relate that to the situation of the developing world. I think we Westerners have to realize what the developing world has to give us. And, the developing world must stand up and find its treasure.

Mohamad Hamaludin:

Madam chairman, I sort of liked how you introduced yourself when you were introducing the panel. I probably want to borrow it. My name is "male chauvinist pig." I was going to talk about some of the things that Jill said. Jill not only stole my thunder, but she converted it into a full-blown Miami hurricane.

My question basically was to Teresa. The imperative of the press today in Canada and in general, and particularly in Regina in terms of diversity, is it that they should bring more women into the media and move them up into management, or should it be native Indians, the first nations people, and give them a chance to move in, even at the lower level? It seems strange to me that you don't have many here in the press, and I understand that they are 30% of Regina's population.

Teresa Mazzitelli:

That's part of the problem. I stayed simply with women and I tried to stress the point that women are just the first step. In other words, if you can't make room for half of the population, then you obviously have not made room for aboriginals or other groups that are part of this society.

Mohamad Hamaludin:

It seemed to me (and this is a dirty word in America) that you seem to be talking something along the lines of quotas. But don't we have a problem? There will be just that number of slots available at one time. All these men are not going to die, they're not going to just fade away. There will be positions. We do have some women who are moving up, but we don't have these other people. Where should the preference be at this point in time?

Teresa Mazzitelli:

I'll address the issue of quotas if you want. I didn't get to that, but there's a Southam task force on women in the media, and obviously it found that there were not enough women moving up the ranks. One of the things that it did; it said merit pay increases are tied to managers' success in promoting women. That was one of the results of that task force. It found, and I invite Scott Honeyman, Norman Webster, some of the Southam people to speak to that, but I found that it was not happening naturally for one reason or another, and so the only way to do that was to legislate.

I'm not a fan of quotas. I would not want to be a woman who was put in that position to fill a slot so as to make the number of women look good. It should be happening naturally, but you're also at a point that if it's not happening naturally, and Southam's just finished doing a vast survey telling you that . . .

Mohamad Hamaludin:

But that task force that you spoke about did not have any First Nations people on it. It seems to me that what they're trying to do is sort of expand the edges of the envelope without opening the envelope. In other words, diversify within a Eurocentric point of view of the country and the city. Because I don't think that any aboriginals were on that task force. I still get to the question, where should the preference be at this point in time if there are openings available in the newspapers and TV, or should the TV stations and newspapers start to offer scholarships that are targeted toward these people and getting them into the media?

Teresa Mazzitelli:

I think you're raising a very good point. There's a lot debate within the Canadian media. Two things have hit us. One is the recession, so there are no jobs for anyone wherever you come from, whatever your background is, and that makes it very difficult for us now to take our good intentions, however we define them, and bring them into reality. The paper I work at has a woman as a managing editor. She's had an enormous influence, not just on the question of women as such, but on exactly the things that you're raising.

She is saying, "Well, we have to look at something past just this white faced female or male point of view, and what are we going to do about it." She's got some very good ideas, and some very controversial ideas. There's no agreement across the board. But the fact is, she can't do anything anyway, because we can't hire. It's a recessionary time period for the media, so whatever we might wish to do, right now it's a very stagnant kind of thing for us.

I think if you talk to journalists at Canadian papers and broadcast media, particularly young people, you'd find they want everybody in. The more the merrier. Because that is what will keep us aware in our country and aware of what's happening out there. Very much, newspapers worry about being isolated from their readers.

Guy Parisram:

I work for CBC Newsworld, and I'm based out in Halifax where we started our operations three years ago. I want to address some of the issues that Elaine raised and some of the fears that Elaine raised. I think that in establishing the 24-hour news network that we are, the CBC may have very well been conscious of some of the concerns that you have raised. What we have done in the three and one-half years that we have existed is to try to widen the scope of our news coverage. Because we are based on the East coast, because we go to air at 7:00 a.m., we have been able to tap the foreign news that seems to be lacking so much in the daily coverage in the National, which has only 22 minutes.

I have been able to bring to CBC a unique kind of experience because I was born and raised in the Third World. I'm from Trinidad originally. I spent fifteen years of my working life as a TV journalist working throughout the Caribbean and some parts of Europe, and as far as India. That was one of the reasons that I was recruited into the CBC because I have the experience and the academic credentials that the CBC was looking for.

Within the 24 hours that we are on the air, we have tried, and we keep trying to expand the depth of coverage, to address not only the international issues that you talk about, but the women's issues, the native issues, the concerns being expressed over and over again in this forum.

What we have found is that we are handicapped, because as a television medium, we have to rely on pictures. Television is about sound and vision. Unfortunately, we have had to become radio on a number of occasions and hang on to the telephone to tell stories about Somalia and South Africa and so many other parts of the world. We're hoping in the months and years ahead that we will be able to tap the resources of television systems in the developing world so that we can tell the developing world's story from their perspective as well. We're hoping that we could depend on your help in the developing world to help us do that.

Carma Livingstone:

I'm a student at the Journalism School here. I'd like to address you, Ernest. You had said that you want women's liberation but not at the cost of Botswanan culture. I don't want to be so presumptuous as to speak for my Botswanan sisters, because I haven't met a woman from Botswana yet, but having chosen to listen to some of my African sisters from other parts of Africa, sisters from Asia and sisters from Latin America, this is how it usually works in patriarchy. You're going to have to go back to the women of Botswana and ask them if this applies to them.

Women's liberation cannot occur within the confines of patriarchy. Your culture, most likely if it's similar to the cultures of my other sisters and our own, is based on patriarchy. So if women are to achieve liberation, it has to be outside the confines of a male dominated structure. I think that's going to cost the culture based on that structure something. I think the first place we have to start is in the newsrooms because we're a reflection of the culture we're reporting on.

Ernest Moloi:

I don't think there's anything to say. I don't think you are against what I said. This transition that we're talking about, women's liberation, it must be in harmony with the culture of the people.

Tina Spencer:

I want to interject in this with an example, and I wouldn't mind your comments. This is a case that happened very recently in Canada. It doesn't have to do with anyone from Botswana, but it has to do with this idea of culture and women's rights. A women came here seeking asylum from Saudi Arabia because she objected to the practice of having to cloak and veil herself. She sought asylum here and the Canadian government basically said, "No," it was simply because she wasn't persecuted. It was simply a case of what the cultural norms were in the country she came from. That stirred a lot of controversy here, and I'm just wondering, is that the sort of thing that you're talking about when you say that women's rights are fine but they shouldn't mess with culture?

Ernest Moloi:

Our Asian brother here was talking about a nation without food. When you start messing with the values and the norms of a society even if it is at the expense of women's liberation, I think you are destroying your nation.

Mike Urlocker:

So, you're expecting the women of Botswana to steal the soul of your nation? . . . No? You're going to give it to them?

Ernest Moloi:

They already have it.

Ngozi Anyaegbunam:

I would like to start by saying that I am relieved when I listened to Elaine. You gave me a lot of hope when you talk about the young journalists itching to move out of their own place to know what's happening in other worlds. That's the only way we can live in a small global village.

I will go back to Teresa. You said something about bias? You said something about women being apologetic when they try to be different, when they have their feminine biases. I would like to talk a little on that. I happen to be the only African woman here right now that has passed through the proper African culture. I know what it means to be a woman in Africa. Therefore, I would like to talk about Theresa, the bias you're talking about: being apologetic for being a woman or for trying to be feminine.

Then I would like to address Ernest on what it means to be a woman.

You see, in my country, Nigeria, we try to preserve our culture (we have culture too!). You know that culture is dynamic and that culture is a growing thing and that you jettison those things that are no longer relevant in your culture. As you're growing you realize that some of those things are becoming very anachronistic and therefore you drop them. You can only achieve this if you have gone through some proper progressive education. I will tell you that in Nigeria, it's still happening.

If the woman is a widow she, most of the time, does not inherit whatever her husband had. It does not matter how many years you lived with your husband before he died, if you are lucky and you had sons, and those sons are grown up enough to protect their mother, then the sons will inherit the property and the woman will indirectly benefit.

Otherwise, if the woman is insisting on having some claims on the husband's property, she has to make herself amenable by being inherited by one of the brothers. In other words, one of your brothers-in-law or even your father-in-law will have to marry you if you want to retain your husband's property. I'm talking to you about culture.

There are so many others. If I begin to tell you, we will waste all day talking about it. Let's move out of that and sound a happy note.

It is happy to note that we now have Western education. But more than 50% of women of Africa (in Nigeria) are yet to get educated. If you know where we are coming from, then you will understand why even the educated women are apologetic about being women. They're apologetic about their feminine biases, even with all the education.

Talking about education for women. I am saying that we are only gradually moving away from these cultures. People cannot move away very quickly from certain things that are reprehensible in their existence because they have been intimidated for too long. That is the same thing that is happening to even the educated woman in Nigeria, in Africa. It is affecting the way even we report in the media. I'll give you one example or maybe two.

There was a seminar that was going on, and we know of one lady who is very candid when she's talking about women's issues. She is lucky that she has a husband who does not mind (he is the man who is liberated) the man is thoroughly liberated, and so he doesn't mind as long as they live in peace and they understand each other.

It was a gathering of women executives. She was addressing the female executives' problem of stress at work. This woman was telling them, for instance, that it is not possible for you to stay at a board meeting all day, get home at 8:00 p.m. and still tell me that you are cooking for your husband. It's just not possible. Let's not pretend. So let us discuss how do we manage this thing so that other people will learn and know how to cope on the job.

In the process, she talked about being able to afford a cook (cooks in Africa are not as expensive as they are here). By the way, in Nigeria, men don't cook. So this woman said that. Then at another conference, because she is well known for such views, as she was mounting the soapbox, one of the ladies, the chairman of the day and who is a professor, started making fun of her, "I hope you're not coming here to tell us not to cook for our husbands." They laughed. In the process they had trivialized what she was going to say before she had said it.

I am trying to say that we have some kind of mentality that has held us back. It's not the men. The problem is with the women.

The other example I want to give you is in reporting. A woman who is very well known in Lagos, we all look up to her, she has been going on effortlessly and coping very well and getting all the promotions. She is chairman of so many banks. How does she do this? One day, I opened one of the glossy magazines on women and I saw her. (I know her very well and I know she does not boil the water for her coffee in her home.) And her husband understands, he is so proud of her. He doesn't mind that she is moving on in the society. The man is also doing well, he is a college professor.

I saw her on the pages of the magazine. They were interviewing her on how she copes. And guess where she was. In the kitchen with an apron around her neck and standing there and showing how she must cook for her husband every morning before she goes to work! And that's not true! She is trying to misinform the younger ones. We all look up to her, hoping that one day we'll be like her, will succeed like her. That is slave mentality. I blame that woman for misinforming us and I blame the journalists for reporting that.

Tina Spencer:

I think that is a very accurate summary of something that women are coping with all over the world right now, psychologically, and I thank you for that.

Mike Erlocker:

I'm a reporter with the *Financial Post* in Toronto. My question is for Charles. You spent a long time in the Soviet Union. I was wondering if you could describe to us your observations of the youth of the former Soviet Union, whether you have seen examples to indicate whether the youth have a desire and an ability to rebuild the society there or whether there is a cynicism and individualism increasing that would not lend itself towards rebuilding that society?

Charles Quist Adade:

I would say that just before I left Russia, I noticed a growing sense of cynicism, not only amongst the youth, but the whole general public. It is because of the chaos, the lack of direction, and the general despondence brought about by the transition to Western style market economy. I would say that a very great number of the youth are now moving into dealing in Western goods, and currency exchange. You find them with tags on their chests saying, "I'm buying dollars, I'm buying marks." Most of them are selling canned beer. Most of them have left the classrooms just to be able to survive. So I would say that there is a sneaky sense of cynicism among the Soviet youth. I'm sorry to say that I'm very pessimistic about what is happening in the former Soviet Union now.

Sue Montgomery:

I'm a former Gemini "fellow." I spent my time in Southern Africa, particularly in Namibia, but I also had the pleasure of visiting Botswana and writing a story about Ernest's aunt, and other women who are involved in the struggle.

I found that when I was interviewing your Vice President, I said to him, "Do you realize that women are taking this law to court?" And he said, "Oh yes, we've got women like that even in Botswana." So there are trouble- makers everywhere I guess.

The point I wanted to raise was the problem I had being in Southern Africa and writing articles was I was always torn between my own Western feminist ideas and the ideas of the women in the countries about whom I was writing. I had difficulty writing about certain issues, such as female circumcision, which seemed to be culturally acceptable. I just wondered what journalists here from the developing world think about that. Should Western feminists be putting their ideas into their stories?

Teresa:

I had a similar experience to yours. I was in Ethiopia for Gemini and gathered a whole bunch of material around female circumcision, spoke to different women, and I think by accident, took the easy way out inasmuch as the story was never written. But even while I was working on it, one of the Ethiopian woman had left Ethiopia, studied at McGill. She, herself, had been circumcised and had come back to teach and study and so on. She spoke to me about the cultural, religious, social implications of it and so on, so I could quote her saying these things. But obviously, you know how prevalent it is in large parts of the continent. You have to take that into consideration, I think, going to both sources or to both points of view would be the only way.

Sue Montgomery:

But there are certain issues that we tend to put under one title like women's issues, which I think is ridiculous when it's men that are sexually assaulting women. That issue, for example, in Namibia where sexual assault was very prevalent, but you couldn't get the women to talk about it because there's the embarrassment for one thing, and the other thing is this idea that their husbands have the right to do this. I, as a Westerner, found this very frustrating. I felt like I wanted to shake them and say that they have to fight against this. It's a point that I wanted to raise. It's a problem.

Teresa:

I think any of us who were there would have that same feeling. I don't know that you can shake them en masse, and I don't know that we have the right to do so. Certainly, individually, you can voice your own opinions, or you can go back to your hotel room and cry. I found that a good way to handle a lot of what I saw and heard in Ethiopia. I also think intuitively you can judge whether the other person, man or woman, is open to conversation, discussion, exchanging different points of view on whether they think it's right or wrong. One of the things I have learned to do is to trust my intuition much much more than a North American society allows us to do.

Unidentified questioner:

Elaine, you talked earlier about the young journalists being disillusioned and about not being able to report on things other than Regina or Saskatchewan. I was just wondering if the onus should be on the system to stroke and nurture the young journalists into being able to report on more, or if the onus should be on the young journalist to say that this is an issue that needs to be reported; this is what we need to do, and not just quit because the system doesn't push them to do that, but to just change things on their own.

Elaine Shein:

I think it's got to be a combination from both sides. From my own experiences, for example, I'm really lucky with my newspaper. Part of it was after I had spent time with Gemini in London, that's when I became more interested in the developing world. Then I joined my paper, the *Western Producer* and I found that if I took the initiative to go up to my editors and say, "This is a really good story" – for example, I might have Gemini stories coming on my desk and I'll say that "I think this is relevant to people that are in our audience." And I can talk other people into taking a second look into it.

We kind of need the encouragement from both sides because I know journalists that have wanted to be doing international news. I've tried even when I've travelled outside the country to approach different editors here in Canada, and we're told they're not interested in taking the stories. So it has to be from both sides.

I guess I want the young journalists not to give up hope because if you believe strongly in something, you can keep working at the system. You can go and travel yourself and see things in other countries. It's too bad that we don't always have the big bankrolls to do it and to learn from other people in other cultures and see things for ourselves. But you can make opportunities happen.

We just need to have more dialogues like this with the people making the decision on what's running their papers. We have to get the message back to them that people are interested in the developing world. I find that when we run the stories on anything to do with the developing world, those are probably the stories that I get the most feedback on. That's when I get the most letters and phone calls. People will phone me and they want more information.

Unidentified questioner:

I feel that young journalists like us shouldn't give up hope if we see that our superiors and the experienced are beating us left, right and centre. I have this strong principal that if there is a better journalist there, I will beat him.

9

Reaching Out: The Western Journalists' Perspective

Introduction

Daniel Nelson,
Editorial Director, Panos Institute

I'm one of the few people that believes that the Cold War was utterly unimportant, and I never concern myself with it in my reporting, and I regard it as a very minor matter of a very short duration, of very little historical consequence – a sort of difference of opinion between two groups of industrial nations which nearly took the spotlight off the most important issue in the world, which is the difference between industrialized and non-industrialized countries, and that that was the important gap, and that the so-called Cold War between these (essentially) two groups of industrialized nations, because I personally think that for the non-industrialized developing countries such as China, their struggle is not a communist-capitalist struggle. I don't think that's of any relevance at all. It's the same struggle that developing nations and industrialized nations are having, and that gap continues.

The panel is made up of: Norman Webster, Bernard Proulx, Scott Honeyman, Patrick Nagle, Barry Wilson and Bill Cunningham.

Bill Cunningham (former television news executive, tv producer and 1991 Max Bell Fellow):

I've been working in television journalism in this country and overseas for thirty years or so, in different capacities: as a correspondent, producer and, at times, a television news executive.

I hope you'll forgive me if I just take one moment to pay a tribute to some of our guests. I've got to say as a Canadian journalist that I've gotten to know a few of you here and have gotten to know some of your stories. In all sincerity, I have to say how impressed I am with your dedication and integrity. I can't help but be in some awe of colleagues like Joe Thloloe or Kuldip Nayar and Luis Tricot, not only for their obvious intelligence, but for their courage in braving beatings, jail, secret police harassment for long periods of time without really making much fuss about it.

I'm rather embarrassed in their presence because of the kind of celebrity status granted the TV war correspondents who are parachuted into one theatre of violence after another in a blaze of publicity. I have to wonder what I could possible say to the Thloloes, the Nayars, the Tricots that could possibly be of any use to them other than to express my profound pride in being a member of a profession that has them as colleagues.

I think the first observation I'd like to make in talking about the inadequacies of Western television journalism is the superficiality of a lot of it's coverage of international affairs. I think of the fact that this conference itself, with the calibre of journalists that are here, is not being covered by national television to the best of my knowledge. That's got to say something about our priorities. And again, to our guests, I have to offer them apologies for this. I think it is pretty shabby.

The topic under discussion today, "Reaching Out: The Western Journalists' Perspective – in the context of the collapse of the "evil empire" and the so-called end of the Cold War. Frankly, in terms of improving the quality of our Western correspondents' coverage of your countries, I'm not sure that the collapse factor is going to make much of a difference.

I'd like to step back a bit and try to explain where some of us older former foreign correspondents were coming from when we were inflicted on your countries. Our attitudes were formed and our perspectives were formed a long time ago. It was a time when some of the West's most liberal leaders, people like Senator Fulbright of the United States, were saying things like, "Of course, African-Asians should have independence – when they're ready."

Many of us took these attitudes and adopted them as our own and really believed in them. That was about the way I was when I was sent to Vietnam. The change in my own views, my own version as it were, occurred not on the road to Damascus, but at the bottom end of the Ho Chi Minh trail. I was probably very typically a white North American carrying all of the cultural and racial biases and baggage that comes with that stereotype. I truly believed that the Americans were justified in their intervention, were certain to win, that God was on our side. All with little or no thought about the people who actually lived in that country. As the war unfolded, I couldn't believe what I was seeing in that it so sharply contradicted my preconceived notions, my cultural and my racial conditioning.

Here you had the most powerful war machine the world had seen up until that time. You had airfields full of multi-million dollar jets; choppers that could hoist tanks; special units: green berets, seals, A-teams, blue teams. You had sophisticated electronics. For example, they'd drop a homing device and the homing device would pick up body odor of troops carrying weapons down the Ho Chi Min trail. From that, they'd have B- 52s come over and they could drop bombs out of the sky and you wouldn't even see the planes and all of a sudden, the world would explode.

Yet in spite of all this, these diminutive people were kicking the hell out of the Americans. They were neutralizing all of this technology, sometimes in very simple ways. For example, I mentioned the homing device. They would get pails of buffalo urine, throw it around the homing device and run like hell and sit on a hill and watch the bombs come in.

Once I started to doubt the God-given superiority of the American position and a lot of my other so-called traditional values that were being challenged – as soon as you started to see what was happening with that war, how all of this effort was being neutralized, it just forced you to examine in a different way what the war was all about – how the West was really misled into that war and the fundamental issues of it.

There's an expression that Westerners often like to use, and it's this: "dead to the world." Well, it seems in reality that we're only partially dead, and that's to half the world – the so-called "underdeveloped" half. Let me give you an incident. When I hear my colleagues here talking about cultural and racial and national sensitivities, I'm embarrassed to tell you this story. During the troubles in Uganda, there was a story on the wire about East Indians who were putting black shoe polish on their faces so they would look like Africans and therefore not be picked out as victims in the strife between the people in Uganda at that time. One of our national newscasts used that as a kicker: "dead to the world."

At times, we seem to be aware of the underdeveloped world, we're there more often as not for your coups, your national disasters, your famines, and oh yes, your tribal warfare. It's funny that we seem to have such affection for the term "tribal warfare," although we never seem to use it in describing events in Yugoslavia, Ireland, or perhaps even here in Canada and the problems we have between French Canadians and English Canadians. There's an awful lot of paternalism, even in the terms we use to describe your part of the globe. We talk about the "developing world." If you look at a city like New York, a good chunk of that city – probably the richest city in the world – the standards of that city would be less than almost any Third World country by the degree of illiteracy, poverty, infant mortality.

In terms of the subject that we're talking about here, how we reach out to our audience, trying to connect our audience and get them interested in international affairs and how to try to improve our coverage of your countries, let me say what can be done about these three problems: the amount of coverage given the so-called developing world; improving the quality of that coverage; and getting North American audiences more interested in that coverage.

Frankly speaking, as a former television news executive, I don't see any light at the end of those tunnels. As the domestic problems of the so-called first world countries increase and demand coverage, there will be less and less air time and resources devoted to the developing world problems.

Just this week, the CBC and the BBC announced a pool arrangement for joint coverage of international affairs. And at the first blush that sounds like a good idea. My concern is that it will eventually mean cutbacks in the purely CBC originated material. I have no quarrel with BBC news coverage; it's among the best in the world in many ways, but it is not Canadian; it is not Canadian originated. I can just see as a television news executive; they kill you with logic. They say why spend money on originating coverage when we can get it off the American networks for little or no cost?

As to the quality of Western coverage of the developing world, an awful lot of things would have to change to see much improvement there. TV correspondents would have to be better trained than they are now; they'd have to be left in their positions longer; they'd have to be granted more air time and facilities to put their reports in context; and they'd have to be assigned more magazine and documentary projects. "And frankly, I don't see those things coming about."

Just take one aspect: correspondent training. As a former news executive, let me tell you that even in recessional times, you can get a hearing for the funding of a new VTR machine that may be as much as a quarter million dollars or whatever; but try to get $10 000 to improve the content by funding a correspondent's special language or historical training.

Which brings me to my last point, the audience and how we engage them more effectively. Part of the problem, it seems to me, has to do with will – the will of the network to make it a priority. I'm ashamed to say again that it wasn't long ago that one of the most powerful news executives in this country looked me straight in the eye and told me, "Canadians just aren't interested in foreign stories." The ratings told him so. Well, in a sense that may be true, although I doubt it.

Canada is a country of immigrants and I cannot believe that the people in this country have no interest in the heritage of the countries that they come from. But, if it is true, what does that say about we've been doing in television journalism over the last 40 years. We've spent millions of dollars on foreign coverage. We certainly, if what that news executive told me was true, we've been very, very ineffective. Even granted all of that, the fact that Canadians may not be interested in foreign news does not get the news executive off the hook from fulfilling his responsibilities to fight for more, better, deeper, less superficial, less stereotyped coverage.

But then we've also spent billions of dollars in television in this country. A lot of it, too, in attempting to explain French Canada to English Canada and vice versa, and let me tell you, we haven't been very good at that either, because anybody who's been reading the papers and knows that probably the misunderstanding between French Canada and English Canada at the present time has never been higher.

So while we may not be completely dead to the world in many ways when it comes to international coverage in both it's quantity and quality, it seems that we're still somewhat sound asleep, and I don't see many prospects for improvement.

Scott Honeyman (*Vancouver Sun*):

I'm here to enhance my reputation of being a man of few words. I have this theory that the more we can deal with people and not with politicians and institutions, the better we're going to do at covering not only our own world, but the Third World or the developing world as well. We are having a huge migration into Vancouver of people from all around the world and it's changing the nature of the city. And I believe that some of our best foreign reporting is being done by some of the local reporters who are out meeting these people who are coming to town.

As an admittedly more or less ignorant person about other cultures, I have to confess that we've been getting some fairly harsh lessons in political correctness from a number of people, so we've decided that what we should do is share that with everyone. We are writing about the various cultures of Vancouver, and I think it's quite a successful effort to celebrate the growing new culture of our city.

I think we've heard here today about sympathy fatigue among other things, and I think the fatigue is a lot deeper than that. I think we're tired of political rhetoric and of endless bad news. Readers eyes start glazing at the steady delivery of disaster, disease, depression. We constantly write about things that are broken. Some people accuse us of breaking things so we can write about them. So I think that our job is not just to focus on what is wrong, but again to celebrate what is right.

I think Joe was right on yesterday when he said that we have to stop taking this official briefing, press release short cut and we need to talk to the real people whose lives are affected by political decisions. We have a readership advisory panel at the paper and we were sitting one night talking about how newspapers cover things. One of the women there said "Newspapers always write for me above the neck." Nothing in newspapers very often hits your heart or your gut. I think that by writing about people wherever they are in the developing world or our own world, we can perhaps get a more visceral reaction from our readers and make them care.

Patrick Nagle (Southam News):

I'm a career correspondent for various newspapers and magazines in Canada and in Europe. I have more than 35 years in the business, 5 years in Africa ending in 1989 and have a continuing interest in the world, developed or undeveloped.

I'd just like to preface my remarks with "How do we reach out?" The newspaper industry in North America is under the most intense stress it's ever been, in my lifetime. The point I must make is that it is a commercial industry. It is not a gift. It is not an institution. You buy it and you pay for it. People are not buying it and people are not paying for it. So, reaching out is a very intense and continuing occupation amongst professional journalists. It's our living, our history, and it's very nearly dying before our very eyes. Anybody who has any sense at all is extremely concerned about it.

Historically, the man from Mars was invoked when senior journalists instructed their juniors about how to report for newspapers. The man from Mars was the icon of ignorance. He knew nothing and had to have all explained. The man from Mars or his earthly counterpart, the Kansas City milkman, dominated newspaper editing and content for the whole of my early career.

Times have changed, but it still a valid concept, given what we know about today's standards of literacy and general knowledge education. Yet the man from Mars has far more tools than newspapers to use today for his global education. The reach of broadcasting into all corners of the earth is undisputed, but as the speed of information increases, the quality seems to deteriorate by some sort of inverse square rule. Just on the rough numbers of the United Nations membership, there are now more than 175 countries related to Canada through the United Nations. Compare this to when Canada joined the U.N. as a founding member in 1946 with 49 other countries; there has been more than a 300% increase in U.N. membership in 46 years. In those 46 years, Canada has taken part in 47 U.N. peacekeeping operations. As Canada's world has grown, regrettably, the country's capacity to cope either intellectually or physically with these developments has declined badly. There are a number of reasons offered for this, but the consequence is that less money is available for manifestly larger problems.

Political considerations have infiltrated Canada's foreign policy to a greater degree than ever before. The immigration information available to the public is being cut into smaller and smaller pieces. For example, the subject of this weekend's seminar is reporting on the developing world after the Cold War. But not one of these formal sessions directly addresses the fact of life that will dominate Canadian attitudes for this topic for at least the next decade.

The end of the Cold War put a whole new series of countries into the Third World. Most of these countries are European by history and have established colonies of immigrants in Canada. These colonies wield influence and will vote for the politicians who promise aid for their homelands. This political consequence of the Cold War's end is far more predictable – and to me far more significant – than any estimate of how much assistance Canada will make available to African development.

Is international news relevant to your audience – the "why should we care" phenomenon? International news is relevant to everyday life the same way domestic news is where it impinges on the individual. This intrusion of the world outside the borders should not be unexpected to the individual, but it invariably is. This is the nature of news and this is where the man from Mars comes in. Three-quarters of a century since the conversion of the communist-capitalist ideological debate into geopolitical warfare has clouded the collective knowledge of what went before. Thus the news from Yugoslavia or from Somalia dismays people as they discover – most of them for the first time – conflicts wider than the consumer economy vs. the centrally planned economy and events deeper than 20th century history.

How are the media to achieve a balance and to ensure people are better and more accurately informed about their fellow human beings? It takes time to build this knowledge and it takes care to ensure the knowledge fits with the reality of the audience. Far too much unwarranted faith is placed in rapid response teams and instant solutions.

The best example I can give you from current history is the United States, where the world's richest and most technologically advanced country could not cope quickly or efficiently with one hurricane in Florida. Compare that U.S. experience with Bangladesh, where several typhoons a year cross the Bay of Bengal and the Ganges Delta. Under the circumstances, it is not surprising the world finds it difficult, if not impossible, to comprehend the huge gulf between the developed and the undeveloped world.

For me, the biggest surprise that the developed world has not grappled with yet is the possibility that some country will make war on the environment. That is what in desperation the Iraqis attempted to do by setting the Gulf alight. If somebody wants to really make it difficult for the first world to continue its existence, isolated from the rest of the world, somebody is going to make a real war on the environment, for which we will all pay desperately. That gulf between the developed and undeveloped world is where we really must reach out to make real information available.

This is the legitimate legacy of the man from Mars metaphor. There are no fast answers; no quick fixes; no silver bullets. People need things explained to them clearly, consistently, and in context. Here on earth, neither governments nor mediums of communication give their constituencies full value if they do not offer that constant of performance.

Daniel Nelson:

Thank you. I must say some of us think that there are a number of countries who already are making war on the environment with their reckless extraction and consumption of resources; but that's another matter.

Bernard Proulx (Radio Québec):

I thought I'd been invited as part of a minority and now that I'm part of the mainstream, I don't know if I ought to apologize or be proud.

If our colleague from China had 10 minutes, maybe in all due proportion I ought to be given 10 seconds. But hopefully I'll get five minutes anyway.

I wonder if you have heard the news about the difficult situation that exists right now for the national symphony orchestra in Nicaragua. They're in dire straits right now because of financial reasons, basically. As a matter of fact, their cellist is not with them anymore. You see, this man has found that he can make more money (three times more), and this is important for his family in Nicaragua, repairing clocks and watches.

This came about because of a structural adjustment program-type situation whereby it was decided to scale down the activity of the government in the public sector. Therefore public servants were offered an opportunity to get training in other walks of life. So this cellist learned how to repair clocks and watches through these programs.

This, I find quite an interesting story. It was told to us by one crew from the program that I happen to work for. The Québecois point of view that was given on this story – the questions were fielded by our journalist who went there – he comes from Burkina Faso, his country of origin – and the director who was working with him on the field comes from Chile originally. Anyway, they brought back this material and I thought it was a great way to inform us about certain situations that develop in a country such as Nicaragua.

If I were to try to put in a nutshell the basic little message that I would like to try to put across, I would say that we are to try to work with empathy more than with pity. By the way, this will be a very brief contribution – a modest contribution.

I will not be dealing with all the media. I'm working with a small television station and I don't like TV very much, I don't watch very much of it. I prefer to read the newspapers and get all the analyses. But TV is a very popular medium, and I think that for this reason it is very important. You may be surprised to learn that there is this program that is now in its tenth season. It's called, "Nord-Sud" which means literally "North-South" and it deals exclusively with those issues which we have been talking about right here.

I'll go on calling it "Nord-Sud" because it has sort of boiled over into English Canada and if you have cable at home, you may see it on Vision television. The producer for North-South is Leo Rampin, and he is here, so if I said that I work with North-South, of course, he would have to say this is not correct.

There's an Angolan who lives in Ottawa now who was very worried a few years back because his country was having a lot of civil strikes, civil war. He said that he was very bothered by the fact that we were always seeing on TV, any time there was mention of Angola, persons who were maimed, people who lost a leg because they walked on a land mine put possibly by the guerilla there. There were a lot of maimed persons going around the country, and this was being filmed a lot; it was sort of an illustration of the plight of the Angolans.

Now this person felt that this was not quite right. He did not want pity. He wanted something else. And he was quite worried when he learned that our program was going to show this again, but he changed his mind because the main character in that story was a young Angolan who was a dancer and he was drafted into the army. He fought, he had a war mishap, and he did lose a leg, and went back to the capital, Luanda, and he kept on dancing on one leg, and he taught dancing to children. He created his school of dancing and he's an extraordinary fellow. I mean that audiences go wild in Angola over him. And, again, this was a matter of creating empathy.

I'm just trying to give a few indications of how in this very small program, we try to cope with these extremely complex issues. I would say that we are still a shoe-string operation given the size and scope of these matters, but we do try to make sure that people get these stories by seeing extraordinary ordinary people. It was great having an interview with Mandela on the program. It was great having Father Aristide before he was President and after he became President. We haven't had him now since the coup, but I think that for most people, it is more important to get the ordinary, every day life stories of Haitians even to understand what Father Aristide is saying, that this comes across much more clearly. And so, I believe it's a matter of trying to avoid the pitfalls in which all you see is a series of catastrophes and extreme poverty, repression and coups.

There are a lot of interesting stories to do. We take the human interest approach. I put it forth to you modestly that possibly this is an interesting approach, because when the TV executives decided that the program ought to disappear for financial reasons, there was enough of a reaction in Québec to have them keep it on.

People obviously felt that this is kind of an institution, that it should not disappear and that although we are not by any far cry in any position to compete with the larger media, the larger television networks (we do not have a newsroom), I still think this has been an interesting contribution and that it's pretty much appreciated by people back home.

Barry Wilson:

I'm a reporter for *Western Producer* which is a farm newspaper based in Saskatchewan with a system of bureaus across the country. I work in the Ottawa bureau, and we have bureaus elsewhere on the prairies as well.

Rather than extend the lamentations about media failures and Western audience ignorance about international events, I'm going to talk very briefly about what might be considered more of a success story – a group of readers who are very interested in world events in this country and who sometimes even get what they desire from the media. For those of you with a low pain tolerance for Pollyanna stories, I'll be as short as I can.

Rather than presume to imagine what media consumers throughout Canada think of international news in general, I plan to talk about the readership audience I know about – the more than 100 000 prairie farm and rural families who subscribe to the *Western Producer* – the newspaper that pays my salary.

Without hesitation I'm prepared to argue that this is an audience eager for international news – developed and developing worlds. There are a variety of reasons for this: commercial, political and humanitarian. I think this is the reason that the *Western Producer* despite very tough economic times continues to spend probably as much or more than most Canadian newspapers on gathering international news, often through staff trips abroad.

International news, at least as it relates to food, farm and rural topics, is not a tough sell at all in prairie homes. Walk into any prairie farm kitchen, and the reading material on the table is as likely to be the *Economist* or the *New Statesman* or the *Christian Science Monitor* as it is the *Red Deer Advocate* or the *Brandon Sun*. This is not necessarily a reflection of a worldly, literate population on the prairies, although some would like to believe that. Rather there are several more mundane reasons why I think prairie farm families have international news interest.

Commercially, of course, farmers in this area of Canada produce for world markets. Political upheaval in Russia or crop failure in Russia could mean the difference between a 5 bushel and an 8 bushel quota for wheat farmers in this part of the world. A famine or political upheaval or revolution or drought in food exporting or food importing areas elsewhere in the world can have a very direct impact on farmers here, so they're very interested in news from abroad.

But I think there are also reasons more gentle than commercial gain as well. Despite vastly different countries and history, I think farmers the world over share a bond of common experience, or at least think they do, common experience and shared frustration. Farmers on the prairies often feel that the plight of one is the plight of all. They can sympathize and maybe even empathize with Zimbabwean farmers who complain about their government's cheap food policy. Or Argentinean farmers who complain about government taxes on their exports. Or the Filipino farmer who complained recently at a conference in Canada about the impact of international subsidy war between the rich countries – the impact of those subsidies on the price of sugar in the Philippines. Canadian farmers can understand those arguments and often sympathize, because they are caught in the same winds of change and pain. So for many farmers here, they actually feel like they're reading about their brothers and sisters in the world when they read about farm experience elsewhere.

There's also an element of humanitarianism, of course. Farmers here support food aid calls and deliver grain to local elevators, which then gets sent to world food hunger spots including, this year, Southern Africa. They engage in exchanges with farmers around the world.

So there is a very deep interest in this part of Canada in international news as it relates to farmers. Farmers want information, but do they get it? I would say the record is spotty, but occasionally it is at least adequate. In the general urban media, of course, there is little in-depth coverage of Third World agriculture and food issues. But then, of course, there's very little in-depth coverage of Canadian food or agricultural issues in the media here either, so, it doesn't make the Third World particularly subject to discrimination.

The prairies does have a band of specialty media outlets which provide in-depth coverage of food and agricultural issues and rural issues; but most don't have the resources to get first-hand information from abroad. Usually, they have to rely on second-hand sources or the wire services. Here, there is a problem with that. Since most of the wire copy is American based or European based, it's certainly American or European influenced.

I'll talk specifically about the American-based wire copy that we get, which is the dominant factor. It's a problem for Canadian farmers and for those Canadian readers who care about this, because Canada and the U.S. look at their capacities to produce surplus food in very different ways, I would argue.

For the U.S., surplus food is another weapon in the battle for world political power. Food embargoes and politically tied food aid really are a part of American foreign policy and always have been since the war, and certainly since they began to produce their great surpluses. The American media reflect this reality, often by adding a touch of what I call an "American superiority" to their coverage of world food and rural issues. Superiority when they're analyzing a crop failure in a socialist country, or when they're talking about food delivery problems in the Third World. "If only they did it as we'd do it, they would do it better."

Not to put too fine a point on it – Canadians have tended to view their surplus food capacity as a responsibility as much as it is a source of power. Of course, there is a commercial interest and I certainly don't want to overstate this and make it sound too altruistic. There is a commercial interest, and Canada pursues that. Canadian farmers care about that. But I think Canadians also have a "breadbasket of the world" mentality about their food and production capacity, which leads to resistance to the use of food as a political weapon in Canadian foreign policy. Sadly, that is changing, and the current government has a couple of times used food as a political weapon, including very quickly jumping on the U.N. bandwagon of a food embargo against Iraq last year, which really was out of the tradition, I would argue, of Canadian foreign policy. But there has been that tradition. This has been one of the few areas in which Canadian governments over the years have consistently pursued a foreign policy that is at odds with the Americans.

All this makes American-based or slanted coverage of world food issues a poor substitute for home grown analysis of the issues offered with some Canadian sensibility. This doesn't mean, of course, that Canadians don't underpin their own food world view with Western assumptions and with a healthy dose of Western arrogance about our good fortune and our advanced farming methods.

But it does mean that Canadian farmers often show themselves willing to learn as well as to teach. Soil degradation on the Canadian prairies and the relentless depletion of the world's plant genetic base in search of the latest high-yielding, hybrid variety, does lead many Canadian farmers to question their own methods of operation and to recognize that agricultural societies hundreds of years older than their own have something to offer. They look to Canadian media for details and insights about farmers and food issues elsewhere. Sometimes they get it. Usually they don't. And for reasons of media priorities, resources and sometimes bias, it is a failing of Canadian media.

But I would also argue that in at least this area, Canadian media, serving the prairie rural and farm audiences, do a better than average job and give a better than average effort to give their customers what they want – a more balanced, sensitive and detailed view of farmers and their problems around the world.

Norman Webster:

I think that when we're among ourselves, professionals all, we should be careful to be a little more precise in our assertions of fact. We heard in one session yesterday that until very recently Zaire and Malawi were "economic miracles and stable democracies" in every depiction of them and that Mr. Mobutu was always glorified as a "good man." I missed that, I must say. This morning we started off with young ladies writing books about Pakistan and ended up with the *New York Times* doing it's Africa coverage with teenagers. Well, believe me, it ain't so.

This afternoon, we heard a lamentation about the retreat of the Canadian media in the way they cover foreign news, and you couldn't find Somalia except on page 52. Not so. In fact, some of us are so old that we remember the good old days, and they weren't that good, believe me. Indeed, when I went to China more than 20 years ago, I was one of only three foreign correspondents in the field for the *Globe and Mail.* When I left the *Globe and Mail* three years ago, they had ten foreign correspondents in the field. We've had more correspondents for the *Toronto Star,* more for Southam, more for CBC and Radio Canada.

We have specialty programs such as the North-South program which has been mentioned here. The Journal is doing documentaries. We are admittedly right now, in a temporary period of great difficulty and there is some pulling back, but I don't think it's permanent, and certainly the amount of good foreign coverage that is done by Canadian media and available to Canadian audiences is miles ahead of what it was when I first went into the field.

I just wanted to make three points. First, we've heard an awful lot about the "Western" media, and I think it's too often being confused with American media.

American media, I think, can take some bashing because they are, more than most other Western media, intensely concerned with American affairs. Indeed, they seem to report foreign affairs only as they affect an American interest. Now, that's a natural thing for all of us, but they carry it to an extreme, and we in Canada know this because most Americans know very little about Canada, their nearest neighbor and biggest trading partner, except that the cold weather comes from here. Surveys have shown that. This is extraordinary. So you're not alone.

And there's some technical things here which have to be acknowledged. One is CNN which, frankly, annoys me as much as it does other people who have mentioned it here because of it's intense American focus. But it's there. And why is it there? Because someone took a very big gamble, spent a lot of money, used the latest technology and got it there first. I'm sorry, but Americans have a way of doing that, and we've got to live with it.

The *New York Time*s has been much mentioned. The *New York Times* is really important. It was mentioned that a correspondent was the second most important person in a country – I believe that, and I've seen that. And indeed, to my chagrin, the *New York Times* has been put to the head of the queue, ahead of me more than once. That is for two reasons: because the *New York Times* is the most important paper in the United States which is "the" superpower of the world upon which we are all remarkably dependent; and secondly, because the *New York Times* is the best newspaper in the world. And I think that's something that we have to acknowledge.

And a third thing that we have to acknowledge is that the Americans, again to our annoyance, are slick and professional and produce things that people want to see or want to read or want to hear. And it drives us nuts in Canada as we're trying to carve out our own identity. We're trying to get Canadians to watch Canadian television, and they turn in annoyingly large numbers to better produced American programming. It's genuinely discouraging. Indeed, if one could perhaps put up a broadcasting wall, as it once was possible to do, one might try to do it, but it can't be done and it's not going to be able to be done anywhere in the world and we're going to have to live with that.

People don't realize the foreign networks of large Japanese papers dwarf anything the Americans have – it's extraordinary. Germans, Spanish, the Nordic countries, and even Canada – there are some good correspondents out there doing not a bad job.

I agree that the Western media can be preachy, self-preoccupied, and often arrogant. And we take some of those attitudes into the field from our own upbringing. We grow up with the idea that we are living in the best country in the world and that things work here and they don't work elsewhere. It is a very useful thing to be sitting one day in a cab in Peking, as we called it then, and to realize that the Chinese taxi driver feels genuine sympathy for you because you're not Chinese and you're not able to participate in the culture – that you're a poor barbarian from abroad and you'll never be able to participate. It's quite a knock to the cultural arrogance to realize that he doesn't look up to you at all – he actually feels some sympathy for you.

I think that the West does impose its own agenda, quite often. This is not going to go away – at least not quickly. A point I tried to make yesterday was that the Western media are in business to inform Western readers and audiences. Connecting with our readers, viewers and listeners – that's what they're doing. They're not there to make Third World audiences feel happy; they're there to inform their own readers and if Third World and, indeed, Canadian audiences are waiting for the American media, certainly, and Western media generally to make them feel happy about themselves and to tell their story to themselves, then they're going to wait a long time.

I think it was mentioned this morning, Ms. Padman said we should stop moaning about the Western media and tell our own story to ourselves. I think she's right. Now, this is easier said than done. One has to acknowledge that, but there are some promising things going. We've heard about the Caribbean experiment; we've heard about an experiment in the South Pacific. There are ways to do things and the technology, wonderfully and remarkably, is becoming simpler and cheaper and it's going to effect a revolution in all sorts of things. It's already doing it here. You used to have to be able to afford $20 million to buy a press to have a newspaper; nowadays, you buy a Macintosh system and you can do it on your desk. And indeed, we're seeing all sorts of alternative publications of every sort in Canada – so you are not dependent upon the mainstream media for everything. Indeed, the specialized publications are taking more and more people's time and attention to the detriment of the big papers.

What kind of correspondent should be out there? The problem, I think, is with the firemen. There's been a lot of talk here about that approach and it is a problem, it does lead to slanted and superficial coverage. These are the people that go out for the coups and earthquakes and that's about it. So how do we address this?

Well, the other pole is to have a local correspondent in all these places filing copy. There is a problem with that, however, and the problem is getting the material that comes from that source used. Mr. Knight of the *Guardian* mentioned this morning that actually getting the stuff in the paper is difficult. And getting material from a series of stringers around the world in the paper is difficult for a couple of reasons. The first is that usually it's not good enough; and second, it doesn't in any case address the concerns of your own reader.

I have a small local example. We're in the middle of a referendum here in Canada. My newspaper in Montreal is going to be sending a correspondent out to British Columbia to tell the story of what's going on there, not because we receive no reports from British Columbia or that there are no Canadian journalists who are any good out in British Columbia, but because he will be able to write a story which in fifty different ways (and I can't pin them down for you) will be relevant to Montreal readers in a way that a story from a Vancouver correspondent would not be.

And the same thing applies in many ways to foreign coverage. So how do we do it? We do it, I think, the best way – resident correspondents. Correspondents resident in a country or resident in a region. These people, if it's done properly, are knowledgeable, are usually sympathetic and understanding. They certainly become so soon after they get there. I certainly look at the whole line of *Globe and Mail* China correspondents and with not a single exception that I'm aware of, they had remarkable sympathy for, empathy with the people of China. Not one of us thought an awful lot about the system or the government, but we certainly felt for the people, and I hope that was reflected in our reporting. Certainly Canadian correspondents in Africa that I know of, they may have been mean to various dictatorships, but they sure feel for the people. Indeed they feel rage at what is happening, and that often comes through in their correspondence and that's a good thing.

But these are not firemen. These are people who are there. They're not there for their lives. Patrick was there for five years and that seems to me to be a reasonable term. You have time to find your feet, you have time to learn what's going on there, and you don't become burned out, which does happen after a time.

How could this be done better? We could increase the time that we give correspondents to prepare. We could increase the education that we let them have, although I must be fair and acknowledge that as opposed to the way, the custom 20 years ago, journalists that go out into foreign countries now are pretty well prepared. They are educated. They have made a study of these countries. They have indeed got the language far better than we ever used to. I remember at one point when I was editor of the Globe, I had four correspondents at the same time in language studies, in Spanish, Russian, Chinese and Japanese, and that was a fairly new thing.

One other way that things might be improved is by increasing the sort of thing that Gemini does. We've seen quite remarkable examples here this weekend of young people who got Gemini fellowships and went into the field and learned a lot, quite clearly. And even if they're reporting in Regina now, they're bringing a whole new perspective which is good for Canada and these are people who are going to be the foreign correspondents of the future.

Open Forum

Unidentified Questioner:

I just wanted to address the point that Canadian readers do want more news from overseas. I work for the Canadian Press in Montreal, and we're closing down our Moscow bureau right now, which seems, to me, ludicrous. But, apparently, the members have told us that they don't want that. They want more sports scores, they want more local color. And it seems to me that the Canadian media are becoming more and more parochial.

Norman Webster:

I know about that decision, and the truth is that the CP budget is being squeezed because all of our budgets are being squeezed, but I don't think that it's being replaced by more sports scores. CP is simply being asked to cut its budget. I didn't say that surveys show Canadians want more foreign news. I don't know. Some surveys show that. I think sometimes people lie because it's more respectable to say that. The surveys indeed show they want more local coverage in their papers. They want to know more of what's going on in their daily lives. However, that said, there is still a substantial interest in the world in Canada. I think Canada is still quite open to the world and the Moscow bureau's being closed; I acknowledge that, but this does not herald a rolling up Canadian bureaus or Canadian foreign coverage.

Unidentified questioner:

Now, we're talking about reaching out. That bothers me because right here in Canada, we have a lot of visitors here, and they should know how the Western journalists work here in Canada because this country hosts this conference right now.

We are not saying that the Third World countries don't have things that are not right, but the way it's been reported! The journalist has to be sensitive. We talk about violence – right now this country has a panel on violence against women because there's violence here on women. You talk about coming out and speaking on this issue. I haven't heard any of these things touched here.

It's like here in Canada things are so rosy. To me, standing here and talking to you, to any one of you on the panel, it is not rosy, and I think we should touch all of it. Western journalists have to be sensitive not only to Europeans but also to other ethnic racial groups.

Mike Urlocker:

I have a question for Norm Webster and Scott Honeyman. I ask this out of self interest because I am the next International Development Research Centre fellow. Do you use the Gemini Service? Yes or No. Why?

Norman Webster:

We buy a number of services; we don't buy Gemini and these are budget considerations. We look at our budget quite carefully.

Mike Urlocker:

In terms of priorities, can you explain what hits or misses?

Norman Webster:

The truth is that our needs for foreign copy are well covered by the services, particularly the Southam News Service, which is our chain's own service of foreign correspondents abroad which costs us a lot of money – far too much money. We pay our correspondents far too much. We feel that we have got enough – it's a simple budgetary consideration.

Scott Honeyman:

We do not at the moment subscribe, but we may consider it sometime in the future.

William Saidi:

I have a lot of sympathy for foreign correspondents because I've been a stringer – in the 1960s I was a stringer for Reuters, the BBC, UPI, and the whole lot.

I think it is unfair for Norman Webster to say that the stringer informs less than the correspondent. I never had my copy rejected by Reuters. In fact, I've a whole file of cuttings on stories that I wrote for Reuters which were used. So I would argue that stringers do a fine job.

I think also the problem that you highlighted is something that we'll discuss in Africa. It is getting the agencies to appoint as correspondents people from those countries. I know that you think it won't reflect well. For instance, if a correspondent writes to a paper in Canada and he's a Zimbabwean and is writing for a paper in Canada, it won't be the same as if a Canadian based in Harare was writing for his paper in Toronto. I think it would be quite an original story if it was written by a national of that country. The advantage is that he would not be writing as if he's simply trying to act as an agent for his country because let's not forget that many foreign correspondents are viewed not only by governments but also by citizens as representing the interests of their country.

Now if you had a Zimbabwean writing for the *Globe and Mail* here, there would be no chance that anybody could construe whatever he wrote as representing anything other than the facts of what was happening there.

When I say I sympathize with them, I take into account the fact that they're not all angels – they're not all angels at all. I remember that in 1964, when there was a coup in Zanzibar, the correspondent who wrote the story which Reuters carried, wrote that story from a bar in Dar es Salaam. This has never been denied. I know the correspondent. He wrote the entire story of the overthrow of the government from a bar because he said, "Look, going across the Indian Ocean, there is no boat or anything – I can't get on a boat, so I'll just sit here." And he composed the whole story while having a drink. Happily for him it came out (it was a coup, all coups are more or less the same), so it didn't make much difference.

I think you ought to campaign to have the nationals of a country become the correspondents. I think it's the best thing all around.

Patrick Nagle:

This is very awkward because I support the notion of getting more African nationals into North American and Western journalism, absolutely, unconditionally and I would be the first in line to get on with that job.

The notion of having a Zimbabwean cover Zimbabwe for Canada is just about as unacceptable as having a symphony conductor write his own review of his concert. It's neither ethical nor acceptable. Once again, we're dealing specifically with North American journalistic norms.

In the case of Zimbabwe, during my time there, Canada had a specific foreign policy in all of the southern Africa region that differed quite drastically from the United States. We differed on Angola, we differed on Mozambique, we differed very, very strongly on the Republic of South Africa. That is the way I reported that – it was from the Canadian perspective – it was essential for Canadians to know where their foreign policy differed specifically from United States foreign policy and how the United States was trying to influence our foreign policy and thereby reduce our independence and damage quite substantially some of the things that Canada was achieving in Southern Africa.

We are not in a country as a foreign correspondent to report that country from that country's point of view. It is our responsibility to report that country for our readers' point of view in Canada and it cannot be otherwise. But I am totally loyal to my newspaper group. It could not be otherwise – I couldn't even claim to collect the picayune paycheque I get, if I didn't carry that loyalty.

Daniel Nelson:

I must say that when I was in the Philippines, I felt that my loyalty was to describe the Philippines to my readers. I felt my first loyalty to the Philippines and actually I was a lousy correspondent.

Unidentified questioner:

I think as someone who reads the result of foreign correspondents' work, I see a number of flaws in Patrick Nagel's argument, but there are two I don't think I should let pass.

The first is that I fundamentally disagree with the analogy that he drew between a Zimbabwean correspondent in Zimbabwe and a conductor writing a review of his own symphony, because that assumes that the Zimbabwean reporter is not a professional journalist, but is rather a flack for his country, and therefore, there should be no foreign journals who have Canadians as stringers writing about Canada, of which there are many. And I don't think that that necessarily makes Canadian stringers for foreign newspapers flacks for Canada.

Secondly, I think that the more fundamental flaw in Patrick's argument is – the point has been made before that while the U.S. tends to look at the world through the eyes of U.S. interests and reports on those areas of the world where the U.S. has commercial or military or strategic interest, Canada is too picayune a country to have that arrogance.

And we don't have interests in all that many countries that are strategic or political. Commercial, yes. So therefore I don't think that every story from Zimbabwe has to have a Canadian slant to it. Much of the reporting they get from outside this country will not have a Canadian slant to it, so I find the argument against local correspondents a bit foolish.

Bill Cunningham:

I wonder if I could take a piece of this and point out that sometimes in certain countries where there are dictatorial regimes in place, it's quite an advantage that the foreign correspondent in there is a foreigner. If he were a national, there is a good chance that he would be killed, where the foreign reporter just gets kicked out of the country.

Patrick Nagle:

The situation is exactly as described. South Africa, for the five years that I was there, was under a state of emergency which very seriously restricted any of the South African journalists, black or white, what they could say. They could not do anything to damage the reputation of the state President – that was in the law. They could not do anything to counsel sanctions. There were a huge number of very specific proscriptions against South African journalists working in South Africa which we defied. We just carried on and dared them to throw us out, and, except in two or three cases, they didn't.

The problem, until such time as a country is free, the problem of a national of a country reporting on that country, is a very dicey one, it really is.

Luis Tricot:

The first thing I want to say is that I have never moaned about the Western press because I have never expected anything from the Western press.

I think it's important to try to determine or define the main issues that those correspondents will have to deal with. I think this is very important because we are living in a world market economy and we also know that there are, more or less, seven main industries which are going to develop even more from now on. Among them are microelectronics, biotechnology, telecommunications, civil aviation. And that will affect our lives.

It will affect the Third World. So I think it's very important, apart from having better trained or bilingual or trilingual correspondents, try to determine now which are the main trends of historical development.

I think it was Patrick who pointed out the ecological problem. I think this is a very serious one. We all know that now, but I don't think we have really understood the dimension of it. We had the Gulf War not long ago, but it's not crazy to think that we will have a water war 30-40 years from now. Water is not a scarce resource yet, but the distribution of it is. Apart from this fact, 90 percent of the world's drinkable water is to be found in the Antarctic, so that's a strategic region from now on. So what can we do about it as correspondents? What can you do in this part of the world to help stop this devastation?

Norman Webster:

You asked a question which has preoccupied us all in modern journalism: how do we look ahead? How do we prepare our people for what's coming? How do we put out ideas that they're going to have to deal with? You've mentioned one clearly. Remember that twenty years ago, the environment was not an issue of real importance to the public. Today it is. I think we're starting to do our job there, but we're always behind, but your question is quite apt; we've got to be thinking ahead and preparing people. That's what good journalism should be doing.

Bill Cunningham:

But how do we do it at a time when our economies are in such terrible shape and all of the news agencies are in many ways cutting back or trying to cut costs?

Mohamad Hamaludin:

The gentlemen up there belong to two camps. There is a sort of a liberal camp and a reactionary camp. Now the fact that I'm going to direct my questions – these are very brief questions – to Norman Webster and Patrick Nagle is quite coincidental, I want to assure you.

Patrick, I wanted to talk to you a little bit about the hurricane (in Miami). You said the response to the hurricane was a little bit ragged because of the economic conditions of the country. So, if that is ragged, imagine what kind of reaction we'll have to Bangladesh. That's wrong. Within two weeks, Congress passed $10 billion to be sent to south Florida for hurricane relief. And the damage was $20 billion, so the private sector is going to come up with the rest.

My question is that at that particular point in time, and even now, the hurricane as Jesse Jackson said, "It was an equal opportunity destroyer." And the conditions the people there are living in are conditions that are perpetual in the Third World – in Bangladesh, parts of Africa, Somalia, you know the score. Did the people in south Florida, or the U.S. or Canada learn anything about what it means to be in a survivalist mode all your life. So that makes you more compassionate or less compassionate. My own interpretation is that it didn't make them less compassionate. In fact, the thing now to think about is "Here we are part of the great part of impoverished people in the world." The thing is, we are going to get our houses back plus some extra money from the insurance company within a year or two, plus all of us are going to get jobs. That is the extent of compassion.

Mr. Webster, reporting, you said, is a matter for your audience – that you report to the people within the context of what their basic background of knowledge is. My consistent point that I've been making throughout this seminar is, "What's that audience?" Who are you reporting to? Both here and in the United States, I find myself being the devil's advocate and I'm criticizing the United States (I'm a citizen), but who are we reporting to? What percentage of Canada is not eurocentric – is not white?

As a journalist, when you are reporting or if you are in a major policy decision making positions, do you try to make it a bit more inclusive – push the society or the community or the nation into becoming a bit more inclusive? Because if you do that and you start to get your First Nations people in and your Afro-Canadians in and you start to see them on TV and you start to report more of the news about them, aren't you then going to have a greater, a wider constituency that will respond a little bit better when you start to report on the Third World?

Norman Webster:

We're after them, that's for sure. That's a very fair point. Canada is changing before our eyes, especially in the big cities: Toronto, Montreal, Vancouver. The immigration now is predominantly non-European. And they mostly come to those three big cities. So in a matter of ten years, there have been enormous changes. Immigration is running at about 250 000 – 300 000 people per year, which in Canadian terms, especially since they go to several population centres only – that's a big change. And those are new readers for us, and we've got to be very nimble in our understanding of the things they're interested in and reporting them.

Patrick has pointed out another thing which we haven't been quick enough on, and that is the disintegration of the Soviet empire does mean that a whole lot of the former peoples who were less assertive under the Soviet yoke are much more assertive now and they're going to want more coverage, so we've got a job to do. You've pointed it out.

Bernard Proulx:

I'd just like to say that a colleague of mine who works on the same program, who comes from Burkina Faso, when he wonders how to tell the story to people here, how to reach out to the public here, he has the same problems that I have. He asks the very same questions that I do, evidently.

Daniel Nelson:

I actually don't think it's valid to claim recession as a reason for not exploring the possible new upcoming stories – investigating them. I think that is one thing that's rather closely linked with developing wider sources than we tend to use. There's all sorts of examples from recent years, including the debt which I and one or two other people were writing about before it officially broke – it was known among a few people that debt was accumulating at an unsustainable way and that something was going to break. I didn't write about it as a debt crisis. I wrote about it as a development crisis, which is what I think it is. Of course, that didn't go down very well. But there were people who'd spotted it.

Similarly, there were people going on about the environment and banging on about it twenty years ago who were dismissed as sort of loonies. But there were people there. And I think if we can widen some of the sources that we use – and I think that is linked with gender and with ethnic people working with us and for us and reporting them, because people do have other viewpoints.

Bethel Njoku:

Somewhere we've dropped the Third World and it became "developing world." Some of us in the Third World have always wondered where the first and second worlds were. But I think more than ever before, we now have a First, a Second, and a Third World. I'm making a plea that "Third World" should be retained. Because with the collapse of communism, we've seen the second world. It's now more visible to those of us from the Third World. The problem is that with resources being so scarce, if you lump the Third World into the bigger developing world it will get lost.

Therefore, I think we should restore the Third World, especially since we now see that reporting the Third World is an extension of the foreign service of certain countries – that you send correspondents out to report about a place to discuss the foreign policy of the country from which they come – not to report the people.

In those circumstances, I think we must make a very strong plea that reporting the Third World, and if the Canadians want to reach out, we should reach out and report the Third World as the Third World, not as explaining your country's foreign policy. I think that's the work of the embassy or the high commission and his information attache.

If you want to talk about what's happening in Lagos, it makes no sense to your reader here if you report it as if it is Regina, because he's never been to Lagos. You have to report it as if it's in Lagos. Then he'll have a concept of what Lagos is and he can then understand what is happening in Lagos in the context of the people who are there. A man laughing in Lagos is different than a man laughing here. He would be laughing for different things.

We had a very funny writer who put together a small pamphlet. He says that when a Nigerian says, "I am coming," it means that he's going. I am coming means he is going. He's going to come. That's what it means. So I don't think that argument is really there.

There is quite a list I wanted to talk about, but I want to stop it there by saying that when we are reaching out to the Third World, and I'm making a plea for the Third World as part of the developing world which I've now said, that you should please reach out to them from their perspective. We know it's your money you are spending.

Those of us who also have run newspapers know this foreign correspondent slot. We know it's a sign to this chappy who should go down there, because it's all amenities and expense accounts. This part of it, let's face it, is not writing better than the local person except of course, in the context I've heard now, that he's reporting the foreign policy of his country back to his country.

Daniel Nelson:

I just like to say that I think you're running against the tide, Bethel, because the Third World by sort of convergence of opinion, the World Bank is and has for several years, been actively trying to stop journalists from using the phrase "Third World," because they say these countries are different economically and you can't lump them together.

I personally think they're doing it for political reasons because they don't want a bloc, but it's been a very active public relations process which is beginning to catch on and there is a sort of alliance with a number of other people from developing countries who have always disliked the term because it's a sort of ranking. "We don't want to be number three, thank you very much." And it's based on a theory of development with number one, number two, and number three, in other words, better than others, so I think you're going to have a hard struggle to retain it.

Incidentally, the countries of Eastern Europe are exactly afraid themselves of being lost in the Third World and now insist on being called "economies in transition."

Allan Thompson:

The trouble is there's absolutely no getting around the fact that what the so-called Western media is doing is spilling over. The satellite dishes are there. People have a desire to learn, and very often the sources of media available to them will be Northern ones. That's not assigning blame; that's just saying there is a reality. I don't think we can just say that it's not our business to worry about whether or not we think our portrayal of your world is accurate because, unfortunately, very often people in the developing world, the Third World, the South, have to learn about their neighbors from us.

And we really have to acknowledge that. And to its great credit, Gemini News Service did that twenty-five years ago and has been doing it with a great deal of success ever since.

In the Cold War era people at least had a choice of interpretations. They could choose to believe what one side told them about themselves, or choose to believe what the other side told them about themselves. So now we have to acknowledge that there's no longer even that much selection available. The West didn't necessarily win, but it's there.

Norman Webster:

I didn't say it's not our business whether the picture we give is accurate. Portrayal is not for Third World audiences, that's clear. It's for our people and I don't applaud all this. Some of it, I think, is just inevitable. CNN drives me crazy too. But as Knowlton Nash mentioned to some of us the other day, CNN is now buying more items from the CBC and that is good, so maybe we will get more, although one suspects they run them in the middle of the night.

Unidentified Questioner:

In Algeria before the elections that were finally never held, but before the first series of elections, the local ones which the Islamic Salvation Front eventually came up the winner in, it was an issue of the coverage that the French television networks gave to the situation in Algeria. And Algerians were picking up on this through the satellite dishes. The world is not isolated anymore.

Dana Bales:

I'm a student at the School of Journalism here in Regina. My question is for Mr. Webster. You stated earlier that the number of correspondents from Canada is getting better. You also conceded though that CNN sells things for a lot cheaper and a lot more glamorously, the way people want to see them, and that it's just easier for the Canadian networks to just buy from CNN. So, that being the case, how is it possible that the number of Canadian foreign correspondents will increase?

Norman Webster:

I was making a comparison between the good old days which weren't so good and currently. Things really have improved now. At the moment, we are in tight budget times and some cuts are being made which I regret and I hope they will be restored, but the CBC is not in the business of being totally dependant on CNN and I hope to God that it never will be.

Patrick Nagle:

I would like everybody to understand that CNN really is a very thin, thin veneer of an information network. They do things on the cheap. They do things in a hurry. They're extraordinarily lucky – at least they have been to date – they're good at what they do, but they should not be confused with a really strong, useful source of information. They're merely a first line of information. You'll perish if you try to take all your information, all your world news from CNN.

Anjum Niaz:

My comments are for Mr. Webster. I would like to set the record straight.

He talks about *New York Times* and he says that *New York Times* is the best newspaper. I think this brings us back to square one. We've been discussing this since yesterday. And we, the people from the Third World, we have a right to our own viewpoint – a right to decide which is the best paper. This view can't be thrust upon us. And I take exception to it, because I think that the *New York Times* has many slants and I don't want to go into those slants, but I think that some of the reporting in *New York Times* is not fair. I think that in a way, these two days have been counterproductive if at the end of this session we are told that *New York Times* is the best paper and you better accept it.

Norman Webster:

Certainly, it would be wrong to interpret my comments as meaning that the whole session was hogwash. However, I was selective. I went through my notes and I found half a dozen ridiculous assertions. Including the one about the anchorperson, you'll remember you prefaced with a remark that ". . the Western media are racist, and as an example . . ." Well, I'm afraid that I don't accept that the media are racist. We can have a difference of opinion there, but I don't accept that. As for the *New York Times*, that's my opinion. That's not your opinion. That's fair enough.

Charles Quist Adade:

My question goes to Norman. Do you think that the media has an agenda setting rule and that the media can influence what the readers read and whether the media can generate interest in readership? If that is the case, then why do you tell us that you write for your readership and that you write things that they are interested in?

Norman Webster:

It would be silly to deny that the media have a role in setting the agenda, but any medium, any publication that gets fundamentally removed from the pre-occupations and interests of its readers or its audience is doomed to die. So it's a two-way process. We have to respond to the interests of our readers, but one hopes that we don't slavishly follow everything that they think. We're trying to educate them as well. That's one of Mr. Tricot's points, that we've got to start to look to the future and tell them things they don't know. But if we suddenly go tearing off on some tangent that bears no relationship to their lives, then we're not long for this world.

Derek Ingram:

I did a story in Indonesia once, and I went around the radio station with a government official who was rather patronizing. It was a local program, but there were no local people participating, but the government was telling local people what to do. And he said that we have to tell people – it's very important to tell people what their problems are, otherwise they don't know.

Shannon Avison:

I work at the Saskatchewan Indian Federated College. I'm a student of native media. I want to tell you a little bit that I know about native media in Canada. There are about 200 newspapers, mostly tabloids, produced by Indian and Métis people in Canada. Most of northern Canada is served by Native Broadcast Service outlets. All these media outlets are struggling. An example is, *Micmac News* has just suspended publication. I think it's one of the oldest native publications in this country. That sort of explains why they're not here – they don't have a lot of money to come to conferences like this and the other thing is that often their outfits are one-person shows, so they really can't spare the people.

We're also struggling at the Saskatchewan Indian Federation College, struggling financially, to deliver training for aboriginal people. The SIFC is based right here on the U. of R. campus and we have a two-year certificate program that leads to the U. of R. School of Journalism Communications degree. We've had a lot of co-operation developing a working relationship.

Also, we've had some meetings with CBC, so I want to acknowledge the people of the Journalism School for their efforts to promote journalism to aboriginal children and aboriginal people and give them a vehicle that lets them not only produce their own media but also start to participate more in the mainstream media. If anybody is interested in knowing anything else about our program or wants to get in touch with aboriginal journalists in this country, I'd be happy to pass on some names.

Unidentified questioner:

There's a concentration on local media because that's what people want to hear – so they say. I wanted to ask the panel if you think that they could create a taste for international news by reporting the ongoing events and not just the chaos, and if it is the media's responsibility to do that – to create a taste for international news.

Norman Webster:

Sure we have a responsibility to do more than the coups and the earthquakes, absolutely. And the developing countries have a genuine complaint when they say you only turn up here for the famines. There's no question. We've got to have a much more balanced and full view of things.

Question Authority

When the man he say war is good
Gonna bring jobs to your neighborhood
Ask him where his ideas come from
You'll find very little in his cranium.

Chorus

So I question authority
You question authority
We question authority
Our life mean a whole lot more.

When the man he say war saves lives
With enought shovels I break into hives
Ask him if he would kindly explain
You'll find that tought for his little brain.

Chorus

When the man he say war not his fault
If he doesn't play he loose by default
Ask him if he ever hear of Kingdom Come
You'll find it's beyond his cerebellum.

Chorus

When the man he want to start a war in your country
Pass you a law, make him a deportee
Don't ask him nice never to come back
You'll find man who make war he is a maniac.

Song by Regina Singer-Songwriter, Noele Hall

APPENDIX

LIST OF DELEGATES

Anyaegbunam, Ngoz
Editorial Board*Daily Times*
Lagos, Nigeria
Address:
Daily Times Nigeria PLC
Agidingbi Road
Lagos, Nigeria. (01) 900850

Behan, Louise
International Development Research Centre (IDRC)
Ottawa, Canada
Address:
P.O. Box 8500
Ottawa, Ontario
Canada, K1G 3H9
Phone: (613) 236-6163 ext: 2564

Bolan, Mr. Kim
Vancouver Sun
Vancouver, B.C.
Canada

Bonneville, Lionel
Regional Director
Societe Radio-Canada
Address
2440 Broad Street
Regina, Saskatchewan
Canada S4P 4A1
Tel: 347-9427

Boychuk, Rick
Freelance (Ottawa)
Office and Home address:
566 Churchill Avenue
Ottawa, Ontario, Canada
K1Z 5E5
Tel: (613) 724 6122

Burt, Mr. and Mrs. Murray
Vice-President, Lazer-fare Media Services Ltd.
Address:
602 491 Portage Ave.
Winnipeg, Manitoba, Canada
Tel: (204) 786-8615

Chabun, Will
Editorial Writer
Regina Reader Post
Address:
Box 2020 Regina, Saskatchewan
Canada.
Tel: (306) 525-8221

Cooney, Roman
Calgary Herald
Editorial Writer
Address:
215-16th Street, SE
P.O. Box 2400 STNM
Calgary, Alberta, Canada
T2P OW8
Tel: (403) 235-7517

Cousins, Brian
Reginal Director
CBC Saskatchewan
Regina, Saskatchewan
Address:
Box 540, Regina, Saskatchewan
Canada
S4P4A1
Tel: 347-9486

Cunningham, Bill
Former Max Bell Professor and TV Journalist
Toronto, Ontario, Canada
Address:
Apt 9, 20 Glebe Road
Toronto, Ontario
Tel: (416) 489-2553

Docking, Alex
School of Journalism and Communications
News Director
CKCK TV (Regina)
Saskatchewan, Canada
Tel: 306 569 2000

Dumelie, Roger
Director, International NGO Division CIDA
Address:
Canadian International Development Agency
200 Promenade Du Portage
Hull, Quebec
Canada
Tel: 997-5578

Ealodona, Joseph
National Broadcasting Commission
Journalist and News Features
Broadcasting Headquarters,
Papua New Guinea
Address:
c/o NBC News
P.O. Box 1359, Boroko, Papua
New Guinea
Tel: (675) 253341

Emery, Jean-Marc
Acting Chief of Media Relations
CIDA
Address:
200 du Portage
Hull, Quebec, Canada
K1A OG4
Tel: (819) 953-6060

Farquharson, Duart
Associate Editor, *Edmonton Journal*
Address:
10006-101 Street
Edmonton, Alberta
Canada
T5J Os1
Tel: (403) 429-5207

Fong, Peg
Vancouver Sun
Vancouver, British Columbia, Canada

**Forrester, Ms. Gillian
Freelance (Regina)
Address:
31 Pappas Cres.
Regina, Saskatchewan
Canada
S4R 7G7
Tel: (306) 543-3418

**Foster, Darren
Communications, SaskPower
Regina, Saskatchewan
Canada
Noele Hall
Common Ground
Resource Co-ordinator/singer-songwriter
Address:
2174 Hamilton St.
Regina, Saskatchewan
Canada
Tel: (306) 522-6619

Gascon, Paul
Society Radio-Canada, CBC Radio
Saskatchewan
Address:
2440 Broad Street
Regina, Saskatchewan
Canada
S4P 4A1
Tel: 347-9540

Green, David
Regina Leader Post
Address:
Box 2020 Regina, Saskatchewan
Canada
Tel: (306) 565-8221

Hamaludin, Mohamed
Managing Editor, *Miami Times*
Address:
900 N.W. 54th St.
Miami, Florida
33127 USA
Tel: (305) 757-1147

Honeyman, Scott
Managing Editor, *Vancouver Sun*
Address:
2250 Granville St.
Vancouver, British Columbia
Canada
Tel: 9604) 732-2457

Ingram, Derek
Editor, Gemini News Service
Address:
9 White Lion Street
London N1 9PD
Tel: (071) 833-4141

Knight, Gerald
General Manager, Guardian News
Service, London
Address:
119 Farringdom Road
London EC1R 2ERUK
Tel: 071-278-2332

**Kossowan, Brenda
Reporter, *Red Deer Advocate*
Address:
Postal Box 5200
Red Deer, Alberta
Canada T4N 5G3
Tel: (403) 393-2400, ext. 244

Kumar, Sat
Director, School of Journalism and Communications
Address:
Univeristy of Regina,
Room 133, Education Building
Regina, Saskatchewan
Canada S4S OA2
Tel: (306) 585-4420

**Langenegger, Stefani
Associate Producer, CBC Radio
Regina
Address:
21-2201 14th Avenue
Regina, Saskatchewan
Canada S4P OX9
Tel: (306) 7575697

Latta, Lori
Saskatchewan Council for International Cooperation
Communications Officer
Address:
2138 McIntyre St.
Regina, Saskatchewan
Canada
S4P 2R7
Tel: (306) 757-4669

Lim, Constance
Program Manager, Corporate Affairs and Initiatives Division, IDRC
Address:
P.O. Box 8500
Ottawa, Ontario, Canada
K1G 3H9
Tel: (613) 236-6163 ext 2430

Marshall, Sharon
News Coordinator, Caribbean Broadcasting Union, Barbados
Address:
"Wilkins Lodge"
Two Mile Hill, St. Michael
Barbados
Tel: (809) 423-9946

Mathieu, Gabrielle
Media Relations Advisor, CIDA
Address:
CIDA
200 Promenade du Portage
Hull, Quebec, Canada
Tel: (819) 953-9505

*Mazzitelli, Teresa
Reporter, *Canadian Family Physician*,
Mississagua, Ontario
Address:
51 Fairbank Avenue
Toronto, M6E 3Y6 Canada
Tel: (416) 783-1389

McClinton, Lorne
School of Journalism and Communications
University of Regina

McKenzie, Professor Jim
School of Journalism and Communications
University of Regina
Regina Saskatchewan S4S 1S8

Moloi, Ernest
Senior Reporter, Botswana Guardian
Address:
P.O. Box 1641
Botswana Road, Gaborone, Botswana
Tel: (267) 352077

*Montgomery, Sue
Journalist, Canadian Press, Montreal
Quebec, Canada
Address:
245 St. Jacques W.
Montreal, P.Q. Canada
Tel: (819) 849 6154

Munamava, Rajah
Editor in Chief,
New Era Newspaper, Namibia
Address:
P/Bag 13364, Windhoek 9000
Namibia
Tel: (061) 34924

Nagel, Patrick
Southam News, Calgary
Address:
P.O. Box 2400, Stn "M"
Calgary, Alberta
Canada
T2P OW8
Tel: (403)272-7073

Nash, Knowlton
Visiting Max Bell Professor
School of Journalism and Communications
University of Regina,
S4S OA2

Nayar, Kuldip
Columnist, New Delhi, India
Address: D7/2 Vasant Vihar
New Delhi 64
India
Tel: (602) 488/688-5450

Nelson, Daniel, Managing Editor
PANOS Institute
Address:
9 White Lion St
London N1 9PD
Tel: 071-278-1111

Nettleford, Prof. Rex
Pro Vice-Chancellor, Director of Continuing Studies
University of West Indies, Jamaica
Address:
University of the West Indies
Mona, Kingston 7
Jamaica
Tel: (809) 927 9953

Niaz, Anjum, Editor
Dawn Magazine, Karachi, Pakistan
Address:
Haroon House, Dr. Zia ud din Road
Karachi, Pakistan
Tel: 2500 83022

Njoku, Bethel
General Manager, Gemini News Service
London
Address:
9 White Lion St.
London N1 9PD
Tel: 071 833-4141

Oguttu, Wufulu, Editor-in-chief
The Monitor, Kampala, Uganda
Address:
P.O. Box 12141
Kampala, Uganda
Tel: 255220

Padman, Padmaja
New Straits Times, Malaysia
Address:
31 Jalan Riong
59100 Kuala Lumpur
Malyasia
Tel: (03) 282-3322 (x) 346

Parasram, Jai
Line-up Editor
CBC Newsworld, Halifax
Address:
P.O. Box 3000
Halifax, N. S.
B3J 3E9
Tel: (902)420 4054

Peterson, Bill
Executive Editor, *Saskatoon Star Phoenix*,
Address:
204-5th Avenue
Saskatoon, Saskatchewan
Canada
J7K 2P1
Tel: (306) 664-8315

Philander, Keith
Director, Social Justice Dept. Catholic Church
Regina, Saskatchewan
Canada
Address:
445 Broad St. N.
Regina, Sask., Canada
Tel: 352-1651

Popoff, Wilfred
Associate Editor, *Saskatoon Star Phoenix*
Address:
204-5th Avenue
Saskatoon, Saskatchewan
Canada J7K 2P1

Proulx, Bernard
Journalist, Radio-Quebec, Montreal
Quebec, Canada
Address:
800 rue Fullum
Montreal, H2K 3L7 Canada
Tel: (514) 521-2424

Quist-Adade, Charles
Freelance, School of Communications
Windsor, Ontario
Address:
Dept of Communications Studies
University of Windsor
Windsor, Ontario N9B 3P4
Canada
Tel: (519) 253-4232

Rampen, Leo, Series Producer
North-South, Montreal
Quebec, Canada
Address:
246 Main Road
Hudson, QC
JOP 1HO
Tel: (514) 458 2733

Risk, Susan
Local Coordinator, Canadian University Service Overseas (CUSO)
Regina, Saskatchewan
Address:
2174 Hamilton St.
Regina, Saskatchewan
Canada S4P 2E3
Tel: 306-525-2900

Ramsay, David
Editorial Writer, *Regina Leader Post*

Russell, Prof. Nick
School of Journalism and Communications
University of Regina
Regina, Saskatchewan S4S 0A2

Saidi, William, Managing Editor,
Sunday Times, Harare, Zimbabwe
Address:
1st Floor, Hungwe House
Jason Moyo Ave.
Harare, Zimbabwe
Tel: 708120/720918

Sanger, Clyde
Director of Communications,
North South Institute
Ottawa
Address:
55 Murray Street
Suite 200, Ottawa, Ontario
Canada
Tel: (613) 236-3535

**Schwabe, Marcus
CBC Radio, Prince George
Address:
1268 5th Ave
Prince George, B.C.
V2L 3L2
Canada
Tel: 562-6701

Scarfe, Brian L.
Vice President (Academic)
University of Regina
Regina, Saskatchewan S4S 0A2
Tel: 306-585-4384

**Shein, Elaine
Western Producer, Saskatoon
Address:
Box 2500 Saskatoon, Saskatchewan
Canada S7JK 2C4
Tel: (306) 665-3540

Siggins, Maggie
Journalist/author
Former Max Bell Professor
School of Journalism and Communications
Address:
2831 Retallack Street
Regina, Saskatchewan
S4S 1S8
Canada
Tel: (306) 586-9505

**Simmie, Scott
Senior Writer, CBC TV National News
Toronto
Ontario, Canada

Spelliscy, Prof. Jill
School of Journalism and Communications
University of Regina,
Regina, Saskatchewan
Canada S4S OA2
Tel: (306) 585-4449

*Spencer, Christina
City Editor, *Ottawa Citizen*
Address:
1101 Baxter Road, Ottawa
K2C 3M4 Canada
Tel: (613) 596-3664

Sperling, Prof. Gerry
Head, Department of Political Science
University of Regina
Regina, Saskatchewan S4S 0A2

Swan, John
Editor, *Regina Leader Post*
Address:
1964 Park St.
Regina Saskatchewan
S4P 3G4 Canada
Tel: 306-565-8242

Tan, Abby
Freelance
Address:
10th Floor, Locsin Bldg.
Ayala Ave. Makati
Philippines
Tel: 8174 784/8178221 (x) 101 3581

Thloloe, Joe, Managing Editor
Sowetan, Johannesburg
Address:
Sowetan, Box 6663
Johannesburg, 2000
South Africa
Tel: (-11) 474-8834

*Thompson, Allan
Toronto Star
Address:
One Yonge St.
Toronto, Ontario
Canada, M5E 1E6
Tel: (416) 869-4468

Todd, Larry
Lab Instructor, School of Journalism and Communications
University of Regina

Traynor, Mr. Dave
Legislative Reporter, *Saskatoon Star Phoenix*
204-5th Avenue
Saskatoon. Saskatchewan
J7K 2P1

Tricot, Luis
Freelance (Santiago, Chile)
Address:
Alvarez 924
Vina Del Mar, DPTO 34-4,
Chile
Tel: 682563

*Urlocker, Michael
Reporter, *Financial Post*, Toronto
Address:
333 King St. E., Toronto, Ontario
Canada M5A 4N2
(for 1993) c/o Gemini News Service
London
Tel: (416) 350-6387

Vanasse, Frederic
Societé Radio-Canada,
2440 Broad St.
Regina, Saskatchewan
S4P 4A1

Webster, Norman
Editor, *Montreal Gazette*
Address:
250 St. Antoine W.
Montreal Quebec, H2Y 3R7
Tel: (514) 987-2500

Wilson, Barry
Western Producer
Address:
402-150 Wellington St.
Ottawa, Ontario
Canada K1P 5A4
Tel: (613) 232-1447

*Wilson, Gavin
Information Officer, University of British Columbia
Address:
Community Relations Office
Old Administration Bldg.
University of BC
Vancouver, British Columbia
Tel: (604) 822-2130

Yinghuang, Zhu
Deputy Editor, *China Daily*
Beijing
Address:
China Daily
15 Huixin Dongjie
Chaoyang District
Beijing, 100029, China
Tel: 422-0544/422-0955

* GEMINI INTERNATIONAL DEVELOPMENT RESEARCH CENTRE FELLOW

** GEMINI UNIVERSITY SCHOOL OF JOURNALISM AND COMMUNICATIONS FELLOW